Passionate Frie

MEMOIRS AND BIOGRAPHY
We Mixed Our Drinks
Come Into The Sunlight
The Escapist Generations

BIOGRAPHICAL NOVELS
Georgian Lady (Fanny Burney)
Poet Pursued (Percy Bysshe Shelley)
Victorian Love Story (Dante Gabriel Rossetti)

CONTEMPORARY NOVELS
Another Man's Poison
Malady of Love

FOR SCHOOLS AND PARENTS
Favourite Books For Boys And Girls

HISTORY
London Villages
More London Villages
The Royal Family and the Spencers

Passionate Friendships

Memoirs and Confessions of a Rebel

Nerina Shute

'This above all, to thine own self be true,
And it must follow, as the night the day,
Thou canst not then be false to any man.'
Hamlet

ROBERT HALE · LONDON

© *Nerina Shute 1992*
First published in Great Britain in 1992

ISBN 0 7090 4962 5

Robert Hale Limited
Clerkenwell House
Clerkenwell Green
London EC1R 0HT

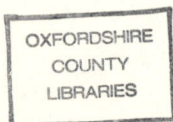

Photoset in North Wales by
Derek Doyle & Associates, Mold, Clwyd.
Printed in Great Britain by
St Edmundsbury Press Ltd, Bury St Edmunds, Suffolk.
Bound by WBC Bookbinders Ltd, Bridgend, Glamorgan.

Contents

List of Illustrations

All photographs courtesy of the author.

Author's Foreword

Why did I write this book?

I have already written a book of memoirs published as long ago as 1973. It was called *The Escapist Generations*. If some of my readers remember this other book they will find repetitions. The basic life story is the same – childhood scenes in California, memories of wartime London – but this time I have written a book of confessions, something I have never done before.

I am a private person. For many years I have managed to keep my secrets to myself, protecting the men and women I have loved. Now all my loved ones are dead, and no longer vulnerable. No one is left who might be hurt or damaged by these confessions unless it is myself. The time has come to tell a story which requires to be told.

I believe there are many women in the world who need the love of another woman in addition to the love of a man. We are bisexual. Usually we hide this fact from our husbands for fear of ending a happy marriage. I made the mistake of telling my husband. It caused a lot of suffering. By explaining how it all happened, and how it ended, I may possibly give help to others. In the end both of us found another partner and mine, strangely enough, was a beautiful and famous woman with whom I spent the happiest years of my life.

1 Childhood

The first home I can remember was a house in Chelsea, 28 Cheyne Walk. I can see myself, a bundle of white muslin, being wheeled in the pram by my nurse. I was a pretty child. Unfortunately I did a lot of screaming.

There was a shameful occasion in Hyde Park, on a Sunday afternoon, when my handsome father, wearing a top hat, took me in a cab to see the riders in Rotten Row. I stood beside him, holding his hand. I waddled beside him in the sunlight, greeted by elegant ladies and gentlemen, my father's friends. For a time all these graceful people were delighted by a little dainty soul called Nerina, who smiled like a doll and politely said, 'How do you do?'

I remember exactly what happened. Like my pretty mother I loved horses. I longed to be old enough to ride as she did in Rotten Row. At the sight of five or six children trotting and galloping their perfect ponies, all of them filled with joy, proud as peacocks, I became jealous and began to scream.

'What's the matter?' said my father.

I went on screaming.

'Is a pin sticking into you?' I shook my head in angry denial. He took the screaming child home, greatly distressed, humiliated, unable to explain what had happened to my mother, who scolded him (out of loyalty to her little girl), his Sunday afternoon quite spoilt by the shock to her nerves.

My mother said, 'You must have upset the child. What did you do?'

About twenty years later I gave him my reasons for screaming and apologized for the scene I had caused on that lovely afternoon. My father laughed at the memory.

It was a time of charm and change. London was altered by the appearance of the motor car. The gay world of King Edward was not quite so gay as before. That was why Renie and Cammy, my mother and father, had decided to relieve their boredom by living in Chelsea. Ladies were taking up sport, becoming suffragettes, even passing the time by opening hat shops, undertaking light jobs, or writing novels, like Renie, which annoyed my father very much.

The first novel by Mrs Cameron Shute was called *The Unconscious Bigamist*. Cammy was horrified. 'If only you had used another name. Why call yourself Mrs Cameron Shute? What will my friends think?'

'I had no idea you would mind,' said Renie.

'All my friends go shopping in the Army and Navy Stores. What will they say when they see that awful poster with your name on it?'

'I don't know,' said Renie.

Cammy was my mother's second husband. (The first had been killed in South Africa during the Boer War. He and Cammy had been friends.) To please Renie my father had been persuaded to leave the army. Now he was growing bored. His attitude to literature, art, sculpture, music and drama was one of distaste. He was beginning to dislike novelists almost as much as artists, sculptors, musicians, actors – and above all poets, who were the worst, he said, of the lot.

'They all,' said Cammy with disgust, 'have long damp curls and horrible ideas. All except Kipling.'

When Cammy's mother came to stay in the spare bedroom overlooking the garden she was enraptured with their London home. Lady Shute thought the drawing-room, with a balcony facing the Thames, was perfect for entertaining. The panelled dining-room on the ground floor was so nice for dinner parties.

'Cammy is like his father, dear. He likes cavalry officers and titles.'

'So do I,' said my mother.

Their combined income was now £600 a year, and on this they could manage with comfort. They had no horses, no car. But my mother was frequently loaned a horse to ride in Rotten Row, and when she was seen schooling it, the owner was able to sell it. Among Renie's admirers was Lord Erroll (father of the famous Lord Erroll, the beautiful young man who was murdered in Kenya). My mother had a gift for sparkle and laughter, enormous blue eyes, a lovely figure, and Lord Erroll often called in the evenings for a glass of port, a light-hearted flirtation. My father did not mind in the least.

Lady Shute still insisted that my father ought to work for his living, an idea which Cammy rejected. My parents were not exceeding their income; cook, parlourmaid and nurse were each paid £25 a year, the 'tweeny' only £14, and Renie had learned to keep accounts.

'How can I cure Cammy's boredom?' said Renie. 'Why is he so

silly about meeting clever people?'

My grandmother said, 'Clever people are boring, dear.'

'But I want to improve my mind. You see,' said Renie, in a tone of apology, 'I would rather like to learn about Rodin, and the pre-Raphaelites, and Ibsen, and things like that.'

'Well, there's no harm in learning things before lunch, dear. Keep your afternoons and evenings for cavalry officers and titles. If you don't,' said Lady Shute wisely, 'you'll lose Cammy.'

'Do you think I ought to give up writing novels?'

'No, dear, I wouldn't go so far as that. It may be rather common,' said Lady Shute, who was always practical, 'but this is your chance to make money.'

My father came of an army family, distinguished and snobbish and pleasantly immoral. Everyone said that my grandmother had a lot to endure. 'Men are different,' she used to say. 'They can't help it. Look what the dear Queen has to put up with!'

Sir Charles (a major in the Inniskilling Dragoons, whose career began in the cavalry charge of Balaklava) expected a lot of his sons. Harry, the eldest, a lieutenant colonel in the Coldstream Guards, with a DSO to his credit, made Cammy feel inferior. Poor Cammy was pushed through Sandhurst, then out to South Africa. He became a major, somehow, in the Second Queen's Royal Regiment. In South Africa he met the fascinating Renie, then married to Captain Ernest Brass, and later, because he was madly in love, he left the army to please her. Renie told me that Cammy was good-looking. She loved his silky moustache and used to say, 'A kiss, without a moustache, is like an egg without salt.'

Even as a small child I could sense the strain between my parents. I was threatened by something. And yet they loved one another, and for me, born of romance and joy after a period of bliss in the Welsh mountains, they both held a feeling of tenderness, almost of adoration. I know now that when Cammy lost all his money on the Stock Exchange, my mother sold her horses and all her possessions to settle his debts. It was the happiest time of their lives. They lived in Maesynrynner, a house on the side of a mountain for which they paid £27 a year.

'Poverty was delightful,' my mother used to say.

They still had quantities of expensive clothes and two faithful servants. I was their first baby. I was conceived during this long honeymoon when they lived in a state of suspended beauty between the clouds and the heather; resting on the rocks below the garden; walking down the narrow path between stones and flowers; driving in the governess cart, drawn by a fat Welsh pony, into Dolgelly, seven miles distant, to do their shopping. And that was why both my parents loved me so much.

But the fashionable life in Chelsea, in the house I remember so well, destroyed something. They were no longer short of money because Renie now received an allowance from her mother. Cammy had inherited from a relative. For the first time they began to quarrel. In the Cheyne Walk drawing-room, spoiled for Cammy by Renie's new-found friends, arty parties, semi-intellectuals, he screwed in his eyeglass, stared at the ceiling and yawned.

'Why must you be so rude?' said my mother.

'Because I can't bear your friends. They make me feel s-s-sick,' replied Cammy, who always stammered in moments of emotion.

He still did no work of any kind. 'Work,' he said firmly, echoing Oscar Wilde, 'is the ruin of the drinking classes. I wish I was still in the army.'

Until the outbreak of war in August 1914 his boredom continued. Renie moved as always within the closed circle of good manners. Her greatest friend was still Lord Erroll. Eventually came news which filled all the papers with angry nervous headlines, sending Cammy to report at the War Office. He was needed by his country. For him it was a happy and purposeful moment. But Renie knew the Edwardian period was finally finished, and so, she realized, was her marriage.

I remember very little about the 1914 war.

For me life really began on a bitter, cold day in February 1920 when a little girl was to leave her father, her baby brother, her nurse, her white rabbit. Soon she would be living in a dreamlike town of great beauty, a town crowded with palm trees and birds of turquoise blue and houses of pink and yellow which stood, like sugar cakes, coloured in sunlight. The name of the town was Hollywood.

'We shall only be away for three months,' my mother said.

I remember my father's sad face on the day we left him at Southampton. Perhaps he knew we would not return. On the great ship, *Mauretania*, we parted from him with kisses and kindness. He walked away from us into the rain, his bowler hat like a helmet on his head.

'Can't you wait,' said my mother, 'until the warning bell for visitors to leave?'

'No, I'd rather not wait. Good-bye, old girl.'

Before he disappeared from sight I saw him open his umbrella. He did not turn to look back, or wave. I know now that he was trying not to cry.

As a little girl I was very much in love with my mother. To journey with her to America was thrilling. I can see now that Renie, in the Ibsen manner, was at last quitting her husband with the intent to lead her own life.

She was forty-two. From a film company in Hollywood she had received an offer for one or both of her novels (*The Unconscious Bigamist* and *The Cross Roads*). In New York she was entertained by friends of the family. For five days we travelled thrillingly on the train to California, arrived one evening in Los Angeles, then drove in an open car to the Hollywood Hotel. After sunset the sky became immediately dark. On the following morning we hurried to the bedroom window. We looked down in wonder at a garden, in the month of February, filled with roses and sweetpeas and stocks.

I remember kissing my pretty mother with a feeling of joy.

'I shall be able to wear my white socks and my blue cotton dress and my sun-bonnet,' I said.

'Well, why not? Life is such fun!' my mother said.

While I sat in the garden among the roses, Renie went to the film studios, where she met Mr Thomas Ince, and actually signed her name to a contract (afterwards cancelled). My loose hair fell to my waist. Among the flowers, with my book on my lap, admiring my new white socks, gleaming in the bright sun, I looked and felt like the heroine of *Alice in Wonderland*.

On one of these enchanted mornings I was found by a dark lady who offered me a part in a film. The lady said she was a screen-writer. What was I doing by myself in the garden? I said I was reading *Jane Eyre*. Would I like to act in a film and earn a lot of money? Unfortunately this exciting offer was rejected by my mother. Film studios might have a bad effect on little girls. My mother kissed me a great deal, we laughed a great deal, and for both of us it was a period of excitement and delight. Renie was later to be involved in a front-page newspaper scandal. It led to a strange story of love and financial ruin by which all our lives were changed. I can still remember how happy she was then, living in Hollywood with me, the little girl who thought she was perfect. She told me all her adventures. She was in love with me and I was in love with her. I can still see her laughing face.

'It's all such fun!' she used to say. 'What will happen next?'

One day my mother had tea with an English lady, well-bred, beautiful, considered more exotic than anyone in Hollywood. Her name was Elinor Glyn.

'She's related by marriage to your father,' Renie said.

I remember the interview as clearly as if it had happened to

myself. I knew that Renie felt nervous. I knew that the famous
writer of passionate love stories was seated at her desk, a long
quill pen in her white hand. I knew that she was wearing a
pear-shaped emerald of enormous value. It was placed like a
third eye above and between her straight black brows. (How
was this done?) Her face and forehead were coated deeply in
white powder. Her silky hair was Titian red.

Elinor Glyn said, 'So you are related to that delightful old
man, General Sir Charles Shute. The wickedest old man in
England, my dear!'

After tea, as one writer to another, she gave my mother
advice, and Renie told me what was said.

'The whole secret is to give the public what it wants. In other
words, love and sex, my dear. Why do you suppose all these
women come to see me?'

She pointed at the door behind which about twenty women
were seated in a small waiting-room.

'They come,' said Elinor Glyn, stroking the emerald with a
loving finger, 'because my book has given them the thrill of
their lives. They sleep with it under their pillows. They enjoy the
purple patches. They are pursued by lovers in their dreams.'

My mother laughed about this, and so did I. We both felt sorry
for the women in the waiting-room. They had been sitting on
hard seats, without a trace of a lover, for several hours.

'Of course I could write something good if I tried, my dear,
but that would be a mistake. I've established myself as the
author of *Three Weeks*, and I've got to keep it up.'

She touched her jewel contentedly.

'Keep what up?' said my mother. 'The emerald?'

'My appearance. My personality. My reputation.'

'Do you mean you don't ever want to write something good?'

'It would probably ruin me,' said the inventor of what
Hollywood then called the 'It Girl'. 'Take my tip as a writer, and
never try to be clever. People don't want to think when they go
to the films. Just give them what they want. Love and sex.'

My mother thought this little story was very funny, and so did
I. It was Renie's first introduction to the world of sex, and mine,
but very soon we were both to begin a full education, I in my
high school and my mother in the divorce courts. My father
heard of the scandal about twelve months later, in his London
club, where he received a letter from an unknown woman in
Hollywood. She said that Renie was living in sin with her
husband. She intended to sue Renie in court. The amount she
required as compensation for a broken heart was one hundred
thousand dollars.

So then my father went to his favourite writing-desk and wrote to my mother. If she was really living with somebody's husband would she please turn the other chap out before he himself arrived in California? Luckily she won the Hollywood court case. She was a fast worker. By the time he left England, Renie had also bought a goldmine, in which both my parents were to lose what remained of their small inheritance.

Renie and I were now living in a bungalow outside La Jolla. Renie's little girl had grown much taller and was developing an American accent. Renie had created a beautiful English garden, ablaze with lupins and delphiniums and roses and sunflowers. Unhappily we had no furniture. All our possessions had been sold, including the grand piano, sent from England to pay our debts. And to make matters worse, the auctioneer had absconded with the money from the sale.

'Oh, dear,' said Renie, 'what will your father say?'

Cammy, wearing his bowler hat, came from San Diego in a hired car, and we went to meet him in the bright sunlit garden. As I then had an elderly admirer, Major Rumsey, who was curious to see my English father, we asked him to give a hand with Cammy's trunk. I can still see my father, slim and immaculate, screwing in his gold-rimmed eyeglass to glare at Major Rumsey, and I can hear myself saying, 'He wants to marry me when I grow up.'

'But you're only twelve,' said Cammy.

I suppose he had been thinking that Major Rumsey was Renie's admirer, not mine. Now he smiled, showing his fine white teeth, removed his bowler hat and gave Renie an affectionate kiss.

The year which followed was not a good one for Renie and Cammy. To be near the goldmine we moved to the mountains above San Diego, to a white-painted cabin in a little place called Descanso. The man my mother still loved, Captain Mallaby, the other woman's husband (although Mallaby is not his real name), was managing the unlucky mine, and of course my father was obliged to meet him.

'He's a bad-tempered chap. I don't like him,' said Cammy to me.

'Why can't we sell the mine, and go away?'

'All in good time. We must get it working,' said Cammy, 'and make a lot of money.'

'Why can't we go back to England, where we belong?'

'I shall take you home as soon as I can. And you,' he told me, stroking his moustache, 'will be a debutante. You'll be presented at Court and have a season in London. Then you'll get married to a nice young chap in the – Guards.'

I knew that my mother still loved Captain Mallaby and for this reason felt sorry for my father. Both of us were jealous of my pretty mother. Each morning Cammy walked up to the mine while Renie prepared lunch and cleaned the cabin. The larger bedroom was shared by myself and my mother. The smaller one was used by Cammy because he preferred to be alone. I could never understand why this should make Renie feel annoyed or hurt. Yet it did. When Captain Mallaby joined us on the front porch for an afternoon cup of tea we were pleased to see him because he brought good news. Sometimes he showed us specimens of galena ore which he said was lead-covered gold. Each of us enjoyed these hopeful conversations. It was a pity they ended as they did. Cammy returned from the mine to find the Captain already on the front porch, and Cammy, between the branches of the ilex tree, saw his wife being kissed. We all knew he was angry about it.

'I'm not a fussy man. Can't you be a little more discreet?' said Cammy, when the captain had left us. 'Why do that sort of thing on the front porch?'

'There was no harm in it,' said Renie.

'Don't make a fool of me. I don't mind a spot of infidelity, but I can't stand disloyalty.'

'So far I've never been unfaithful.'

'Well, I have,' said Cammy, who was equally indignant, 'but I've never been disloyal, and I never shall.'

Soon after this Captain Mallaby was killed. In my heart of hearts I was not sorry to lose him. First he had the great misfortune to be caught on the wheel of the engine at the mine, and then, a crippled man, he was killed while driving with a woman friend in his car. At the time of death Cammy was in Hollywood. Renie was rushed into hospital at San Diego. I knew she had drugged herself with a bottle half-filled with aspirins and nearly ended her life. I felt sick and bewildered.

Since then I have read the plays of Henrik Ibsen and have learned that my mother was in spirit an Ibsen heroine, a Nora from a house of dolls, an escapist, one who was seeking to herself to be true, one who believed less in her duty to society than her duty to her own heart, one who despised the conventional forms of polite hypocrisy.

But the young girl who went to dances at Descanso could only see that her high-spirited mother was unhappy and misunderstood. Somehow men had betrayed her. My father was a man, and somehow he had betrayed her too. I felt hurt because my mother felt hurt.

To add to my personal problems I had long pigtails instead of bobbed hair like American girls. After one year of co-education in the La Mesa High School (where young girls rouged their faces and occasionally had babies) I persuaded Renie to let me stay at home with her. This was because I hated Latin almost as much as I hated the idea of sex. American children laughed at my accent (which was neither English nor American but a mixture of both) and also my pigtails. So now I began to use rouge and mascara in an effort to conform.

While my mother heard only the pop-pop-pop of the engine which had made a cripple of Captain Mallaby, I was listening to the music of the Ford cars, driven at speed, by the boys and girls with their arms round each other's necks; to the honking and rattling and screaming and giggling which accompanied romance on the dusty mountain roads in the heat of summer. I decided to improve my American accent. It was better to be like the others.

'Promise you won't let those awful boys kiss you. Don't you see, they aren't your class!' said my mother.

'But there *is* no class in California. Oh, you make me tired,' said this new Nerina, in the idiom. 'Gee, I wanna have fun like the other kids.'

Cammy divided his time between Hollywood and Descanso. On his final visit to the mountains he was wearing a pearl-grey flannel suit, a light blue tie with silk handkerchief to match, an elegant pearl-grey hat. He discovered Renie, with cups of tea, waiting on the front porch. His much-changed daughter was in the bedroom. When she appeared at the door, Cammy screwed in his eyeglass and said, 'Good God! Is this Nerina?'

'She's taken to using cosmetics,' said my mother, in a tone of apology.

'What's that thing on your left cheek?' said Cammy, after gingerly kissing me.

'It's a beauty spot. Everyone says it looks cute. Gee, don't you like it?'

'I think it looks horrible.'

'So do I,' said my mother.

'But this is your daughter,' said Cammy reproachfully. 'Why don't you tell her to wash her face?'

'Why don't you tell her yourself?'

'Nerina, go and wash your face.'

The American Nerina, smiling, sat down between her father and her mother, in the rocking-chair. As she spoke she played with her long pigtails and rocked energetically.

'I don't wanna be treated like a little kid any more. Listen, folks, whose face is it? Gee, what's going on around here? Who do you think you are?'

'I'm your father.'

'Gee, that's too bad. You oughta be more careful.'

Cammy considered this astonishing remark. 'Well,' he said at last, 'I suppose we can't force you to wash your face. But when you return to England I do hope,' he said gently, 'you won't think it necessary to wear a – beauty spot.'

At the gentle rebuke we both smiled. My mother laughed.

'This isn't England. This is Descanso. And here comes Bob Benton,' Cammy was told as a tall cowboy, wearing a black sombrero hat, appeared between the branches of the ilex tree.

'Hello, Bob. Meet my poppa.'

'Pleased to meet you, Mister.'

'He's my feller,' said I proudly.

'We're going steady,' added the cowboy.

'You're doing *what*?' said Cammy in dismay. He screwed in his eyeglass. He gazed at the young man as though unable to comprehend.

'Come on, Bob, let's go.'

The cowboy and I walked over to the store to buy bottles of soda pop. We sucked it through straws. When I returned to the cabin, feeling less English than ever before, I knew there had been a quarrel between my parents. Renie had refused to return to England. She wanted their baby son to join them in California. Cammy did not. Their son, as he often said, must be educated at Eton. (Why was Eton so special?) I can see myself, the uncouth Nerina, as I smiled and said, 'What's the matter, folks?'

In the end my parents decided to part. They sat for days beneath the ilex tree drinking tea on the front porch.

Cammy said, 'Come home, old girl, before it's too late. Say good-bye to Descanso. After all, the engine has stopped.'

'Because Mallaby is dead!'

'Never mind Mallaby. I'm asking you to give up the mine, and bring Nerina home.'

'I'll bring her home when she's old enough to marry. Not until then. I shall find someone to manage the mine. I shall make it pay.'

'I'm going home. You'd better come too.'

'But you don't love me.'

'You can be unfaithful. There's no need to t-t-tell me about it.'

'But I want to be loved,' said my mother, wanting the best of both worlds.

In the end my father returned to England, and my baby brother was sent to Eton (as a scholar) and given a home by a wealthy spinster, who loved him and cherished him. Finally he became a Cambridge professor. And I, when I left my mother, became a London journalist.

2 My Brilliant Career

My mother ran beside the train, waving her white cotton gloves, the tears running down her face.

'Come back soon! Good-bye! Good-bye! Give my love to your father! And don't,' shouted Renie, 'cut off your pigtails!'

Of course I did. Within a week of my arrival in London the pigtails were off. At first I stayed with my mother's wealthy sister in a vast house in Eaton Square. This was alarming. The front door was opened by a footman in claret-coloured uniform. I remember how glad I was to join my father in Devonshire. I now wanted very much to be part of my father's life, an English girl, a well-trained Nerina, belonging, as he did, to the dignity of old houses, loving, as he did, the beauty of green English lanes, those places where primroses grew beneath peaceful hedges and nobody, or so I hoped, was interested in petting parties or sex.

It is difficult to describe the transition period between life in Descanso, life in Devonshire, and life as a journalist in London. At this time I really adored my mother. I left her because she had married an actor from Hollywood, a hot-tempered Irishman, and I was extremely jealous. My father's friends were conventional. Soon I was wearing dingy dresses and trying not to say 'Gee!' They made me see for the first time that my mother was a bigamist. She was married to my father and also to a penniless actor. She had abandoned her baby son.

To avoid hurting my feelings they sometimes said, 'Please, Nerina, don't let's talk about your mother.' When I continued, which I usually did, defending my mother, I forced them to say unwise things.

'She's a bigamist. She deserted your father to live with people beneath her class. She deserted her baby. Her poor little son had to be adopted.'

'It wasn't her fault. She *had* to do it. There was no other way!' I protested. How could I make them understand that my mother had tried, in her own special way, as my father had done, to face life with courage and gaiety?

Cammy found me my first job in London. I started as a typist in the Times Book Club. From this humble beginning I managed to raise myself. I became known as the Studio Correspondent, writing for *Film Weekly*.

'I think you're wonderful,' said Cammy.

'I expect I shall get the sack.'

'Oh no, you won't. You've got a head on your shoulders.'

One day the editor sent a message that I was wanted at once in his office.

'You have a very impertinent pen, Miss Shute!'

'What do you mean?' I said nervously.

'You described Nelson Keys as a Baby Austin lady-killer, and Madeleine Carroll as a ruthless Madonna.'

'Well, are you going to give me the sack?'

'Certainly not,' said the editor. 'I'm going to give you a contract and a rise in salary.'

From the dazzling sum of £4 a week I was now lifted into the heights of glory with a contract for one year at £6 a week, rising the second year to £8 a week.

'Considering you're only nineteen,' said the editor, 'you're making a lot of money. Go ahead and write some more of these impertinent articles. They're good.'

At the age of twenty-two I found myself a successful young woman but extremely lonely. I was still a virgin, writing my first novel (about my mother), and deciding to call it *Another's Man's Poison*. Both my parents lived abroad, my mother in California with her fourth husband (there were two more to come) and my father in Belgium in a place called Le Zoute, a small escape hole for impoverished gentry. From time to time, separately, they visited me in London.

My novel was published by Grant Richards. In front of me now is the blurb, which was signed by my publisher himself, and printed in postcard form with a picture of the author.

Miss Shute brought her manuscript to my office, told me I must read it myself and confessed that she was only twenty-two – not a very promising beginning from a hard-boiled publisher's point of view, especially as she added that I should find the story very frank and downright. However, I said that I would read it myself and I forthwith proceeded to do so. Now it waits the approval of the world. To be honest it has been edited here and there, but very little. It is in my opinion a story very much out of the common. It is vital; its characters, whether in the English countryside or in Hollywood or in the Californian hills, or in London, breathe.

Of course I was flattered by his praise of my book. Here is a piece of dialogue, taken from it, in those days considered shocking, defending the morals of my mother and my highly-sexed friends in London. It led to trouble with my father's generation, hurt feelings all round. How innocent it all seems now!

The speaker is a girl called Melis (myself).

'Oh, shut up! You don't realize how much this means to me! What d'you think I felt like when I came to England and found my mother – who I'd always thought was the most marvellous thing on earth – supposed to be wicked? *She* could be put in jail, according to English law, for committing bigamy. A different standard again! She's done all sorts of things worse than that, things even I could see were terrible. I couldn't do them myself. But I loved her just the same. I thought it all out, not in words you know, but just *inside* me. And the more I thought, the more I *knew* she wasn't wicked. She's never done anything *she* thought was wrong. Why, she'd be frightfully shocked if she knew about Paula!'

(Paula was what we then called ambi-sextrous.)

'That kind of thing seems as wrong to her as the things in her life seem to you. But I know she isn't wicked. Just as I know Paula isn't wicked. They both do things that I wouldn't do. But I love them. Yes, and respect them. They *think* they're right, so they *are* right. Their codes are different, that's all. Or call it their standards if you like. It seems so plain to me now. I could put it into one sentence, I think.'

'What's the sentence, my wise little infant?'

Melis drew in her breath. Scarcely she dared to say this thing, for it seemed so important ... so vastly important.

'It's – it's a proverb,' she said at last, 'just a proverb.'

'Well, what is it?'

'One's man's meat is another man's poison.'

There was a silence. There were frowns on their faces and they sat without moving. *Had she made them understand?*

At the time it was published no one had any idea what it cost me to write such a troublesome novel. My father's friends were not impressed. They were offended. Imagine a young girl, a lady, writing about lesbians and bisexuals!

I must explain that in London, in those days, we talked a great deal about homosexuality. It was illegal. Occasionally a nice young man would be caught by the police and sent to prison. Of course we talked about it. I remember saying to Aimée Stuart, my greatest friend, a well-known dramatist (author of *Nine Till Six*), 'What do you think about homosexuals?' Aimée was about twenty years older than myself, with white hair and the figure of a girl.

Said Aimée to me, 'I like homosexuals, don't you?'

'Yes, but what will happen in forty or fifty years' time? Will pansies be acceptable? Or will they still be called perverts?'

'Let's hope they'll be acceptable. After all, why not?'

'I think it's terrible to call anyone a pervert, don't you?'

'I think it's unforgivable,' said Aimée.

As I write I am trying to capture the charm and challenge of the thirties, the staccato style of London life. We were starting something. We did not then know what we were doing or where we were going. I know now that we were giving birth to the permissive age, something we had never heard of. We were trying to discover and assess the 'brave new world' described in different ways by Aldous Huxley and Miles Malleson, H. G. Wells and D. H. Lawrence, and many others.

We could all see that London was changing.

We visualized a new London, a place where civilized men and women would live together with love and tolerance and understanding, whether married or not, whether 'normal' or not, whether heterosexual, homosexual, or bisexual, or ambi-sextrous, as we laughingly called it.

We did not foresee the advancing drug addicts, the hippies, the final punishment of AIDS.

It was a pleasant little world of laughter and lust and love and it was led by such charming people as Noel Coward and Cecil Beaton. Aimée Stuart used to say, when describing an actor, or paying someone a compliment, 'I believe he's very bedworthy, dear.'

It was a world of escapists.

They were objecting, like my much-married mother, to the hypocrisy of the conventional world into which they had all been born. The changing Nerina, the would-be intellectual, the girl in the black hat, was struggling to become an adult.

As a bright young journalist, a writer of pen portraits and interviews with film stars, I greatly enjoyed my exciting profession. Every week I had lunch with famous people at the Ivy Restaurant (where Noel Coward could sometimes be seen) unless we went for a change to the Savoy Grill. It was fun. It was hilarious. To tell the truth, I was secretly embarrassed by so much talk about sex. To be a virgin was horrible. I really must put an end to my virginity.

Charles was my first lover. My age was twenty, when I met him, and to me he seemed a bit elderly. His age was thirty-two. He was tall and slim, with a shock of bushy mouse-coloured hair, rising up in frizzy rebellion from a high forehead. His intelligent face and chiselled nose (with a high nostril, like my mother and myself) was spoilt a little by his wild and wiry hair. There was something raffish about him. His pale blue eyes were shifty. I never knew when he was telling me the truth.

Once, at a petrol station, waiting for the garage man to fill the tank of his car, I heard Charles holding what appeared to be a vital conversation. When he returned to the car and drove out, laughing at something, I said to him curiously, 'What on earth were you talking about?'

'About man-eating tigers.'

'What do you know about tigers?'

'Nothing,' said Charles, 'but the man believed every word I said.'

'Why did you tell him all that?'

'I don't know. He enjoyed it, and so did I. I'm a very good liar,' said Charles. 'Haven't you noticed?'

I found him more amusing than anyone I had ever met but I had no wish to sleep with him or any other man. He told me smutty stories in a soft cultured voice, an Oxford accent, laughing until his eyes filled with tears.

'I've never met such an ignorant young woman, and yet,' said Charles, 'you're bursting with intelligence. Why is it?'

'I've had no schooling. I was in California, going to dances with cowboys. I've got a lot to learn.'

'It's a good thing you left your mother and came back to England,' said Charles. At the end of one of our long discussions he said: 'Do you really believe in free love? Or are you pretending?'

'Of course I'm not pretending,' I said indignantly.

'Would you be shocked if I took you to a Chelsea party and showed you how the real free-lovers behave?'

'Of course not,' I said.

I felt nervous when we arrived at the house in Chelsea. My hostess was wearing nothing but a pink silk vest.

'Are you going to take off your dress like the others?' whispered Charles.

'Certainly not. Are you going to take off your trousers?'

'Certainly not.'

This settled, we sat for a long time in a corner of the room drinking beer with a dash of gin. The truth is that the new, modern, free-thinking Nerina, the bright young journalist, was not at her ease. In fact I was profoundly shocked by the horseplay of men and women, permissive, unpleasing, dressed or partly dressed in ugly underclothes. Was this what was wanted by D. H. Lawrence and Aldous Huxley and Miles Malleson, my three heroes? Was this a glorious bawdy exhibition, or was it, could it be, something nasty?

In the end, to my relief, we were told by our hostess to leave the premises. To see this lady so angry, still in her pink silk vest, made me smile for the first time. She ordered Charles, in violent language, to remove his impossible girlfriend.

'You're not a gentleman,' said the lady in the pink silk vest, 'or you wouldn't have brought her to my home!'

'No,' said Charles amiably, 'I'm a nature's non-gentleman.'

Not long after this he asked me to marry him. Charles made me feel that life, however serious, was a thing to be enjoyed. For this I really did love him with all my heart. Charles. Dear Charles.

At the time when this courtship was going on my father was visiting London but I thought it better not to mention Charles until very much later. Charles was not my father's type!

On Sunday mornings, unless it was raining, my father liked me to walk with him in Hyde Park. As he and I strolled beneath the plane trees, passing Stanhope Gate, he was remembering the pretty ladies of the past; the trailing silks and muslins, the big leghorn hats with drooping brims and ostrich feathers, the cherry-coloured parasols, the fascinating groups of elegant ladies and gentlemen who gathered, and flirted, after saying their prayers in church.

But I, at that time, was not interested in the past. I was thinking about myself and my secret problems connected with sex. The ignorant girl in the black hat had never even heard about something which my father called 'church parade'.

'Those were the days,' said my father, in his elegance. The bowler hat was trying to communicate with the Bloomsbury black hat.

'Your mother and I were a good-looking couple. We always came here on Sunday mornings. We used to wait,' he said happily, 'to see Queen Alexandra. She and the King used to drive by, you see, in a barouche. They always did it just before lunch.'

We sat on the seat where my father used to sit with my pretty mother. We watched the stream of cars and the unknown badly-dressed people. Couples lay on the grass, tightly clamped in each other's arms. I could feel Cammy's loneliness, and he could feel mine.

'I really must divorce your mother,' said my father, 'in case she decides to settle in England.'

'Is divorce necessary?'

'We can't have a bigamist in the family.'

'Why not?'

'It isn't d-d-done,' said my father, with his charming stutter.

So my mother was divorced by my father in England (with me as a witness) long after my mother had divorced him in California. Bigamy was ended. We then had a letter from my mother to say that she had parted from her third husband and so another divorce was in the offing, and another marriage.

'Good God,' said my father, 'your mother really is a wonderful woman! As a matter of fact, she was very nearly a very g-g-good sort!'

At this remark we both laughed.

Cammy did not like my first book, *Another Man's Poison*, but he tried not to hurt my feelings.

'We all know these things happen, but why write about them?'

'Because it's important. Don't you see how important it is to tell the truth?'

'No, I don't,' said Cammy, 'I never have. I think I'll go back to Belgium for a bit, and save up some money.'

I was comforted by Grant Richards (my publisher) who kindly wrote: 'I do believe in this novel. It seems to me to be a story of unusual vitality. It has, surely, an electric quality.'

This was not the opinion of Rebecca West, who wrote in the *Daily Telegraph*: 'Miss Shute writes, not so much badly as barbarously, as if she had never read anything but a magazine, never seen any picture but a moving one, never heard any music except at restaurants. Yet she is full of talent.'

Here was a lucky review. As a result of it I received immediately an offer of ten guineas a week to write a series of articles for the *Sunday Graphic*. I was advertised as 'The Girl With The Barbarous Touch', which, of course, made everybody laugh, even my father.

And then something wonderful happened.

I was summoned by one of the newspaper tycoons, the great Lord Beaverbrook, and commanded by his secretary to visit him in his country home.

At Leatherhead Station I was met by Lord Beaverbrook's car. At the door I was greeted by a magnificent butler and was taken grandly and silently into a vast room of dazzling white, having a white carpet, a white sofa, and white armchairs. The only contrast in this early Hollywood room was a touch of scarlet. It only added to the startling whiteness, and I, when left by the grand butler, felt as miserable as a bat in a snowstorm. He came back at last. I was invited to the drawing-room, large and unpretentious and comfortable. At one end of it stood a small man who looked important, full of authority, as a schoolmaster might look. This was Lord Beaverbrook. The fat pupil who stood nervously in front of him, reading aloud something he had written for the *Sunday Express*, was Lord Castlerosse.

I sat down by the fire. Presently the reading stopped, both men turned round with a look of enquiry, and Lord Beaverbrook said gruffly,

'Who are you?'

'I am Nerina Shute.'

'Who is Nerina Shute?'

I explained that I had come by invitation because Lord Beaverbrook had read and enjoyed one of my articles in the *Sunday Graphic*. Lord Beaverbrook then remembered my name. Lord Castlerosse lit a long cigar, sank heavily into an enormous armchair, arranged his pink bald head on a cushion and turned his pink face to the ceiling, so that all I could see was the long cigar rising out of him like a chimney on a red roof. Then it started, a cross-examination. This was his way of discovering new writers for the *Daily Express*.

Lord Beaverbrook wanted to know what I thought of the National Government, why I disapproved of the Means Test, exactly what I thought about religion. Presently Lord Castlerosse woke up and said with a smile: 'I am a Catholic.' He closed his eyes and went back to sleep.

I remember that interview vividly. When I had been with him for about forty minutes, Lord Beaverbrook enquired if I was a virgin. Then he wanted to know what type of man appealed to me as a lover or husband. He gave me the impression that each question was important. When answered it was followed by another. He instantly wanted to know what I thought of modern painters, Epstein, modern literature, pacifism, nudism, symbolism, education, the English class system, and finally, more important than anything else, the new sex life in London.

I said: 'You've got to be true to yourself. What's right for you might be wrong for me. One man's meat is another man's poison. That's the title of my first book. *Another Man's Poison*.'

'What do you mean?'

I tried to explain about the difference between right and wrong. To give unhappiness by living in sin was wrong. To give happiness by living in sin was right. Needless to say I began to talk about homosexuality. Would Lord Beaverbrook be shocked if I told him that in theatrical circles, among people like Aimée Stuart and Miles Malleson, we believed that homosexuality was permissible and normal for those who liked it? He was not shocked. He was interested. The trouble, I said, was that men who preferred men, and women who preferred women, were made to feel guilty by the lucky ones who happened to be heterosexual.

'You must have the courage of your convictions,' I said bravely. 'You must always be true to yourself.' Lord Beaverbrook nodded.

I found myself telling him, as I told Charles, that homosexuality had probably been practised by Shakespeare, Caesar, Socrates, and Michelangelo. It was not a bad thing at all. But secretly I felt insecure. Where was the link between Shakespeare and Caesar and the little elegant boys who twittered in West End grills and lisped in Chelsea clubs? Was Shakespeare a pansy?

Lord Beaverbrook continued to listen. I told him him that Sappho and Christina of Sweden were quoted as lesbians by young women with closely cropped hair who strutted down the King's Road, Chelsea, dressed as men. (Secretly I detested these masculine women.) To be a lesbian, I told him, was not illegal, not condemned in the Bible, and since the Great War, as Lord Beaverbrook agreed, there were not enough Englishmen to go round. 'What was wrong,' I said, 'with being a lesbian?' Again he nodded. He had read *The Well of Loneliness* by Radclyffe Hall. So had I. At that time everyone I knew in London was reading it, or discussing it. I had never met Radclyffe Hall, and neither had he. But I had known several men who were proudly homosexual. So had he.

'Well,' said Lord Beaverbrook at last, 'I suppose you think you're a typical modern girl?'

I did think so. I was a mixture of innocence and sincerity and half-baked permissive ideas.

'Of course I'm a modern girl,' I said.

After three hours of questions, followed by long discussions, Lord Castlerosse woke up with a start.

'Are you still talking about religion?' he said.

After that the three of us had tea together by the fire. I began to feel almost at ease. Before I left him Lord Beaverbrook said, in one of his kindly moments, as a father might have said it: 'I believe, some day, you might be a great journalist.'

'Thank you,' I said.

He invited me to visit him the following week. 'Bring your riding breeches. We'll go for a ride, have lunch, and then we can talk things over.'

I remember the parting very clearly indeed. Lord Beaverbrook took my hand and I, to my surprise, found a piece of paper folded between my fingers. It turned out to be a five-pound note.

The money was useful. I spent it on a new pair of breeches, and wore them proudly, a week later, when I rode in Lord Beaverbrook's private park. This time he was not in a good mood. 'I only do this because it's good for my health,' he said. At lunch he was irritable. Afterwards, in a bored voice, he asked me to join the *Daily Express* as a reporter. Then, as I said good-bye, he paid me a flabbergasting compliment.

'You know,' he said, 'you're a beautiful woman.'

Seeing my look of astonishment, as though he had offered me ten thousand pounds, or proposed marriage, he added thoughtfully, 'But very few men will realize it.'

He spoiled the compliment, at the same time giving it more interest.

'Good luck to you on the *Daily Express*. One of these days you might be famous,' Lord Beaverbrook said.

In this he was quite mistaken. As a reporter, in Fleet Street, I was soon found to be useless, and was given the sack at the end of six months by my editor, Beverley Baxter. No one could understand what Nerina Shute was doing among brilliant young writers like Margaret Lane. Why had I been selected? Who had given me the job? The unlikely story about Lord Beaverbrook I kept to myself, only telling close friends. Of course Aimée Stuart was told, and so was Charles, with whom I now decided to live in sin.

It must have been the loneliness that made me join him in Liverpool. I belonged neither here nor there, not in Fleet Street among the writers, not in Elstree among the film stars, not in the old-fashioned finery of my father's well-born friends, not in California, in my mother's world of Hollywood actors and quick-changing husbands.

I have suffered from loneliness all my life. It has nothing to do with not being loved. I was then idolized by my father, who thought of me as something beautiful and brilliant (which I was not), by my mother, who thought of me as someone who understood her (which I did not), by Charles, who thought of me as an ignorant child with the power to reform and inspire him (which I never could). He very much wanted me to marry him. I loved him, knowing that marriage would be wrong. As I told him, it would lead to divorce. Yet I needed his help with my secret sex problems.

Let me quickly say that Charles was a man of quality, good,

bad, unpredictable. There were many sides to his character.
There was the Charles who loved me so tenderly, the other
Charles who lied, enjoyed a fight in a pub, hated authority,
belonged in his heart to the underworld. He might have been a
poet. He might have been a gangster. Again there was Charles,
the doctor, who had been struck off the medical register for
performing an illegal abortion. There was also the playboy, the
scrounger, the nature's non-gentleman.

For me his greatest charm was his gift of conversation, his
ability to understand, and explain, to exchange ideas. Charles
spoke several languages, French, German, Flemish, with a
smattering of Spanish and Italian, and this impressed the
ignorant Nerina who could only speak English.

Charles was such good company. Charles enjoyed talking.
Better still, Charles believed in asking questions and listening,
and learning to understand the thoughts of others, even a
modern girl, complicated and confused, like myself.

So when I joined him in Liverpool we talked about
international politics, about poetry, about English literature,
about psychology, about medical problems, about religion,
about philosophy, and finally about homosexuality. Charles
listened, lit a cigarette, considered my thoughts, and then began
to question me.

'Why do these sex problems upset you so much?'

'I don't know.'

'You seem to have a guilt complex. Why do you feel guilty?'

'Because in my heart I find women more attractive than men.'

'Have you ever been to bed with a woman?'

'Only once or twice. With the same girl.'

'Was it a success?'

'I don't really know. I felt it was wrong.'

'Did you like it better than going to bed with me?'

'In some ways it was more pleasing. But I like going to bed
with you now. I hated it at first.'

'I know you did. Sex is like chess,' said Charles. 'There's a lot
to learn.'

'Supposing I fall in love with another woman?'

To my amazement, he laughed. 'I can't take it seriously. What
does it matter?'

'Aren't you jealous?'

'Jealous of another woman? Of course not!' Charles laughed
again. 'Come on,' he said, 'let's have another game of chess.'

'All right,' I said, 'let's have another game of chess. By the
way, do you remember our honeymoon?'

At this we both laughed. About six months before, in the

summer of 1931, I had said to Charles, 'Let's do it, and get it over.'

'Don't be so unromantic!' retorted Charles. 'Why don't you think of me as a thrilling admirer with whom you are hopelessly in love?'

'I am deeply in love with you,' I said with annoyance, 'and I wish it was hopeless, but it isn't.'

Soon after that Charles had compelled himself to accept a temporary job as a courier for a tourist agency. To his surprise I agreed to join him on one of his trips abroad, travelling as his wife. It was quickly decided that Charles would spend two weeks in France, conducting Americans round cathedrals, and I would leave him after one romantic week-end.

'By the way,' said Charles, 'are you still a virgin?'

'Of course I am,' I said.

On a bright summer morning, with a new hat, a brave smile, and a Woolworth wedding-ring on my finger, I appeared in Coventry Street to find a crowded coach waiting outside the tourist agency, and Charles, in his old grey hat, talking in a professional way to an agitated American woman who said she was sick at her stomach and would certainly vomit unless she sat in the best front seat.

Charles whispered: 'How can I show cathedrals to a woman like her?'

'It isn't cathedrals I'm worried about, it's the honeymoon,' said I.

Unfortunately the coach was very late in arriving at the little hotel in Amiens, by which time Charles and Nerina were both feeling tired and cross. In a double bedroom with a worrying wallpaper Nerina went through the usual routine of washing, powdering, and combing, thankful that Charles was still downstairs passionately arguing in French with the hotel manager, who said the coach party was too late for dinner. The whole adventure seemed sordid and horrible.

Later that night I remember saying to Charles: 'For physical pleasure I would rather go to the dentist!'

I remember thinking that a love affair was not what it was cracked up to be, not by a long chalk. I had wanted to feel inspiration. I had hoped for a sense of beauty. One day, perhaps, I would be able to understand the deep, turbulent happiness of D. H. Lawrence lovers in disagreeable bedrooms, and also the sweet exotic tortures enjoyed by Huxley lovers in extremely swagger bedrooms, but meanwhile the whole thing was a grave disappointment. Charles tried to comfort me. He said, amongst other things, that the heritage of woman was pain.

'You see,' said Charles, when he saw my distress, 'sex is like

music. You have to get used to it, and study it, and try to
understand the difficult bits.'

'Do you think I shall learn to like it?'

'Of course you will. It isn't nearly as awful as you think.'

In the thirties, in London, young people despised convention
as they do today. For this reason it was a great relief to stop
being a virgin, because virgins were not acceptable to Aldous
Huxley and D. H. Lawrence and Richard Aldington and Miles
Malleson, still my favourite authors.

All the same, we behaved like hypocrites. In Liverpool,
in March 1932, I bought myself another Woolworth wedding-
ring. Charles, poor Charles, had accepted a job as a commercial
traveller, hating it, doing it, he said, to prove his love. I
pretended to be his wife. If it became known that he and I were
living in sin, Charles would lose his job! Or so we believed.

I remember thinking it was bad luck to be cast in the role of
housewife. What had I done to deserve it? My black hat was
gone. So was my self-respect. Charles kindly said he would
teach me to cook. I would soon overcome my hatred for the
kitchen as well as my dislike for sex. Adding insult to injury my
so-called marriage was made public. A notice in the *Daily
Telegraph* was followed by a wedding present from my generous
aunt in Eaton Square, my mother's sister. My father's sister had
told the press, my mother's sister had sent the present, and
now, as Charles said, I had brought respectability upon myself.

As usual we both laughed. He and I had no roots. We were
social misfits. We were escapists.

'As for me, I'm a rolling stone,' Charles used to say.

'I don't know *what* I am,' said Nerina, 'I'm still trying to find
out.'

'Why don't you solve your problems by getting married? Let
me make you an honest woman.'

'It might not work. Let's just have a trial marriage,' I said.

The first few weeks in Liverpool were surprisingly contented.
The warm weather came in April and May. I felt less like a
housewife as we sat blissfully in the sunlight, on a small
balcony, bronzed by the sun, reading aloud, laughing, sharing
the stories of O. Henry. Charles had found us a very nice flat
overlooking Sefton Park. He spent most of his time talking and
reading and playing chess with Nerina. He named me his
concubine. There was, he said, Nerina's education to be
considered. He would teach his concubine about poetry and
politics as well as about sex.

At this time a fascist movement in Germany, headed by a man
called Hitler, was threatening to repudiate the Versailles Treaty.

'Every country in Europe is broke,' said Charles. 'Nobody wants to buy goods from anybody else and so now we have an international crisis.'

'What about Germany? If Germany can't sell her goods, how can she pay reparations?'

'Exactly,' said Charles.

Germany's payments were now reduced, but Charles continued to talk in an angry voice about the Versailles Treaty. Germany would rearm because the young Germans would be filled with a sense of shame and indignation. War was coming. War was bound to come.

We had the same feeling of insecurity from which young people are suffering today. Where was the purpose in life?

Charles taught me to play chess (at which I was quickly able to beat him) and tried to explain the charms and changes of Rupert Brooke, the icy fascination of T. S. Eliot. Poetry gave us both a small sense of purpose. Eliot's manner, but not his religious feeling, was copied by the new poets. We told ourselves that we belonged to a godless generation. Instead of God we were offered communism by poets like Auden, Day Lewis, and Spender. But Charles was not a communist. If anything he was a romantic. The poet he taught me to love most was Yeats.

In those halcyon days of mental happiness, and finally physical happiness, my love for Charles became deeply dependent and in many ways very exciting. At last I was fulfilled. At last I felt like other normal women who loved their husbands with no desire to conceal or deceive or seek tenderness from female companionship. Thank goodness I was not a lesbian. This was a wonderful feeling. I could tell Charles all my thoughts, all my temptations, all my secrets, with no sense of shame, or reserve, or regret, no deception or discrimination of any kind.

'Are you happy?' said Charles.

'Very happy.'

'No sense of guilt?'

'None at all,' I said, 'when I'm with you.'

'Are you still worried in case you're a lesbian?'

'Well, yes, a little bit worried. Do you think I'm normal, or not?'

'Of course you're normal.'

'I know it's not wrong, and I like lesbians, but I don't want to be one myself.'

'There's no need to worry,' said Charles. 'Forget it.'

'I can't help feeling attracted by women. Are you sure you don't mind?'

Charles laughed. 'How can I take it seriously?'

He encouraged me to spend the afternoon in bed with a

girlfriend while he, Charles, went out with friends. When he
returned we both laughed about it. There was certainly no need
to feel guilty. Life was a joke and sex was a joke. Even love was a
glorious, happy, hilarious joke.

In Liverpool, with Charles, as I now understand it, there was a
great deal of laughter but also there was a great deal of drinking
and quarrelling. When I saw Noel Coward's comedy, *Private
Lives*, I recognized myself and Charles. We behaved like
children. We fell on the floor, fighting, and ended up making
love and laughing. There were many lovers like ourselves. We
lived wildly, as if each day might be the last. It seemed right
because I loved Charles, and he, like my mother, was an
escapist. That was why it hurt so much when my trial marriage
came to an end.

I remember so well how it all happened. After a game of
chess, and a few drinks with some friends, Charles said he
would drive them back to their various homes.

'I won't be long. Don't go to sleep,' he said.

When at last he returned, I created a scene because he was
late and drunk. I behaved exactly as my mother would have
done.

'Have you gone mad? Thank God we're not married,' said
Charles.

After that our trial marriage was finished. Wondering what I
had done, not understanding Charles, the escapist, nor why the
happiness and joy had mysteriously left us, like the end of a
song, I began to see, after weeks of loneliness, that I had lost my
lover.

'I must be able to feel free. I've always been *free*,' said Charles.

'Why?'

'Because I'm a nature's non-gentleman. That's why.'

He said it half in anger, half in anguish, without amusement,
deprived of something, frightened of me and afraid of himself.
To drink with his Liverpool friends he now left me alone. To
punish me he now spent week-ends in London. I paced up and
down the sitting-room, caged in Liverpool, longing for London.
The flat was outside the town and at night there was nothing to
do. Where was Charles?

At the end of six months, still believing that no other man
could ever take his place, I packed my bags and returned to
London to look for a job. (I always return to London.) Charles
drove me to the station, helped me to arrange my possessions in
a third-class carriage, stood foolishly on the platform, his old
grey hat between me and his pale blue eyes. I knew that he
wanted to cry. Instead he made jokes.

'Never mind, Nerina. Love is only sublimated sex, isn't it?'

As the train moved away from the platform, I saw Charles lift his hat, waving good-bye, smiling, and I looked with a pang of jealous love at his wild untidy hair, his thin disappointed face. Then I sat down to read a newspaper, trying not to remember his expression of sadness. Presently I got up and threw the Woolworth wedding-ring out of the window. I could always buy another. In London, of course, I did. It was not a happy time. I now had only £20 in the bank. I belonged to no one, not even to Charles.

3   Love

Nothing had changed during my absence.

Young people continued to gather in Aimée Stuart's flat in Carlton House Terrace. Edgar Middleton, author of a famous play called *Potipher's Wife*, often came with Yvonde, the famous photographer (his wife). I frequently met Kay Hammond there, a brilliant comedy actress who later married John Clements, one of my favourite actors. Everyone knew that remarks made in Aimée's kitchen or sitting-room might later be used in a light-hearted comedy written by Aimée and Phillip (her husband).

For example, the characters on the stage might greet one another by saying, as we sometimes did, 'Hello, darling, how's your sex life?' or better still, 'Hello, darling, are you married, or have you turned into a lesbian?'

These were good openings to a bright conversation. Remarks like these belonged to the thirties. As I tried to explain to my father and mother, we moderns were against hypocrisy. We believed in honesty. No doubt the older generation enjoyed sex, as we did, but they liked feeling guilty about it. Guilt and secrecy increased their pleasure.

But there was no guilt or secrecy in Aimée's flat.

At Carlton House Terrace the bathroom and lavatory faced the front door. A visitor might enter the flat and immediately start a conversation with the person sitting on the lavatory. Of course these things were done with laughter. The white-haired Aimée brought her husband to look at me in the bath. It was perfectly natural. I might have been a puppy, or a baby, or a young seal.

In Aimée's little world, a new world which was throbbing away at the heart of London, we continued to talk endlessly about free love and homosexuality as they talked in my father's world about politics and cricket and the servant problem.

I remember that wonderful story about Tallulah Bankhead. Tallulah, with her deep voice, silky blond hair, eyes like beautiful poached eggs, was like no one else on the stage. Most of her fans were girls. Every night they queued at the stage door, clamouring for autographs. But men liked her too. According to the story, a married man fell in love with this witty and glamorous beauty. At the end of a passionate evening he suddenly said: 'Tallulah, I want you for my wife.'

And Tallulah replied: 'Fine, darling, bring her along.'

Among my normal friends were two very pretty young women who married homosexuals. How could I explain such things to my father, or even my mother? My parents spoke a different language.

When I returned to London in November 1933 I managed to find a bed-sitting-room in Elgin Crescent for the sum of 27s. 6d. a week, including breakfast of tea and toast and marmalade. It was fitted with a gas fire, a gas-ring for the kettle, and a shilling in the slot machine which always hungered for another one. The room had a large window overlooking the chestnut trees, the lilac bush and the fresh green of a London lawn, not to mention the two fat pigeons I grew to love.

I had, of course, only £20 in the bank, but I reckoned I could live on this for at least six weeks, and then, of course, I would find a job in Fleet Street.

Encouraging letters came from Charles. He was missing his concubine very much. One of these days he would join me in London because Liverpool without Nerina was boring and hateful.

I discovered that six months in Liverpool had added the final shabbiness to my small collection of cheap sweaters and skirts. This was a nuisance. I walked up and down Fleet Street with a heavy heart, wearing my black hat, enquiring for jobs, visiting the offices of the *Daily Express* and the *Sunday Graphic*, each day feeling unwanted.

Returning one evening from one of these bad interviews in Fleet Street I was met by my landlady on the doorstep.

'Cheer up,' she said kindly, 'there's a letter from Liverpool waiting on your table.'

I remember running upstairs, two at a time, and there on the table was a great bulky envelope addressed in the beautiful copperplate writing of Charles. I lit the gas fire. I sat in the shabby chair, holding the letter, until at last the fire, which needed another shilling, went out with a pop. I found a shilling, lit the fire, and later it went out for the second time, but still I was reading his letter, the long bits about his frustration, his loneliness, his disappointment, and the finishing bit, with tears running down my face, which said that our trial marriage was a great mistake. Charles never wanted to see me again. It was like a physical blow.

This was a sad period in my life.

I managed to find enough work as a freelance journalist to pay for food and rent and a few more sweaters and skirts but no one in Fleet Street would give me a permanent job. Without Charles I was lonely. I missed the long conversations. What would Charles say about Hitler? What would Charles say about all these London lesbians I was now meeting at parties?

Hitler was clearly a dirty dog but nobody took him seriously. He was a little house painter with a funny moustache. Even the Reichstag fire was greeted with indifference. Hitler blamed the Communists and the Communists blamed Hitler for the fire. What nonsense! Just imagine the Prime Minister of England ordering a British General to burn down the Houses of Parliament! Could anything be more absurd?

I remember saying to a Fleet Street journalist, 'Do you think the Nazis really did it?'

'Of course they did, and a good thing too. It might save all Europe from Communism,' I was told.

At the time when these things were happening in Europe I applied to the editor of the *Sunday Referee* for the job of film critic. Instead of spinning a long tale to explain my poverty and the difficulty of finding a job after many months away from Fleet Street I told him the truth, including the unhappy story of Liverpool.

'You see,' I ended, 'I'm down and out, but I used to be a damned good journalist. Would you like to see my press cuttings?'

'I've read your film stuff,' said Mark Goulden, the editor, 'and I'll take a chance on giving you a job.'

'What about salary?'

'Only five pounds a week but you're lucky to get the job.'

'Yes,' I said, 'that's only too true.'

Five pounds a week was less than I had earned at the age of nineteen. At the age of twenty-five I felt grossly underpaid and yet, as compensation, I found myself drinking cocktails at noon, champagne at lunch-time, brandy after dinner. From exquisite supper parties at the Savoy Grill I returned in a taxi to my bed-sitting-room, where I hunted anxiously for a shilling to drop in the gas meter. It was a strange life. Never mind. I was the film critic for a well-known Sunday newspaper. At 10 a.m. or 10.30 a.m. I joined the other critics at the Tivoli Cinema or the Carlton, shabbily dressed, wearing my black hat. If it was a comedy the critics seldom laughed. If it was a tragedy they sometimes laughed a good deal.

I believe I was the youngest film critic in Fleet Street.

One of my colleagues, a little older than myself, was a sad young poet called John Betjeman. One afternoon, looking untidy and badly dressed, with a broad smile on his face, as though laughing at a secret joke, he arrived in a great hurry at the Carlton or the Tivoli Cinema (I forget which) for a private showing of a very important new film from Hollywood. I greeted him with pleasure at the entrance.

'I am supposed to be meeting my wife,' said John, 'but of course she's late. What shall I do?'

'I think you'd better go in by yourself.'

John had recently been engaged as film critic by the *Evening Standard* which the rest of us considered rather strange. How could a highbrow poet become a lowbrow film critic?

'Look here,' said John, 'you must help me by meeting my wife and bringing her inside. Do you think you can find me in the dark? I shall be in the Dress Circle.'

'Yes, yes, but how can I recognize your wife?'

'She's very ugly!' said John, with his broad smile.

'Lots of people are very ugly. How can I tell which one is your wife?'.

'I know what to do,' said John. 'I'll draw you a picture of my wife.'

He then drew a quick sketch of an ugly lady with a big nose on the back of an envelope.

'You can't mistake her,' said John, as he left me to join the other critics. 'Thank you so much, Nerina.'

'Not at all,' I said, clutching the envelope. 'See you later.'

Soon after that poor John was fired by the *Evening Standard* for refusing to meet a film star at Southampton. 'I don't like film stars and I don't like Southampton,' said John.

In the evening, as likely as not, I would find myself dining at the Savoy Grill, in company with a film star, or a famous producer like Herbert Wilcox, drinking champagne until midnight. It was not until I found myself back again in my threadbare sitting-room, no longer under the spell of these magic evenings, the perfume of wines, the delicate glasses full of colours, the strange loud gaiety paid for by Hollywood, that my longing for Charles returned. Where, oh where, was Charles?

And then, quite suddenly, with no warning of any kind, he appeared in my sitting-room. 'I've come back,' said Charles briefly.

'But why?'

'Because I couldn't bear it any longer without you.'

Charles continued to visit me whenever he could find the money for a week-end of pub-crawling and quarrelling in London. During that time we drank quantities of beer, and sherry, and gin. During that time my mother arrived from California and did her best to separate me from my difficult lover because he was not, as most people thought, my husband. I remember her indignation when she found out the truth.

'Do you mean to say that your father encouraged you to live in adultery?' said my mother. Her hair was now silvery grey and her head was bound with a blue ribbon to match her eyes.

'Nowadays people don't live in adultery, they live in friendship.'

'It's the same thing. I can't understand why your father allowed you to do this.'

'He couldn't stop me. Any more than he could stop you.'

'But I never lived in adultery – or in friendship, as you call it. I've made a point of marrying my admirers.'

'You can't be expected to understand. You come from a different generation.'

'I don't see what difference that makes.'

'You break the conventions in your way. I break them in mine. But we both break them,' I said with affection, 'because you and I are alike.'

'I do what I believe to be right.'

'So do I.'

'I make mistakes,' my mother admitted, giving me a smile, 'but I don't care in the least what other people say. That's where I'm different from your father. I believe we should have the courage of our convictions.'

'So do I.'

'Then why on earth don't you have the courage to marry your lover?'

'It's asking for trouble to marry a man you hardly know. It's like buying a car without driving it first. No one in their senses would do that.'

'But a man is not a car.'

'The principle is the same. If you buy the wrong car, or marry the wrong man, it's your own fault.'

'I really can't agree. I think a woman should come to her marriage pure in heart.' My mother gave me another smile. 'If the marriage is a failure she should *immediately* get a divorce and marry someone else.'

'But that might go on forever. Now you,' I unkindly pointed out, 'have had four husbands at the age of fifty-four.'

'I see no harm in that.'

'Neither do I, but I don't want to do it myself. And I'm glad I'm not married to Charles. I still love him but I don't at all want to marry him.'

'What an extraordinary girl you are! How you've changed!'

'Not really. It's just that the world has changed. You can't help being a romantic, and I can't help being a realist.'

'I hope,' said my mother, more in sorrow than in anger, 'that you're not proposing to live in friendship with every man who takes your fancy.'

'Certainly not. Only if it seems a sensible idea.'

'How can you be so prosaic? Have you no sense of romance, or beauty, or adventure?'

'You don't seem to realize how different things are. London has changed. England has changed. The world I live in is a working world. How can I help being prosaic?'

'Yes, I see what you mean.'

We smiled at one another.

'It must have been a shock when I told you my marriage was only a trial marriage. Thank you,' I said, 'for taking it so well.'

These things happened long ago, in the early thirties, but the memory is vivid. I can still see my pleasant bedroom, furnished by my mother, who had lived in the flat herself, then grew tired of it, then suddenly returned to her fourth husband in California, leaving her London home to me.

This was a big room with a green carpet and a big bed. I also had a small sitting-room crowded with pretty things; ornaments, pictures, a chintzy sofa with a big armchair to match, all provided by my mother. Beyond the sitting-room was a tiny kitchen, side by side with a tiny bathroom, then the front door and the staircase, old-fashioned and narrow.

Every morning I waited to see the two fat pigeons through my bedroom window. They twisted and turned on the branch of a chestnut tree in the gardens of Elgin Crescent, courting one another, the male bird puffing out his chest to the size of a huge powder-puff, bowing his silvery head many times, the female bird turning her tail in silvery surrender. If they failed to appear because it was raining I felt disappointed. Somehow the presence of those two pigeons was necessary to relieve my loneliness. Like my mother, and like Charles, they came and went.

Just before she departed, my mother persuaded Cammy to leave Belgium in order to rebuke his obstinate daughter. They wrote one another long letters. Cammy soon arrived and I was invited to dine with him at a small hotel in Old Quebec Street, near Marble Arch.

When the meal was over, Cammy said: 'I gather you've been quarrelling with your mother.' He filled my glass with port. 'What's the trouble, old girl?'

'I don't know. I think she wants me to marry my lovers.'

'Why?' enquired Cammy, screwing in his eyeglass.

'That's what she does herself.'

'Yes, I know she does, but you can't keep on getting married time after time. It doesn't do,' said Cammy.

'That's what I think myself. Five lovers and one husband is better than six husbands. Why have all those divorces?'

'On the other hand, dear,' said my father, defending my mother, 'she has only had four husbands so far. It's natural that she should be anxious about you.'

'I suppose it is.'

'Have you,' said my father delicately, 'a lover at present?'

'No, but I'm looking round. I wish I could forget about Charles.'

'In my young days,' said Cammy, 'it used to be thought that a man never married his mistress.'

'That's what my mother says.'

'I believe she's right.'

'You're as old-fashioned as she is. In these days,' I told him impatiently, 'a man *prefers* to marry his mistress. Then, don't you see, he knows what he's got.'

'Well,' said Cammy sadly, 'I suppose this is progress.'

After another glass of port, feeling more and more friendly, I made a confession. 'Sometimes I don't know what to think because attitudes keep changing. How can you tell the difference between good and evil when everyone says something different?'

'It's very simple, old girl, just ask yourself if you've done any harm. If you haven't, you're not evil.'

By this I felt strangely comforted.

'Have another port, old girl.'

My nice father belonged in a different world. He belonged in those elegant London houses in garden squares, served by parlour-maids and house-maids, drinking port after dinner by candlelight, visiting the opera sometimes, appearing at Ascot and Lord's, attending the theatre in full evening-dress, being seen with pleasant people at the Royal Academy. It still existed, even in the thirties, a small world of rules and ritual. London was still dominated by it. The older generation was still in charge.

I missed my mother's laughter. I thought about her as I lay in bed, watching the pigeons making love in the chestnut tree. I missed Cammy, away in Belgium, saving his money. Above all I missed Charles. My lover had been right about Hitler. War was on the way. Everything was happening as Charles had predicted.

In this mood, lonely and heartsick, thinking about my sex problems, I went to bed early one night and lay in the darkness with a throbbing headache, unable to sleep. The telephone rang. A woman's voice said: 'May I come round, please? I want to talk to you, Nerina.'

'What is it about?'

'I've fallen in love with you. May I come round, please?'

This was the beginning of a long love affair and a faithful friendship. I shall call her Josephine, which was not her real name. She arrived that night in evening-dress, having been to a smart little party with a group of people who loved dancing, as she did, and I noticed for the first time that she was slim and extremely elegant.

Where had we met?

In her hand she carried a single flower, a tall red rose, and this she presented to me with a laugh.

'I fell in love with your photograph,' she said. 'I've been in love with you for quite a long time.'

'Where did you see the photograph?'

'Oh, on somebody's dressing-table.'

'A woman's dressing-table?'

'Yes.'

Since the separation from Charles I had allowed myself to be consoled by a woman I had met at one of those gay homosexual parties when not being entertained at the Ivy or the Savoy Grill by my rich film friends. The experiment was disappointing and better forgotten. Homosexuals were still called 'perverts' by the older generation, even by my father, and by this I still felt hurt and diminished. I wanted to escape from passionate friendships.

But Josephine was not at all like the others. To begin with, Josephine was deeply religious, a Catholic, and I presently discovered that she went to mass for pleasure, once a week, as other people went to the cinema. She lived with her mother, to whom she was devoted. She had numerous quite wealthy friends, as smart and elegant as herself, some normal, some homosexual, but for private reasons she had never been to bed with a man.

'I like men very much but not for sex.'

'Could you fall in love with a man?'

'I don't think so.'

'Why not?'

'Because sex with a man would be disgusting.'

Josephine now came frequently to my little flat, quite often at night, bringing me a single rose, or an orchid, sitting or kneeling beside my bed when I was feeling tired, or depressed, or half-asleep, telling me that she loved me, caressing me, fingering my hair. I began to enjoy these romantic visits. After a while, surreptitiously, a long, slender, manicured hand found its way beneath the bedclothes. An exciting new happiness came to us both.

Josephine told me that she had read my book, *Another Man's Poison*, because it was supposed to be shocking.

'Were you shocked?'

'Of course not.'

'Did you like the bit about lesbians and free love and all that?'

'I loved it. You only said what I have always believed to be true.'

This endeared her to me at once. Had I found a soul mate? A fellow escapist? A female Charles? No, certainly not, and yet Josephine, my passionate friend, was good and kind and gentle and loving and utterly enslaved by her growing devotion to me.

I remember explaining to Josephine my reasons for writing *Another Man's Poison*. It was partly to justify free love and partly to justify my much-married mother. I continued to love my mother. She was not, I said, a wicked woman, any more than Josephine was wicked. All three of us were courageous people with a sense of romance and idealism. All of us, in different ways, tried to do what was right and good and brave.

'Do you see what I mean? What is right for you can easily be wrong for me. We must *not* try to change one another.'

'Is it wrong to be a lesbian?'

'Of course it isn't wrong,' I said. 'No more wrong to be a female homosexual than a male homosexual, or a pansy, or a queen, or a queer, like Cecil Beaton and Noel Coward and all the others.'

'But they put men in gaol for doing it.'

'I know, I know, but it isn't wrong from a moral point of view. Thank goodness they don't put lesbians in gaol.'

'There's nothing in the Bible against lesbians,' said Josephine.

'Of course there isn't. How dare they call women 'perverts' just because they happen to love one another?'

I remember these youthful conversations very well. Today there is no need to be indignant. The world has changed. The practice of homosexuality between consenting adults is no longer against the law. And yet, and yet, I happen to know an attractive young woman, aged about thirty-five, who is now suffering from much the same problems, feeling guilty, not wishing to be a lesbian, unable to change, unable to find a suitable partner. *'Plus ça change, plus c'est la même chose.'*

Anyway, I still have a copy of my first novel, considered so shocking. An outrageous book for a girl to write, let alone a lady, said my father's friends. Today it seems quite a babyish book, pathetically innocent and totally immature.

The truth is that when I was young I hated to be seen as a member of the homosexual world. I was haunted by the word 'pervert'. Where was Charles? How could I explain my need for Charles to Josephine, or my need for Josephine to Charles?

In this mood, lonely and heartsick, I went with Aimée to a Bloomsbury party, and there I found someone whose lively conversation reminded me of Charles.

'Be nice to him, darling. He's a poppet,' said Aimée.

I can see my dear Aimée, the motherly bohemian, with her smooth white hair fitting her head like a cap, her long earrings, her sympathetic face. She wanted me to find another Charles. This one was a Russian. He was wearing a white linen embroidered smock with a high neck. He looked clean and elegant and distinguished. The others by comparison looked scruffy and arty, untidy women with fringes and beads, untidy men with beards and pot-bellies.

Said Aimée to me: 'He's attractive. I do so wonder if he's bedworthy. What do you think?'

The Russian turned out to be very entertaining. He said he had not quite recovered from a love affair with Elsa Lanchester (before she married Charles Laughton). His family had escaped from Russia at the time of the revolution. And yet, he said, he felt a deep admiration for the Soviet government, his heart was in Russia, his greatest desire was to return to the country of his birth. He suddenly said, as Charles might have done, 'What is your name? Will you come with me to Moscow?'

Thinking of Charles, I smiled at the Russian.

'As a London film critic you ought to visit Moscow,' he said. 'Don't you know that the best films are made in Russia?'

Thinking of Charles, I nodded my head. 'All right,' I said, 'I'll go.'

No one was more surprised by this decision than the Russian himself. Aimée was delighted. 'What you need,' she said, 'is a love affair with a nice man.' She began immediately to insist on thick woollen underclothes and snow-boots and flea powder. I must buy them at once. If not, she would buy them for me herself. Everyone knew that Russia was full of fleas and fearfully cold.

My new friend, Josephine, was far from pleased.

'Must you really do this, Nerina?'

'I'm sorry but I really must. It's a wonderful opportunity to see what's happening in Russia.'

'Have you fallen in love with this man?'

'No, of course not,' I said.

'Please be careful. Please come back soon. I love you so much.'

In those days Russia was not a country to be visited for pleasure by an English girl. I was advised to stay at home. I remember speaking to my father's friend, Leslie Davies (mother of Leslie Mitchell, who later became so famous on films and television), who seriously said: 'Don't go, Nerina. You'll only be raped! Your father will be furious!' I laughed at her fears. To annoy her I said: 'Don't you know the old Chinese proverb?'

'What proverb?'

'When rape appears inevitable, relax and enjoy it.'

On a cold morning in January, muffled up in a borrowed coat, loaded with flea killer, soap and disinfectant (provided by Aimée) I set out for Berlin, the meeting place arranged by my Bloomsbury Russian while wearing his high-necked linen smock. As the train moved out of the station I opened a new book about Soviet Russia, glanced at the young Frenchman on the opposite seat, then closed the book and stared into space. Where was Charles? Why was I going to Russia without Charles?

The Frenchman said: 'Will you have a cigarette?'

'Thank you, I will.'

Lately, in a fit of irritation, I had told the hairdresser to cut my hair quite short. The style was then called an 'Eton crop'. It was boyish, not in the least attractive, and I knew, without much caring, that I now looked hard and cold and untouchable. There was no Charles to please, no reason to bother with my appearance (except Josephine, who thought I was beautiful even with an Eton crop).

'Are you travelling far?' enquired the Frenchman.

I wondered why he was interested. 'Moscow,' I said.

'Moscow? They tell me Russia is a dangerous country. Why are you going to Moscow, mademoiselle?'

Because he was so charming, and talked with a burning vitality all the way to Dover about his need for an English girl as well as a French girl, I said I would write to him. (Afterwards I lost his address.)

It was a bitterly cold day. The sea was rough. Having parted from the Frenchman at Dover I now had a chance to walk by myself on deck, feeling the wind ripping through my short hair, nearly tearing it off my head. The weather was so wild and furious that most of the passengers had disappeared from sight. To my surprise I was joined presently by an elegant gentleman with a waxed moustache. He was wearing a black London hat and carried a walking stick which he twirled gracefully.

'Do you feel sick, mademoiselle?'

'Of course not.'

'What a pity. I would like to look after you,' he said pleasantly.

It was odd, I thought, that in one day two Frenchmen should wish to look after an unattractive English girl who could obviously look after herself. I found myself alone with him on the Ostend platform. I was not at all pleased when told by the porter that the Berlin train would not leave Ostend for two hours. Furthermore, he said, the train could not possibly be lighted until the time of departure.

'Never mind,' said my elegant friend, 'we will sit in the dark, mademoiselle. There is nothing else to do.'

'How boring!' I said.

To sit in the dark with a Frenchman could never be boring. It turned out to be violent exercise. While fighting for my honour I forgot about Charles. I remember feeling quite desperate.

'Won't you please stop while I'm talking?' I said.

'I can't stop,' he replied.

At long last the carriages were lighted up and other passengers began to enter the Berlin train. By this time I was worn out, crumpled, indignant. My elegant friend was calm and smiling. When the lights were on, as naturally as day follows night, he engaged me in a formal conversation about politics and art.

Presently he said, 'Are you tired, mademoiselle?'

'Very tired indeed.'

He told me to lie full length on the wooden third-class seat. Very kindly he made me comfortable with a folded coat under my head, then ordered me, in a fatherly voice, to go to sleep. I did so at once. A few hours later I woke up with a jerk to find the train had stopped in a station, strangers were entering the carriage, and the Frenchman was in need of his coat.

'Good-bye, mademoiselle. Thank you for a pleasant evening.'

'Thank you for looking after me,' I said.

Of course I never saw him again. The following day, when the train arrived in Berlin, I suffered youthfully. Where was my Russian? Supposing he behaved like the elegant French one? How was I to cope with all these determined foreigners? At last I saw him wearing his tall fur hat, making his way to my carriage, and he seemed in very high spirits. He had spent Christmas with friends. When he had explained about his holiday in Moscow, about the English girl going to travel with him, his friends were astonished.

'Why?'

'Because English girls are supposed to be old-fashioned.'

At this point I decided to tell him what had happened on the dark train, and to make it clear that I objected strongly, whether he considered it old-fashioned or not. 'You must have given the Frenchman a bad impression,' said my Russian with a laugh.

'Well,' I said, in a tone of asperity, 'I hope nobody else gets a bad impression.'

I returned to my thoughts about Charles. In my present mood it was impossible to think about anyone else. At Warsaw, in a Russian train, we were given sleeping-bags. The arrangements for passengers were very hygienic and no flea powder was necessary. In each compartment were four wooden bunks. No curtains were provided because men and women were not expected to wish for privacy. I was the only woman in the carriage, possibly in the train, and yet no one had the slightest desire to rape me, as prophesied in London. How Charles would have laughed!

I longed for Charles to be with me in the New Moscow Hotel. Here I was given a luxury bedroom with central heating and a private bathroom. It was tastefully furnished, with a writing-desk, even a vase of flowers, but no wardrobe, no chest of drawers. Hoping to find a hook on the back of a door, I walked into the bathroom. There was no hook. The walls were charmingly tiled in pale green but one of them had collapsed on the floor, and on top of a huge pile of bricks and rubble I noticed three large beetles. In addition to beetles I had a washing problem. The cold tap, most alarmingly, gave out a sudden volcanic stream of scalding water, and the same thing happened when I turned on the hot tap. In those days, in the New Moscow Hotel, a visitor was expected to fill the bath, or wash-basin, and then wait for fifteen minutes for the water to cool. After all, there was no hurry!

As the days passed I continued to think about Charles. To fall in love with my Russian friend was out of the question. I had come to Russia because I was charmed by the man and how I was charmed by Russia and bored by the man. To be quite honest I went to bed with him once. Afterwards I felt miserable. Where was Charles?

The news went round that a London journalist was staying in the New Moscow Hotel. I soon had numerous friends. They arrived every day at 4 p.m., smiling broadly, to eat an enormous meal of soup, meat, vegetables and soggy pudding. They ate like wolves. Most of them had been working at university, or in factories, or swinging a pick and shovel to help build the Moscow Underground.

In Moscow money meant nothing. I was told that nobody wanted fame or reward. There was not even the hope of some vague heavenly happening in another existence, because they despised religion. And yet they were more like believers than pagans. They were inspired. I listened in wonder to their glorious talk of struggle and sacrifice and hunger. I felt inspired too.

One evening I met a girl called Tania Tretiakov, daughter of a well-known dramatist. She had just passed a vital exam. She announced with pride that in five years' time she would be a qualified aviation constructor. Lucky Tania! What could be more desirable?

Tania believed in what she called 'factual marriage'. In Russia, said Tania, you had only to cohabit with a man for a certain period of time and the union automatically became legal. I told her about Charles. In Russia, she said, I would be forced to pay Charles alimony because I had left him!

Then I heard about Vera Inber. She had written a book called *The Place in the Sun*, an autobiography, printed in several languages but not in English.

My guide, who spoke perfect English, said to me: 'She is one of our leading writers. I would like you to meet her.'

But the interview went badly. In her little home, when I sat down with her to talk, glancing quickly at a toothbrush hooked on the wall, noticing a hair-brush, a sponge, a hand mirror, all so neatly arranged by the owner, I thought of my own home in Elgin Crescent, a palace compared with hers.

I said to my guide, who repeated it in Russian: 'I feel perfectly certain that religion in a new form will come back to Russia. It will take about fifty years.'

Vera Inber looked furious. This was a stupid and churlish thing to say. It was like announcing to a London hostess that the United Kingdom would soon be overrun by black magic.

Later I offended all my Russians by writing about them in the *Sunday Referee*. 'They have been told,' I wrote, 'that religion is bad for them, just as the early Victorians were told that sex was bad for them. So they believe it.'

In London, when the holiday was over, I found Josephine waiting for me with love in her eyes. She was giving me the tenderness my mother had given me as a child.

'Were you faithful to me?'

'In my fashion,' I said.

I was now a person of special interest. I was invited by *Gaumont British News* to appear in a five-minute news film to speak about the women of Russia. A few days later, on a platform, I was talking to a large audience of women, telling them, among other things, about Tania and Vera Inber.

By my friends I was not taken seriously. 'What nonsense you talk about Russia! Of course you only saw what the Russians wanted you to see!'

But Josephine said: 'I think you're wonderful!'

I was certain that she loved me. At that time I needed the love of another woman very much indeed.

4 Marriage

I worked for three years as film critic for the *Sunday Referee*, and then I was sacked by the editor, reluctantly, because he liked me, and I was good at my job. (I am coming to that later.) For three years the fabulous parties continued, and the drinks, and the bright lights, and the razzle-dazzle of love and sex which came to us like a breath of stale air from Hollywood and Elstree. I visited Russia for the second time. I read and talked about Hitler. I made friends with Aleister Crowley, the black magic expert, and had a meeting with H. G. Wells.

These two men were considered important and interesting. They were adored, hated, admired, feared, envied; so different, so attractive to women, each one part and parcel of the sex-obsessed thirties I am trying to describe and recall. One or the other was constantly in the news. I liked them both. But much more important and interesting was my long friendship and love affair with Josephine.

It lasted until my marriage with James Wentworth Day. Even after that Josephine was faithful and adoring. For several years I was given a sense of stability and permanence by her love.

What is more she took me in hand, the untidy Nerina, persuading me to dress with care, as she did, in beautiful tailor-made suits, worn with silk shirts, and nearly always a gardenia, or a carnation, in the button-hole. We both looked immaculate and extremely smart. Josephine had discovered a tailor who charged us only £10 to create a superb coat and skirt which fitted like a glove.

Josephine was tall and dark and deliciously slim and wore, I am sorry to say, a monocle, which she said she needed, having poor sight, but which gave her a slightly lesbian look. I was tall and blonde, having changed my hairdresser and bleached my hair, and Josephine made me have photographs taken because, she said, I was beautiful.

It was always a happy relationship. Josephine was a good and stabilizing influence on her difficult companion but we both knew that I was missing Charles. How could I talk to a girl like

Josephine about poetry and English literature and architecture and politics and history and even chess?

She and I never talked about books but we talked a great deal about love and romance and homosexuality and the need we both felt for the tenderness of a passionate friendship with another woman. At night, in my little flat, we lay in bed after making love, deeply content with the touch and smell and quick response of the loved one. Relaxed and satisfied and happy, we held long and intimate conversations. We asked one another questions.

'Why are we different from ordinary normal girls?'

'I don't know. Does anybody know?'

'Is it to do with childhood and mother love and all that?'

'Maybe it is. Why do you hate the idea of being a lesbian? What does it matter?'

'It matters very much. Anyhow, I'm not a lesbian. I'm in love with you but I'm also in love with Charles.'

'Why don't you forget about Charles?'

'I wish I could, but I can't.'

After about twelve months of faithful devotion and gentle affection, which was touched quite often by physical passion, I made a proposal to Josephine. I needed her love so much. I begged her to leave her mother and to live permanently with me. Josephine refused.

'How can I possibly leave my mother?'

'Why not? Other people leave their mothers. I left mine.'

'That's quite different. Your mother doesn't need you. Mine needs me very much.'

'Will you think it over?'

'Yes, but I can't let my mother down.'

'One of these days you will have to chose between me and your mother.'

'What do you mean?'

'I may decide to get married.'

'To Charles?'

'No, not to Charles, but I might find somebody else.'

'Do you really want to get married? I thought you were happy with me.'

'I hate living by myself. It makes me feel lonely and sad.'

'You ought to have stayed with your mother. Why did you leave her?'

'Because I hated her Hollywood husband. I was jealous.'

My mother's Hollywood husband had been a highly-sexed Irishman, half in love with my mother, half in love with me. When my father invited me to England I accepted with joy. At the end of six months I knew I would never return to my mother. In London, at the age of eighteen, totally untrained, I took a job as a typist.

These things were not easy to explain. When Josephine left my bedroom, sometimes calling a taxi by telephone at three o'clock in the morning, my loneliness returned. If Josephine had accepted my proposal I would never have married Wentworth Day.

I remember that Josephine objected to my friendship with Aleister Crowley. So did my Fleet Street friends, who described him in newspaper headlines as THE WICKEDEST MAN IN THE WORLD. I heard that he was looking for a journalist to write his memoirs, a ghost writer.

He was then living in a boarding-house in Kensington, sharing a room with a woman friend who happened to be an alcoholic. I remember the surprise I felt on entering the boarding-house, led by a down-at-heel domestic through a dining-room which smelt of onions, divided from the dingy hall by long lines of dangling brown beads, up a narrow staircase to a dark landing. There stood Aleister Crowley, once a rich man, looking like an angry Prime Minister, in striped trousers, tailcoat, silk cravat, a top hat clenched in his hand. He always looked angry. He seemed to radiate anger as some people radiate happiness.

'Come in,' he said. 'We're staying in this place because we have no money. No money at all.'

At our first meeting, after gravely shaking hands, he led me into a bedroom. In the double bed, drinking gin out of a tooth glass taken from the wash-stand, was a middle-aged woman. She looked at me with suspicion. 'I'm pleased to meet you,' she said, which was obviously untrue. We shook hands in a formal way. Aleister Crowley placed his top hat on the dressing-table, gave his woman friend some more gin, then sat hugely on the bed, looking at me with anger, and embarked on the first of many interviews.

'There's only one chair. Won't you sit down?'

'Thank you.'

'Are you a good journalist?'

'Not bad.'

'I am a celebrity. Are you willing to write my memoirs and wait for payment?'

'I don't know yet.'

'What do you mean? Are you afraid of me, like everyone else?'

'No, I'm not afraid of you.'

'Are you sorry for me?'

'No.'

'Well, you ought to be. Because everyone hates me.'

'Why do they hate you?'

'Because they don't understand me. They're frightened of a man who believes in black magic. They think I'm evil.'

I was to spend about three months trying to understand Aleister Crowley, this tall, ugly, bald-headed man who held a fascination for women. At the first meeting he offered me a half-finished autobiography, written by an American journalist with a taste for what Crowley called 'purple patches'. They had quarrelled before the script was finished.

'It's horrible and vulgar,' said Crowley, 'but you'd better read it, because it's true.'

'Thank you, I will.'

'I want to make a telephone call but I have no money. Can you lend me some pennies?'

'Certainly.'

With an angry frown he accepted all my pennies, and left me for ten long minutes with the gin drinker in the bed.

'He's wonderful,' she told me. 'There's no one quite like him. Without him I should be dead.'

'How is that?'

'I was drinking myself to death. He cured me.'

'How did he cure you?'

'By giving me so much gin that I hated it.'

'Do you still hate it?'

'I drink a little now and again,' she said, and emptied her glass with a smile.

That night, in my bedroom, I read the Crowley script from cover to cover. As a little boy (I forget his age) he decided to kill the cat. Having learned from his nurse that cats have seven lives he decided to kill it in seven different ways, to include burning and drowning. I believe he cut the cat's throat after drowning it. Anyway, the story of the murdered cat made me feel sick with disgust. I told Aleister Crowley that I did not feel able to write his memoirs.

'Why not? Don't you like me? Is it because they call me "the wickedest man in the world"?'

'I feel sorry for you.'

'Then help me.'

'How can I help you?'

'Introduce me to your friends in Fleet Street.'

'All right,' I said, 'I'll give a party. You can be the guest of honour.'

He frowned angrily. 'Thank you,' he said. 'You seem to be a

kind sort of girl.'

'I do hope they like you.'

'They won't,' he said furiously, 'your friends will dislike me as much as I shall dislike them.'

In this he was perfectly right. He had a genius for making enemies. My Fleet Street friends saw him as a scholar, a poet, an artist, a man of intellect, and yet they hated him. I heard him say to a room full of people that he could, and sometimes did, make himself invisible with the help of black magic. He had walked down Piccadilly stark naked. Nobody had turned to look because nobody could see him.

His temper was not improved by the arrival of his alcoholic friend. She had come uninvited, very drunk, to take him home. When he had gone, I apologized to my friends. 'He's unhappy,' I said, 'that's why he's rude.'

Aleister Crowley had the unhappiest face I had ever seen. It was a tortured face. Whatever he had done in his search for occult knowledge, good or bad, he had suffered for it. I never understood his attraction for women. Perhaps an escapist is a form of lame duck. Women love lame ducks.

At any rate, I could do no more for Aleister Crowley. I now became involved in some half-hearted flirtations with nice young men. When Charles was in London he always visited me for a cup of tea or a drink. I told him about my flirtations. We swapped stories and laughed.

'Are you still in love with me?' said Charles.

'Yes, I'm in love with you, but I'm also in love with a very nice girl.'

'You'll get over it,' said Charles.

'I need the love of another woman,' I said, 'but I don't want to become a lesbian. I want to be normal. I want to be like everyone else.'

'How dull!' said Charles.

One day, during this period of loneliness, divided between Charles and Josephine, uncertain of myself, frightened of the future, I received a telephone call from my editor, Mark Goulden. When I went to his office in Tudor Street, a turning near Fleet Street, I was hoping for a rise in salary. Instead he said quietly: 'I'm sorry, Miss Shute, but you're fired. I've been trying to defend you but it's no good.'

Sitting crumpled in the office chair, feeling crushed and defeated, knowing that my cheeks were flaming red, I listened while the situation was explained. The *Sunday Referee* was owned by the same company as *Gaumont British Films*. I had insisted on criticizing pictures produced by my editor's boss. Now the axe had fallen.

'You're a good film critic, Miss Shute, but there's nothing more I can do. I'm very angry about it. You've been sacked against my wishes.'

Sadly I left his office. On the verge of tears, I telephoned the *Sunday Dispatch* offices, made an appointment with the News Editor, and then walked across the street to ask him for a job as a reporter.

Not everybody has been dismissed by two firms in one week. This happened to me. I was sacked by the *Sunday Referee*, engaged by the *Sunday Dispatch*, and then sacked by the *Sunday Dispatch*, all within five days.

I knew I was in the wrong. On Sunday morning at 7 a.m. I was to join a riding party with some friends. At 1 a.m. the telephone rang. A friendly voice said: 'This is Britain calling ... editor of the *Sunday Dispatch*. There's been a railway crash. Big story. Would you like to cover it, Miss Shute?'

'No, thank you. I'm very tired.'

'What did you say?'

Half-asleep I stupidly repeated: 'Sorry, but I'm too tired. Sorry, but I've got to ride a horse before breakfast.'

The editor was stunned. An angry voice said: 'I'll get somebody else to cover the train crash. Good-bye, Miss Shute.'

So then I was fired for the second time, and of course I deserved it. The news editor liked me. 'I can only suggest,' he said, 'that you put things right by handing in a front-page story. An interview with H. G. Wells, or something like that.'

Not only was he the author of *Outline of History* (my Bible at one time), he was admired by all of us as a leader of permissive society, father of Rebecca West's illegitimate son, himself the son of a gardener and a house-maid, the greatest free-thinker of them all. I remember feeling nervous at the prospect of meeting so great a man. He agreed to see me because I was in trouble with the editor. No wonder I was frightened, an inky-fingered reporter, not yet the Bond Street blonde I became about six months later.

This is what I wrote about H. G. Wells:

> He is nervous, impatient, and his high-pitched voice is a surprise when he first speaks. His eyes are full of interest and humour, and must be described without apology as 'twinkling eyes'. He has a peculiar walk. His walk reminds me of a young woman hurrying into a hat shop.
>
> He is, I believe, a great admirer of women, but he treats them

with that mixture of amused affection and impatience with which a schoolmaster might treat a child.

'Well,' he said, 'I have always said that a great war will come in 1940. In my film *Things To Come* you will get an idea of this war. It is followed in 1963–68 with pestilence, fearful disease and suffering.

'Did you know, by the way, that in 1918 more people died of influenza than were killed in four years of warfare?' I did not know. H. G. Wells smiled. 'After that the film becomes an exciting fantasy and you see the world being cleaned up and put straight, all sorts of extraordinary changes taking place.'

I pelted H. G. Wells with questions about the women in his film of the future, but I found him hard to draw out.

'One thing will not change. Women will be no more important a hundred years hence than they are today. They will be as charming as they are now, but they will never hold the important jobs held by men.

'Even in Russia today, where you have women engineers and women soldiers and there are no domestic ties whatever, you still find that men do all the responsible government work.

'In my early books I was always writing of women being the "mates" and collaborators with men, but I doubt if that is the way things will go.'

'Are women inferior mentally?'

'I would not call them "inferior". Women use their brains differently and see things from a distinctive point of view. The main trouble with you,' he added, 'is that in respect to sustained persistent effort you're lazy. All women are lazy when it comes to serious work.

'The big problem, I think, is to get a woman to co-operate honestly with a man, or a man to co-operate honestly with a woman.

'You can't escape the sex and flirtation business, which makes it so impossible to treat you as another worker.

'You find it easy to use that charm of yours. Of course it is difficult for a woman to achieve anything important and not to be lazy when men are always flattering and trying to amuse her. She gets demoralized when she is young, and when she gets to forty the habits of charming evasion are ingrained ... Winston Churchill is as interested as I am in the film industry. It was he who insisted that *Whether Mankind* was a bad title and should be changed to *Things To Come*. In the end we had to change it. He was right, I think, and anyway he gave us no peace.

'And now,' finished Mr Wells, rising briskly, 'have you got enough stuff to concoct your interview, or not?'

It was published on 7 July 1935.

But this interview marked the end of my life as a freelance reporter. From the insecurity of Fleet Street I moved into Bond Street. I had had enough. The black hat of bohemia was discarded. I decided to become a Bond Street blonde and to escape from the escapists. The change was not difficult. After a few months in the service of Max Factor, the Hollywood beauty firm, I looked with surprise at my own reflection in the mirror. Was this painted patrician with the canary-coloured hair and tailored suit, gardenia firmly in button-hole, cigarette in long holder, the untidy journalist who had visited Lord Beaverbrook? I was now a publicity manager. In a little while I was walking to my office followed by a white poodle, beginning to enjoy myself in a new role, escaped from Fleet Street, hoping to return, with dignity if I could, to my father's more conventional world.

By this time I had formed several serious friendships with men. I believed that I had now escaped, or nearly escaped, from the dangers of homosexuality. I was even considering marriage. I did not know it, but the famous Cecil Beaton, society photographer, was finding himself in the same situation, forcing himself to fall in love with the opposite sex. He managed rather well, later persuading Greta Garbo, of all people, to go to bed with him!

But Josephine, who loved me so dearly, seemed to know what was happening. Josephine was still my partner, my dearest friend. In the thirties we still had a sense of elegance and we managed to enjoy life very much indeed. Nobody took much notice of Hitler. Mr Baldwin was our Prime Minister and Mr Baldwin said with conviction: 'It is not the case that Germany is rapidly approaching equality with us. Her real strength is not fifty per cent of our strength in Europe today.'

So Londoners were lulled into sleepy security by nice Mr Baldwin. We amused ourselves at parties and dance clubs and first nights. There was always the ballet and the music of Ivor Novello, not to mention the comedies of Noel Coward and the exhibitions of Cecil Beaton. We loved these three. They were as pretty and charming as butterflies. We liked the Victorian styles in dress, the Victorian furniture, and even the Victorian jokes. The one I liked best, and repeated to all my friends, was the one about Mrs Patrick Campbell, when asked what she thought of marriage.

'Oh, the peace of a double bed,' said Mrs Patrick Campbell, 'after the hurly-burly of a chaise longue!'

Josephine thought this was very funny, and so did Charles, who enjoyed the hurly-burly as much as anyone. In my heart I still loved Charles. In an effort to change my life style I decided to leave Elgin Crescent, to part from the fat silvery pigeons, still in the branches of the chestnut tree when the season came to make love. And then, to the distress of Josephine, I shared a flat with a woman friend (a platonic friend) living in Bury Street (close to St James's Street, handy for Bond Street) and Charles decided to spend a night in my friend's bed. Neither of them knew I still loved him. In the morning Charles entered my room to tell me all about it. He was naked, laughing, perhaps wanting to hurt my feelings, to show his independence. To him it was a joke. To my woman friend it was just an experience.

'Shall we have a threesome?' said Charles.

'No, thank you,' I said.

I told Charles to leave my room. I never wanted to see him again. Perhaps that was why I decided to get married, hurting the feelings of Josephine who wept bitter tears, separating myself from Charles and the other escapists by an act of escape.

Josephine said: 'What on earth do you see in him, Nerina?'

He was a well-known journalist and he belonged to my father's world, the establishment, the Conservative party, the world of elegance and good behaviour. My father was delighted.

The most unreal thing of all was probably the wedding. My mother returned to London for this event, and appeared at the reception triumphantly in powder blue. She looked remarkably pretty, ornamental, charming. It was almost the first time she had spoken to Cammy since ending their marriage, several husbands ago, and now, in their beautiful London clothes, my parents smiled and chatted quite naturally, as though they understood one another, which in some ways they did.

They stood apart from the other guests, each with a glass of champagne, watching their changeable daughter with pride and interest as she cut the wedding cake.

'I knew she would settle down,' said Cammy with satisfaction. 'She told me once she would rather have five lovers and one husband than six husbands. That was a cut at you, old girl. I think she takes after me.'

'What do you mean?'

'She's more of a realist than you are. She may have lovers but she won't insist on marrying them.'

'There's no need to have lovers,' said Renie indignantly, 'if you're happily married. I hope Nerina won't ever have them again,' she added, as though lovers were as troublesome as fleas.

'I hope so too.'

'But we mustn't be surprised,' said Renie suddenly, 'if she kicks over the traces. In some ways she's very like me.'

'I hope not,' said Cammy.

'So do I,' said Renie.

I believe they enjoyed the wedding much more than I did. I remember feeling that all of it was happening to someone else.

5   *The Escapist Generation*

My marriage to James Wentworth Day lasted for only one year.

All the same there were good things about that marriage (as my mother would say), and I can see now that Jim was at heart a nice person, a hot-tempered Conservative, an ugly man of considerable charm, with a bald head, a neat moustache, a surprising sense of humour, peering at the world through thick unpleasing spectacles. In those days I was an ardent Socialist. Now I am an ardent Conservative, an admirer of Margaret Thatcher, and Jim would find me a better companion.

Jim lived in a squat old house in King Street, beautifully panelled, several hundred years old, close to St James's Palace. In Jim's sitting-room, furnished with bright scarlet curtains, was a soft green sofa and armchair, an old refectory table, an old farm dresser with blue china and pewter, and on the walls, in every room, old guns and swords, stuffed birds and antlers, and stag's heads and stuffed fish.

He loved duck shooting. He loved the smell and sounds in the salty marshes in Essex, the whicker of a wild duck rising unexpectedly, the feel of a small boat bumping on the waves, the sight of marshy flat fields, the call of a peewit.

Here, at least, was something the difficult Nerina could understand.

I was back in my father's world, soothed and surrounded by gentle voices and mannerly ways. One did as the others did. One allowed Jim to laugh at the Socialists. One even allowed him to call homosexuals 'perverts'. When he imitated their voices and gestures one smiled with tolerance and amusement. After all, Jim's world was my father's world. It was better than Josephine's world, or the homosexual world.

Some of it was very nice indeed. In my new bowler hat, my beautiful hand-made black boots, I went fox-hunting for the first time. (In California I had ridden with cowboys, which was not at all the same thing.) I was photographed at Ascot in a huge hat, smiling like a film star. I believe everyone thought my married life was good, and glamorous and gay and exciting. Everyone except Aimée Stuart, who knew me so well, and Josephine, who still loved me.

Aimée said: 'Do you love your husband?'

'No, I'm afraid I don't.'

'Why did you marry him then?'

'Because I was lonely. Because he insisted.'

'Did you tell him you didn't love him?'

'Of course.'

'Did he still insist?'

'He said it would be all right. I would learn to love him.'

'Is it going to be all right?'

'No, it isn't. Well, who knows? Maybe it *will* be all right.'

'I think you were both out of your minds,' said Aimée.

At that time, at the end of the thirties, as we all grew closer to war, feeling more and more fearful for the future, we made dozens of silly marriages. Some of us were slightly hysterical. We laughed at ourselves and our mistakes. We were waiting for something, on the edge of a precipice. It was a period of marriage and muddle and madness. When we greeted one another, instead of saying: 'How is your sex life, darling?' we now said: 'Hello, darling, who are you married to now?' Marriage was a joke. Sex was a joke. Even war was a joke.

Jim thought little of the new young King, with his night-club ideas. Jim's wife defended him passionately, remembering with real emotion the day in January when she had stood in the Strand to watch the funeral procession and the white-faced young man who was following his father's coffin. I thought I had seen great loneliness in the young man's face. The new King, with his white unhappy charm, was loved passionately by his people, and yet, as Jim said, he represented bottle parties, and milk bars, and steel tubular furniture, and talking pictures, and jazz, and ugly steel and concrete blocks of flats, and cocktail parties, and film stars, and a general feeling of noisy excitable people, frightened of the future.

To Jim, who disapproved of the young King's friendship with Mrs Simpson, I said heatedly: 'Well, why shouldn't he be in love with an ordinary American woman? What does class distinction matter?'

'I'm a die-hard Conservative,' said Jim, 'and I don't believe in these damned newfangled ideas.'

After my wedding, to the delight of Josephine, it was necessary for Jim to spend a month in Egypt with a group of journalists, leaving his new wife in London. There was no honeymoon. That would come later.

Josephine said: 'How wonderful! At least we have one more

month of happiness together.'

While Jim was in Egypt the storm broke in the Press and the English public were told for the first time of the love between Mrs Simpson and the sad-faced young King. It was 3 December 1936. Until now the man in the street had never even heard of Mrs Simpson. He was told the truth. The King, the much-loved King, was proposing to marry an American woman, twice-divorced.

Aimée said, 'Poor young man, why don't they let him get married?'

Josephine said, 'How wonderful to be so much in love! I know how he feels!'

On 4 December Mr Baldwin announced that the Government would not consider the King's marriage to Mrs Simpson. On the same day Mrs Simpson left England for the south of France. Then we found ourselves listening to the farewell broadcast. The King's voice was thick and tearful. It rose in a boyish way at the last sentence. I remember thinking it was like a shout of defiance.

I can remember wiping my eyes when he said:

'But you must believe me when I tell you that I have found it impossible to carry the heavy burden of responsibility and discharge my duties as King as I would wish to do without the help and support of the woman I love. And I want you to know that the decision I have made has been mine and mine alone. This was a thing I had to judge entirely for myself. The other person most nearly concerned has tried up to the last to persuade me to take a different course.'

At this point I began to cry.

  'I now quit altogether public affairs,' the emotional voice continued, 'and I lay down my burden. It may be some time before I return to my native land, but I shall always follow the fortunes of the British race and empire with profound interest, and if at any time in the future I can be found of service to His Majesty in a private station, I shall not fail.'
  'And now we all have a new King. I wish him and you, his people, happiness and prosperity with all my heart. God bless you all.' He raised his voice. 'God save the King,' he shouted.

It was the public death of one King and the cruel birth of another. It was a shock. It was an unforgettable broadcast.

Aimée said afterwards: 'What did you think of his farewell speech?'

'It made me cry. It made me feel small.'

'Me too,' said Aimée. 'I wonder why?'

'Because he gave up everything for love,' said Josephine.

The words used by the poor young King were typical of the new generation of escapists. He opted out. My women friends admired him greatly and my men friends despised him. 'Selfish young devil! Supposing we all gave up our jobs for the sake of a woman?'

In an age of escapism he was supreme. That was why the Archbishop of Canterbury was so angry with him. With scorn he said: 'From God he had received a high and sacred trust. Yet, by his own will, he has abdicated – he has surrendered the trust. With characteristic frankness he has told us his motive. It was a craving for *private happiness*.'

I can see now that our ex-King was a royal drop-out. (I still love him.) At that tragic time London was full of escapists, and a drop-out was a King to be admired. In London, waiting for war to break out, we said, like Aimée, 'Have a good time, dear. If you can't be good, be careful.' Or we said, like Charles, 'Don't cry, Nerina. Love is only sublimated sex, isn't it?' Or we said, like my mother, 'Life is such fun. Let's run away, and get married!'

My mother, needless to say, was not on the side of the Archbishop.

'I'm furious with him,' said Renie. 'He has no right to talk in that sanctimonious way about a craving for private happiness. Don't we all want to be happy?'

'Of course we do,' I said.

'How many people have the courage to do what they think is right if other people tell them it's wrong?'

'Well, *you* have,' I said, 'even if *I* haven't.'

'I can't stand the Archbishop,' said my mother.

We were still feeling angry with the Archbishop when Jim returned from Egypt, and Jim, of course, was full of scorn for the new Duke of Windsor, the ex-King.

'He always was a bit of a cad. I never thought much of his clothes. Much too flashy. The chap didn't look like a gentleman,' said Jim, and it might have been my father speaking.

I was still working as publicity manager for Max Factor, with Josephine as my assistant. The money was useful. In my father's world you needed money as well as good manners, and now I had both. I was beginning to dress well. I no longer looked like a journalist. Sometimes I heard myself called a beautiful woman, which made me feel like somebody else. It was a strange life. On Tuesday evenings, by arrangement with Jim, I went out with my

Fleet Street friends, or Josephine. (Jim was good about that.) Then I had another idea, a better one, to make marriage less boring.

I said to my husband, 'I want you to find me a tutor.'

Jim laughed. 'Male or female?' he said.

'I've never had time to study,' I said with embarrassment. 'Don't laugh. I'd like to have a tutor and read English literature.'

'All right,' said Jim, 'Why not?'

He recovered quickly from my extraordinary request. Indeed he was very kind about it. A telephone call to an agent brought a stream of potential tutors to King Street, so that Jim, whose husbandly wish was to find a man with good references but no sex appeal, interviewed two or three unattractive gentlemen each day. Young and old applied for the job. Their coats were shabby and their eyes glittered at the prospect of a few guineas for teaching Jim's wife. At the same time they were puzzled. Was Jim's wife bedridden? Was she mentally defective? Why did she require a tutor?

Finally a woman applied for the job and was engaged immediately by a thankful Jim. We both liked Susan. Out of my Max Factor money I paid her £3 a week. Each morning for two hours, Max Factor's publicity manager would listen contentedly while Susan read aloud the diary of Swift, or the early novels of Richardson and Fielding and Fanny Burney (whose name I had never heard until then) or the essays of Doctor Johnson, or the eighteenth-century poets. Sometimes Nerina appeared for her lessons in a dressing-gown, very tired, suffering from a headache after a late supper party at the Savoy Grill.

'Anybody looking less like a student of English literature I never saw!' said my tutor.

It bothered her when I refused to make any notes.

'I don't want to pass an exam. I just want to enjoy myself.'

'What do you get out of it?'

'Happiness,' I said.

By this time I knew that my marriage would not last. How could it possibly last without love? But two hours with Susan, reading old books about pleasant people in a sweet world of dignity and security, was a glorious way to start the morning, like two hours in the sunshine, listening to the sound of the sea.

At 11 a.m., the lessons finished, I sailed along King Street into St James's Street, arm-in-arm with my tutor. We parted in Piccadilly. Feeling comfortably full of reading, like a dog after a good meal, I would arrive at my office to find a pile of letters, half-a-dozen telephone messages, a note from the managing director to say I was wanted in a publicity conference. This was not bad at all. At 1 p.m., I would meet my husband for lunch, either at Prunier's or the Savoy Grill, or perhaps we would lunch at home, for we had a well-trained housekeeper, Mrs Cameron, a motherly old Scot who was fond of us both, especially me. In the afternoon I would write an article about make-up for the eyes. At 6 p.m. I would rush home, swallow a cocktail, change into evening-dress, and then go with my husband to a reception at Grosvenor House, a private party, an expensive supper. We would drink champagne. At 2 a.m., excited and fretful, we would return home and relentlessly quarrel. What did we quarrel about? It might be politics, or modern books, or modern art, or homosexuality, or nothing at all. Some of the quarrels were violent. I remember hitting my husband with a cheap hand-mirror, which immediately broke in half. Being a gentleman, he replaced it with a beautiful silver mirror, and said with a grin, 'You can hit me with this. I don't think it will break.' (I still have it today.)

Jim used to say, in a furious voice, 'You Communists talk nonsense! Thank God, Communism will never happen in England!'

'But I'm not a Communist. I'm a left-wing Socialist.'

'It's just as bad,' shouted Jim. 'The trouble is you read too much. You read the wrong books!'

One day Lord Lloyd came to lunch at the King Street flat. To my husband he was a shining hero, the man of the future, the only man in Government circles with any real force or courage, in fact a die-hard Conservative.

'Please be charming,' said Jim.

So the great man came to lunch, small, dapper, with quick bird movements and a clean-cut smart face, full of charm and kindness. To me he was delightful. I saw the man whose name was once the terror of Egypt as a little dapper man whose ways with women were gentle. To please me they talked about horses and hunting.

With a smile Jim said: 'My wife is a Communist.'

Said Lord Lloyd: 'Good heavens, I never met a hunting Communist before!'

After lunch I walked up Bond Street to my office in a mood of pleasure. I might be a bad wife but at least I was helpful to Jim as a kind of decoy duck. Also, fortunately, I was a good publicity manager for Max Factor. A few days later I was interviewed by my boss, who offered me a rise in salary.

'We like your work. We want you to give us more of your time. How much money do you want?'

'Fifteen pounds a week in salary and five pounds a week in

expenses,' I said. (It seemed like a small fortune, the equivalent to £20,000 a year at the time of writing.)

When Susan was told about this new arrangement she was astonished.

'Imagine making all that money with so little effort!' said Susan. 'Here am I, with an Oxford degree, and I'm working myself to death for half your salary.'

'It's damned unfair. You ought to be a publicity manager like me,' I said.

In the summer of 1937 my play was produced at the Kew Theatre for the usual try-out. It was a comedy. On the opening night my mother had the shock of seeing herself portrayed on the stage. She took it very well, and laughed loudly. It was viewed by three West End managers but in the end they decided against it.

I began to feel increasingly unhappy, knowing that my marriage was a failure. Jim belonged to my father's world and this had been my reason for doing such a stupid thing. How could I have married without love?

Then came the death of Cammy. He did not realize that my marriage had failed. He died as he wanted to die, quietly and tactfully, leaving his friends when his money came to an end. For some time I had given him a small allowance, taken from my earnings. It was not enough. My father no longer wanted my help, nor the help of anyone else.

'I'm seventy, old girl. I've had a jolly good life and I shan't be sorry to go. After all,' he said amiably, 'I haven't done a stroke of work since I was forty. How many men can say that?'

His death, when it came, was a blow. I missed the elegant Edwardian figure and the gentle, amiable sayings. Before he died he said for the last time, 'Your mother's a wonderful woman. She makes mistakes, dear, but she's very nearly a very g-g-good sort. What's more she's a lady,' he added, 'and so are you, whether you like it or not.'

'Do you think so?' I said with surprise.

'Well,' said my father with a smile, 'not quite a lady.'

His words were like a gentle caress from a man who forgave when others did not. (After all, my mother had ruined his life.) They comforted me when my mother suddenly married a white-haired old banker from Crawley, Sussex. The previous American husband had died in a mining accident but the new one took me by surprise. He was the fifth husband and his age was seventy. Renie, when she married him, was nearly sixty. Had she made yet another mistake? Of course she had, but never mind that.

I found her at Rottingdean. After a secret marriage she had brought her latest partner to a large expensive hotel, on the edge of the Downs, for a honeymoon. 'Well,' I said, when her husband, Arthur, had tactfully left the room, 'why didn't you tell me you were planning to get married?'

'What was the good of telling you a thing like that?' said Renie. 'I knew you would advise me not to do it. Besides, dear, a runaway marriage is much more fun. I feel ten years younger.'

'How do you manage to amuse yourself?'

'I ride on the Downs every morning. It's wonderful. I haven't been so happy for years.'

'What does your husband do?'

'Oh,' said my mother, 'Arthur reads the paper. When he's bored he goes to the churchyard and looks at the tombstones.' She laughed in her youthful way. 'Arthur loves doing that. Aren't men extraordinary?'

'Do you think this marriage will end in divorce?'

'What a question! You should learn to enjoy life as I do, and stop worrying about the future. Come to the stable,' said Renie, 'and see the horses.'

'I do hope you won't have another divorce.'

'Considering I'm still on my honeymoon,' said Renie indignantly, 'it's ridiculous to talk about divorce. That,' she pointed out, 'comes later.'

So we looked peacefully at the horses, and gave a lump of sugar to Renie's chestnut, which she rode and jumped every morning. We had tea in the hotel lounge, talking in loud voices to Arthur, who was rather deaf but extremely polite. Renie whispered that Arthur was very romantic. He had loved her from afar (over the counter of the Crawley bank, that is to say) when she was a girl, living at the family home in Sussex.

'I'm glad you're happy,' I said, before leaving. 'I only hope it will last.'

At that moment I felt older than my mother.

'I know you pretend to be a realist, but there's no need to be so depressing. My latest marriage,' said Renie cheerfully, 'is bound to last for two or three years. Why not enjoy a marriage until it comes to an end?'

'Mine,' I said, 'has come to an end already.'

'What did you say?' Renie was full of sympathy. 'So that's why you look gloomy. It's horrible, isn't it? I know exactly how you feel. Why didn't you tell me before?'

'There's nothing to tell. I didn't love him. He said it would be all right but it wasn't all right. Do you know what I mean?'

'The only way to learn about men,' said Renie, from long

experience, 'is by trial and error. Never put up with unhappiness for the sake of appearances. What I advise you to do, dear, is to grasp the nettle. Be like the Duke of Windsor!'

I returned to London with a feeling that Renie, like the romantic ex-King, had been gifted with a greater courage than some of us, more meek in spirit, who envied and criticized, unwilling to praise. In this world you must do what you want to do, said Renie, and prove afterwards (if you can) that you are right. Well, the Duke of Windsor had given up his job, his friends, his responsibilities. And now, poor man, he was a social misfit. Perhaps, I thought, all escapists are social misfits. They are escaping from the social background which others enjoy, or endure.

In a state of gloom and foreboding I went, as usual, to Aimée Stuart for council. 'I don't like marriage. I shall never be happy with anyone. What am I to do?'

'Have a drink, darling,' said Aimée, 'and find someone else.'

My marriage was not quite over, but it was certainly coming to an end. For six months Jim had been out of a job. How could I leave when my husband was unemployed? One day he said to me: 'You and I are going to Egypt. It's a gamble, but I think we shall make a lot of money out there.'

He explained that Seddik Bey, Minister of Tourism, had offered him a free visit to Cairo in return for publicity services. He explained that he had an idea for creating an enormous duck shoot in Egypt by flooding the lands according to his own pet theory and thus offering a new attraction for tourists.

'All right,' I said, 'when do we start?'

If asked by friends why we were going to Egypt for a month I told them lightly (in my mother's voice) that my husband had a plan for flooding the entire country and making it a refuge for wild ducks. Even the pyramids would be flooded if my husband had his way, and so, naturally, I wanted to see them before it was too late. The story went well. Jim had decided to make Egypt the playground of the world. Well, why not?

So my husband and I, with our bags addressed to Shepheard's Hotel, Cairo, set out on a cold day in February 1938 with the light of adventure in our eyes.

'Supposing the trip is a failure?'

'It won't be,' said Jim.

'Have you prepared your scheme for flooding Egypt yet?'

'No,' said Jim, with his broadest smile, 'but I'll think it out by the time we arrive in Cairo.'

The result of this mad trip was not the filling of Egypt with ducks, as Jim hoped, but it led to a big publicity contract with the Egyptian Government. Also it proved a very nice holiday. Since Nerina was a blonde her success was immediate, for the Egyptians loved women with golden hair, even brassy hair with peroxide streaks, and I found myself in great demand from the moment I arrived.

Jim said: 'It's a help to have such a popular wife.'

Soon I found myself riding beautiful Arab horses on the desert around Menahouse, and flirting outrageously. When the excitement was over, at home in London, we walked up the Haymarket on the way to Jim's bank, smiling at poverty as my mother would have done. Jim had spent his last penny in Egypt, and the Egyptian Government had not yet coughed up. Jim was not worried.

'I told you the trip to Egypt was a gamble,' Jim said, 'but I knew it would turn out all right, and it did.'

The break came in the summer. One night in August there was one more violent quarrel and the following morning, quite silently, I packed my suitcase, called a taxi, and departed for good. Jim was now on top of the world, financially safe and strong, full of plans for the future. Apparently the Egyptian Government had coughed up. No one could say I had left him in the lurch. No one could say I had left him for Josephine, or anyone else. I gave the taxi driver Aimée Stuart's address, then sat back in the cab and cursed myself for being a fool, for making a loveless marriage, and finally for indulging in self-pity. I had no right to feel sorry for myself. What had happened was well deserved, and it was happening all around to my friends.

'Well,' said Aimée, when I arrived at her flat, 'I was afraid it would turn out like this. Never mind, darling. You can stay with me as long as you like.'

I can see now that I married Jim in a wild attempt to escape from the homosexual world. In my case the whole operation was a dismal disaster. On the other hand, having left my husband, rejected him, run away from him on grounds of incompatibility, I had no wish to become a lesbian. I had escaped from marriage and also, I hoped, from the bondage of passionate friendships. No more women lovers for me! No more Josephines!

'What have I done?' said Josephine.

'You refused to leave your mother when I asked you to be my partner.'

'But I love you.'

'Not enough,' I said. 'I want to escape. I want to be free. Besides, you're too young.'

And so now the decadent laughing thirties were nearly at an end. The mood of London was cheerful. In his New Year's message to the people Mr Chamberlain summed up the year, 1938, giving us new heart.

'A year marked by such underlying goodwill,' he said, 'is one which leaves behind it no grounds for pessimism.'

Mr Eden said, 'War can be averted.'

'Mr J. H. Thomas said, 'I believe there will be no war.'

General Smuts in South Africa said, 'I think we are in for years of peace and quiet.'

Sir Samuel Hoare said on 10 March, 'I am convinced we could not be defeated in a short war by any knock-out blow, and that in a long war our almost inexhaustible resources will ensure the final victory.'

A few days after this last encouraging speech came the news that Hitler had broken his word to Mr Chamberlain. German tanks smashed into Prague. Quite suddenly British statesmen began to talk about the 'rape of Czechoslovakia'.

At last they were telling us the truth. Winston Churchill had warned us, and now it was happening. We would soon be at war, and we knew it.

Once again, feeling lonely, in a mood of black depression although smiling brightly, I paid a week-end visit to my mother in Rottingdean. By leaving my husband I had followed her example. I was living by myself in a flat in Hanover Square. My mother was living by herself in a small brick house above the sea.

I remember the house very clearly. It was high on a hill, overlooking the main road; a cheerful house, it was filled with the sounds of wind and waves, like a small ship, and Renie was given immense pleasure by the Sussex Downs which lay behind it. Twice a week she hired a horse. She loved the green sea-scented turf; she enjoyed finding new tracks, jumping the fences, exploring the sweet green hills between the grey churches.

Renie was sixty-one. She looked much younger. On a horse, she still wore the riding-habit and bowler hat she had worn at the age of twenty, and she was still a magnificent rider, braver than myself. At home, looking healthy and happy, she still wore a blue ribbon tied tightly round her curled grey hair. Once again she was a merry widow. She had lost the deaf old banker from Crawley. (Possibly she had tired him out, poor man.)

'Are you missing your husband?' I said.

'I can't honestly say that I am. Are you missing yours, dear?'

'I don't like living alone.'

'You must find someone else, dear.'

'I'm glad you didn't get another divorce. I suppose you would have done,' I said, 'if Arthur had lived. Do you think you will marry again?'

'I expect so, if I get the chance.'

'You're bound to get the chance. You always do. But do you really want to do it again?'

'I enjoy it, dear. I love getting married. It relieves the monotony,' said Renie, 'and it takes your mind off politics and war. What's the good of being miserable? Find another husband and cheer up.

'Husbands don't cheer me up.'

'Husbands cheer everyone up. What you must do is to fall deeply in love and get married. It's not right for a woman to spend her life alone. You must learn to enjoy yourself, dear. Don't forget,' said my smiling mother, 'there's always something round the corner.'

We had supper together in Renie's little kitchen. The next morning I hired the horse usually ridden by Renie and went out alone. In the distance I saw two female figures riding slowly, with an escort from the livery stable. For no particular reason I followed them and heard myself shouting, 'Good morning. Do you mind if I ride with you?'

One of the women turned out to be a gynaecological surgeon, and the other, which surprised me, was a dental surgeon. Their names were Helen and Andy. A few months later I was invited to live with my new friends at their beautiful house in Portland Place. I accepted with pleasure.

6 War!

I loved the dignity of the tall old house in Portland Place. They gave me a large and beautiful room at the top, with a private bathroom. There I slept and worked at my desk until the bombs drove us out.

My windows had a fine view of Georgian buildings with elegant front doors and gleaming brass knockers which reminded me of smart old ladies in poke bonnets, for they looked so extremely prim beside the modern block of flats facing me from across the road. I loved this broad and benevolent street. I loved walking round the corner into Park Crescent where the white houses which were built by Nash to please King George IV were still the most beautiful group of buildings in London. Whether walking in the rose gardens or watching the swans on the little lake in Regent's Park, or staring in wonder at the quiet graceful houses arranged in patterns like ladies in a pageant, I always thought lovingly of King George IV. His friendliness was here in each house. To me he was more real than Hitler.

The new life was wonderful, even though war was declared two weeks later. I now had two good friends, a background, a perfect home. In this magnificent old house, lived in by hard-working women who prided themselves on their wine cellar, their perfect dinner parties, I had found something solid and substantial.

Helen and Andy were distinguished people, well known in the medical world, but to me quite new. They were many years older than myself. They danced, they played cards, they went to the opera, they held large parties in the big old-fashioned dining-room, the table glittering with silver, lighted by candles. They took pride in the choice of wine. They were amused and pleased by everything around them, from the dachshund puppies to the elderly butler whose hair grew long and grey from the back, and came forward over his bald head like a lid.

I loved watching the butler. When called to the front door on a windy day he used one hand to hold onto his lid of hair and the other to operate the door or unload the car. To him the lid of hair was more important than anything else.

My new friends owned, among other things, a magnificent blue Rolls Royce, also a Baby Austin, used by Andy for shopping and visiting the hospital. They spent their week-ends at a flat in Brighton. They went riding, as I did, on the Downs near Rottingdean, but they were not good riders. In this, at least, I was more accomplished than they were.

On the morning of 3 September 1939, Helen and Andy were enjoying a Sunday treat in the shape of breakfast in bed. I can see the group clearly. Nerina, in a dressing-gown, sprawled in an armchair, reading the paper. Opposite was Helen, lying in her bed, a long lanky figure with sandy hair and a smiling Irish face. I can see Andy through an open door, small and plump, with appealing brown eyes, eating a box of chocolates.

'What do you think of the news?' I said anxiously.

'Awful,' said Helen.

'Turn on the wireless,' called Andy from the next room.

At 11.15 a.m. the voice of Mr Chamberlain filled the bedroom at Portland Place. He spoke in a tone of sadness. He had asked Hitler to withdraw his armies from Poland, and Hitler had refused.

In a broken voice Mr Chamberlain said: 'I have to tell you that no such undertaking has been received and that consequently this country is at war with Germany.'

About ten minutes later, while all London waited for further news, a sound of wailing started in the streets.

'What the hell is that?' said Helen.

It was the first sound of London sirens, the first air-raid alarm. Helen took charge at once. 'I'll give you five minutes to get dressed. Hurry up, both of you. And Nerina, don't forget your gas mask and torch!'

I can see myself as I was then, slim in a summer dress, clutching gas mask and torch and handbag, hurling myself into Andy's little car, the Baby Austin, being driven by my frantic friends to the Elisabeth Garrett Anderson Hospital (where they were both on call in case of emergency), dashing with them through back streets, taking a corner on two wheels. My heart was thumping. My gas mask was clutched to my bosom. We expected the bombs to hit London. On that day we expected to be killed.

We laughed about it afterwards. At the time it was horrible. I was filled with senseless forebodings, hating the medical smell of things, confused and bewildered by stretchers and trollies and nurses and rows of empty beds waiting for casualties. I remember feeling sick in the lavatory. I stayed there all the afternoon, unable to get out when the door jammed, almost weeping with misery.

Helen, who loved puns, laughingly said, 'Poor Nerina! I hunted for you high and loo!'

Later I took my training in First Aid. I received a most becoming uniform as a Red Cross nurse. Then we moved from London to a mental hospital in Bedfordshire, a casualty centre, waiting for casualties who failed to arrive. Somehow I became an Assistant Almoner.

'Luckily,' said Helen, 'there are no patients for Nerina to assist.'

'In the end, in a state of boredom and frustration, we returned to London. There we had to wait until the summer of 1940 when the Battle of Britain suddenly began. The waiting period was a time of uncertainty. It was the spiritual bridge between the old life and the new life, the past and the future, Cammy's generation and my generation. We all knew that our dear familiar world would never be the same again. What would the brave new world be like?

I learnt such a lot from Helen and Andy. My two distinguished friends had no inhibitions. Their enjoyment of life included everything skilled, from sex to surgery. Andy was a highly qualified gynaecological surgeon, Miss Anderton Sharpe, FRCS, MRCP. Helen Mayo was a dental surgeon, older than Andy, well known in the medical world as the third qualified woman to practice dentistry in London. By this I was very impressed. I soon found that their lives had been carefully planned. Marriage had never been part of that plan (although Helen, through the years, had been three times engaged to men who were killed by the Germans, and Andy, with an independent income, must have had many offers), because things like surgery had always intervened.

These two women could not possibly be called spinsters. They were professionals. They were doctors, friends, originals, joyous hard-working women with a strong sense of humour, to be envied, to be loved, but not to be married.

I loved them both. While waiting for the Battle of Britain to hit London we began to know one another very well, working, dancing, talking, laughing, soon becoming close friends. For the first time I possessed a home, I possessed a family, I belonged to Helen and Andy as I had never belonged to anyone else.

I remember Andy saying to Helen: 'Let's give her a good old-fashioned Christmas holiday. She's never had a home, or a family, and she's never had a real Christmas.'

Of course Helen and Andy were ahead of their time. They had lived together for ten happy years. They had numerous men friends, rising medicals, attractive men aged between thirty and forty, most of them good dancers as well as good doctors, a type I had never met before. With these young men we dined and danced and drank, laughing, buffooning, flirting, refusing to be serious. Helen said she was engaged to marry one of these men, a veterinary surgeon, but there was no hurry. He might or might not get his divorce from a difficult wife.

Helen was much older than the rest of us. All the men enjoyed her company. They talked shop with Andy (who might be called away in the middle of a party to attend a patient in hospital) and then turned to Helen, listening to her jokes, having fun, sharing her gaiety, amid shouts of laughter.

The one I learned to love most was Helen.

I remember the nervous feeling when Helen took me for a week-end in Brighton. I knew that she intended to make love to me. She had kissed me many times and once, on the first occasion, she had said: 'You make me feel young again.' So now, sitting beside her in the Rolls Royce, I said nervously:

'Are you a lesbian, Helen?'

'Of course not. Lesbians are women who don't like men.'

'Do you believe in homosexuality?'

'I believe in friendship,' said Helen. 'I believe friendship leads to love and love leads to sex, but it ends in friendship. Andy believes the same thing. As you can see, we're very good friends.'

I discovered that Andy had prepared a hamper filled with beautiful food; sandwiches, salad, fruit, cheese, a cooked chicken, and that Helen had provided several bottles of champagne. We stayed in their delightful flat overlooking the sea.

'Can you cook?' said Helen.

'Definitely not. Only a boiled egg,' I said.

'This time it doesn't matter because we can always get a meal at the Ship Hotel. Next time we'll bring Andy with us and make her do the cooking,' said the smiling Helen.

'Oh yes, that's a good idea,' said the nervous Nerina.

It turned out to be a happy week-end with moments of conversation in addition to walks by the sea, much laughter and a lot of champagne. I remember saying to Helen: 'I really don't want to become a lesbian, I want to be normal.'

'But there's no need to give yourself a label. Just allow yourself to love people. Fall in love with someone, and sort out the sex afterwards.'

'Is that what you and Andy do?'

'Of course it is.'

'Does Andy feel jealous of me?'

'Not in the least. She likes you very much. That's why she gave us a cooked chicken!' said Helen smiling.

She was a tall woman, ugly and attractive, as the French say *jolie laide*, with an aristocratic face and a gift for laughter. Everyone noticed her hands, so long and strong and slender, with delicate fingers, so light in their touch, so finely shaped. With these beautiful strong hands she had pulled out the teeth of many well known people who later became her friends. I discovered that her beautiful hands were equally good at pulling out teeth and making love. Her delicate fingers knew exactly where to go and what to do.

Yes, it was a happy week-end, and it led to a long story of love and friendship and laughter. Helen was easy to understand, with her Irish temper, her gorgeous sense of humour, half-Irish, half-Mayfair, and her noisy flamboyant character, more sympathetic and less hard-headed than clever little Andy. Helen had been born and bred in London, Andy in Yorkshire. They had both been to public schools. Helen had been presented at Court. Her father, the Revd John Mayo, was the well-known Rector of Whitechapel. (For many years we had listened to his broadcast on Christmas day.) Andy's family was enormously rich but Helen's family was a little more upper-class. I discovered that Andy was the practical one. She looked after us both like a couple of children.

Helen once said, 'I enjoy quarrelling. I like a good row.'

'Why?'

'It's like taking off a tight pair of shoes and wearing an old pair of slippers. It does you good.'

Anyway, I managed to find a job (having left Max Factor when war broke out), and earned a few pounds a week writing publicity paragraphs, using an office in the Strand. During the winter months, in the black-out, I walked home with my gas mask dangling on my arm. Sometimes I forgot the torch and lost myself in the blackness of spongy streets. I remember feeling afraid to cross the road for fear of being killed by a car.

To relieve boredom there were supper parties and night clubs and harmless flirtations and a lot of dancing. The only one who never paid a bill was myself. But then I was, as Helen made them all understand, between husbands. 'Yes, she's between husbands. It's like falling between two stools,' Helen said.

Sometimes I thought about Josephine. Compared with my medical friends, so much older, so much wiser, so much more distinguished and worldly, Josephine began to seem like a young child. She was now far away, in Barbados, having found work with some friends, but Jim, my persistent husband, was still in London. He called at Portland Place two or three times, was received by Helen, who made him laugh, and was sent away with his tail wagging, as Helen said.

'I told him you would never return but he didn't believe it. Of course he left you some orchids,' she added.

This is how things were going on the day when Hitler's armies marched over the frontiers of Holland, Belgium and Luxembourg, the day when the Chamberlain government fell and Churchill at last came into power.

Within three weeks we knew the tragic story of the Dunkirk beaches. Hitler prophesied 'total annihilation'. Mr Churchill warned the British people to be prepared for 'hard and heavy tidings'. The waiting period was over.

When I think of the Battle of Britain I can see at once the pink and beautiful sky over roof-tops and black chimneys in Portland Place, and the black outline of Broadcasting House at the end of the street.

The sky was coloured almost every night by the fires in burning London. I remember listening for the next crash, and hearing it, and later, in September, wondering where the next bomb would fall; perhaps on Broadcasting House, perhaps on my new home. I was frightened. Sometimes I was terrified. London was being consumed before my eyes. My marriage and my past life had already been destroyed. There was probably no future for any of us. And yet the pink sky remains more vividly than anything else.

I remember looking up at the black chimney-pots on the tops of brown brick Georgian houses in Portland Place. I loved them. I loved Helen and Andy. I loved the pink sky, knowing that one life was over and another was about to begin. Surprisingly there might not be time to love and be loved by another man. A bomb might end it tonight or tomorrow night.

The madness of destruction was thrilling.

I had always loved that crescent of Regency houses at the north end of Portland Place, the ones built by Nash, a white semi-circle of smooth and shapely buildings with similar beautiful faces. One night a German bomb removed one house. The other houses, poor things, were bereaved. Hitler had taken it out, as Helen said, like a front tooth. Nash must have turned in his grave.

When it happened we were still living at 92 Portland Place but now the butler and the maids had disappeared. We were sleeping in a row of beds in the basement. That particular bomb made a sharp and shattering crash because it fell so close, and all of us were frightened sick. 'Where's the gin bottle?' said Helen. 'Nerina, find me some gin!'

When the gin had at last been found we all had a drink. We heard a banging on the front door. In came Willie, a young doctor, living in the house next to the one demolished, demanding to sleep in one of our beds for the rest of the night.

We gave him a glass of gin.

'It's the first time I have slept with three women,' said Willie, as he closed his eyes.

'We all knew that Broadcasting House was one of the targets. It was not far away. Portland Place, although wide and spacious, leading to Regent's Park, used in the old days by Queen Alexandra when driving in her carriage, was a short street, a dangerous street. That was why we had so many visitors a night. Sometimes all the beds were borrowed by friends.

'The gin bottle is empty!' said Helen, sometimes in despair, 'Nerina, who drank all the gin?'

'You did.'

'Did I? Well, find some more!'

It was difficult to sleep, even with the help of gin.

In the mornings we listened to the sound of tinkling glass. It became so familiar, like music, a little tune, half gay, half tragic. It was the silvery sound of the sweepers in the London streets. They were cheerfully sweeping up broken glass from windows and skylights smashed in the night.

I used to telephone around. 'Are you all right? What happened your way? Anybody hurt? Well, good luck.'

Sometimes I telephoned my mother in Rottingdean to tell her I was still alive. It became a ritual. It was rather like wishing your friends and relations a Happy Christmas. It was always done to the tinkle of glass.

'What happened your way? Anybody hurt? Well, good luck.'

One night in early September I had a typical experience. Helen and Andy were both sleeping at the hospital so that I was in charge of the Portland Place basement, with a woman surgeon to keep me company. It was a noisy evening. More disturbing than usual was the friendly racket caused by the anti-aircraft barrage, the familiar guns which I grew to enjoy because some of them had high-pitched nasal voices and others banged away in growling gutturals. They were like a pack of dogs. I knew their voices.

That night I heard a number of whistling bombs. Each time I ducked my head foolishly. Then came a nasty spluttering sort of bang and I knew that hundreds of nearby windows and doors had been in that moment splintered and shattered.

I was right. A few moments later I heard a noise in the hall overhead, no longer a hostile sound, just a warning that the wardens had arrived to make enquiries, or that someone wanted shelter for the night. I dashed upstairs. In the hall I found an excited party of women. As the front door had been blown open by the last bomb, the lock neatly removed and placed on the doormat, they had entered at once. The leader, a friend of Helen's, was a well-known woman doctor, a heart specialist. Followed by her secretary and her maid, she had come from Park Square East, only five minutes from Portland Place.

'We've been bombed out!'

'There's a time-bomb in the kitchen!'

'We ran all the way because the bomb might explode any minute!'

They had been sitting in the servants' basement, they told me, when the Regent's Park explosion suddenly happened. In that moment all the doors and windows seemed to fall down simultaneously, but what surprised them was the behaviour of the lighted gas fire, which detached itself from the wall and jumped into the centre of the room.

As they rushed out of the house, not even stopping for their tin hats, they encountered some wardens.

'Do time-bombs tick?' said the woman doctor, 'because if they do, I've got one in my kitchen! I distinctly heard a ticking noise!'

They had left no fewer than five wardens bravely listening to the ticking noise in the kitchen. By now, perhaps, they had all five been killed, poor things.

'Well,' I said, after much excited talk, followed by some gin, 'shall we all go to bed?'

When the light went out I suddenly remembered my manners as the basement hostess. 'By the way,' I heard myself saying, 'I don't know the name of the lady in the bed opposite mine.'

So the courtesies were exchanged in the darkness.

'Really, this is a silly war!' said the woman doctor, turning her face to the wall.

I am happy to say that her house in Park Square East was not demolished, and the next morning, when she made enquiries about the five wardens, she was told that the sinister ticking noise in her kitchen was caused by the blast damage to the kitchen clock. Apparently there was nothing wrong with her beautiful house except that it had lost all its doors and windows and a few ceilings.

And yet I loved Portland Place in the mornings.

Opposite my window the grand old houses, like warriors, stood smiling in the sun, or frowning in the rain, chipped and scarred and mutilated, waiting for the next attack. In these old houses had lived the fine people of the past. They were brave and contemptuous houses. They scorned Hitler. Near the crescent, someone had built a block of modern flats without any beauty at all, and these flats, of course, were much less dangerous to live in.

One day Helen said sadly, 'I'm afraid we shall have to move. If we stay here we shall all be killed.'

So we left the tall thin house with its large and lovely rooms, moving our beds and possessions and a few bits of furniture unwillingly to a modern flat on the first floor.

'We shall now get more sleep,' Andy said.

'And less gin,' said Helen.

The move took place at the end of September 1940. And it must have been then, or a little earlier, to the sound of sirens, at the time when London was burning and all our lives were dramatically changing, or ending, that I was invited to take part in a radio programme at Broadcasting House. The man in charge was Howard Marshall.

7 'The Voice of England'

On the day of the programme, very nervous, I was met by Sunday Wilshin, a BBC producer, whom I remembered at once as a pretty young actress in a play called *Nine Till Six* by Aimée Stuart. Her blonde hair was now cut in a masculine style, very short, and she was wearing a tailor-made suit which added to the boyish effect. In her friendly way she told me that the famous Howard Marshall was easy to work with, not conceited, not gay, not a womanizer, a man of great charm. She had an air of excitement, as though working for royalty.

When he arrived he looked twice as big as anyone else in the studio, an enormous man with a deep, velvety voice. Sunday introduced me to him. It was done with a quick glance from one to the other, each of us aware that something was happening.

Howard said: 'Is this your first broadcast?'

'I've done a few commercials for Radio Luxembourg.'

'What did you talk about?'

'Film stars and fashions.'

'Are you nervous?'

'Very.'

'It won't be difficult,' said Howard, smiling at me. 'I shall help you as much as I can.'

Nowadays the name of Howard Marshall is almost forgotten. In those days it was a household word. His name held a special meaning in the Commonwealth and for English people all over the world. They called him 'The Voice of England' and they listened with rapt attention to his weekly programmes about cricket, or fishing, or his home, or his family. Sometimes, to make a change, he interviewed a girl like me. Almost everyone who owned a radio knew and enjoyed his velvety voice. It gave importance and beauty to the things they understood, green fields and cottages, a country walk with a dog.

I remember thinking that Howard was like a large golden Labrador, gentle and kind, protective and slightly majestic. Sunday Wilshin managed to increase the feeling of his bigness and importance and fame by her attitude of reverence. (I believe that his weight at that time was eighteen stone.) I remember thinking he was handsome in a melancholy way. To me he looked more like a poet than a rugger blue. His large eyes were tired and sad.

We had no script, and I have quite forgotten what we talked about. He rehearsed me, and helped me, and made something out of me. When it started, still nervous, I replied to his questions and even made a crack about his huge size. Howard smiled at this. I remember his enquiring eyes. When it was over I felt the enquiry again and nodded my head and returned his smile.

This nod of understanding started it. He told me afterwards it was a signal, an answer, a moment in time. I only knew that I liked his pale sad face. Two days later I was greatly flattered when I heard his deep voice on the telephone. He was inviting me to lunch at the Berkeley Grill.

'Can you come? How nice. I look forward to seeing you.'

He told me afterwards that had I been late he would not have waited more than ten minutes. Fortunately I was early. As I write I can see his face on the other side of the table. I can feel the disturbing sense of enquiry and hear his voice plainly, even now, quoting lines from an old love poem. At once it held a new meaning.

'When can I see you again?' he said.

Helen and Andy were quite astonished at the turn of events. It all happened so quickly. It was bound to cause trouble.

Helen said, 'Be careful, Nerina. He's a lot older than you. He's at the dangerous age.'

'He's younger than you are.'

'Don't be rude.'

'It's true, isn't it?'

'The truth is always rude. Besides,' Helen added, 'I'm ageless. Like the Sphinx.'

Strangely enough my two passionate friends had the same initials. Helen's name was Helen Patricia Mayo and Howard's name was Howard Percival Marshall. They liked one another but in character they were totally different. Helen loved music, Howard was bored by music. Helen loved parties, Howard hated parties.

One night, in the old-fashioned dining-room at 92 Portland Place, we gave an exciting party. It began with champagne cocktails. Andy took part in it. She entertained her guests with an African dance, wearing a short skirt, rolling her hips and belly, which was always a success, as we knew by experience, because Andy had appealing brown eyes, an attractive little body, and a gift for moving it beautifully and voluptuously in a weird tribal dance invented by herself.

Everyone laughed except Howard, who began to look uncomfortable. Most of the others were light-hearted medicals. In the end, because there were no air-raids, they decided to play games, behaving like students. I remember laughing when one of them picked up a chair and gave us a joyful display of drawing-room acrobatics. A middle-aged man, one of Helen's patients, followed his example. I was breathless with laughter, and so was Helen, but Howard was embarrassed.

He said afterwards: 'I have never been to a party like that. How did I seem?'

'Miserable.'

'Perhaps I'm too old for that sort of thing.'

'You're not so old as Helen.'

It seemed to me that his only fault was a slight shortage of humour. Helen was very much an extrovert, and Howard, I suppose, was an introvert. I only knew that I loved them both.

At that time, in all parts of London, frightened by air-raids, men and women were behaving as we did, holding parties, playing childish games, falling feverishly in love, forgetting our marriages, dancing, laughing, refusing to be involved in the future, having fun, living in the present, some of us loving deeply, perhaps for the first time.

Helen thought our romance was a risk. What about Howard's wife and his two sons in America? How would I feel when Howard's family returned?

No one enjoyed the pleasant and civilized sins more than Helen. But, she said, there was a proper way to do things. Loyalty was important. Cruelty was unforgivable. To make a man happy and then hand him back, uninjured, to the other woman, was sometimes permissible in war time. On the other hand you must not, repeat *not*, muck up a marriage.

'So you see what I mean, Nerina?'

'Clearly.'

'Then why don't you take my advice?'

'I can't.'

'Why not?'

'Your advice is untakable.'

'You mean you're too much in love?'

'Yes.'

'Love is like an aching tooth.'

'What do you mean by that?'

'You should have it out.'

'Is that a pun?'

'Yes.'

'If it's a front tooth, you refuse to have it out.'

'All right,' said Helen. 'You win.'

Sometimes I did take her advice. Helen understood me better than Andy, who was more critical, and I knew very well that Helen loved me. Her father had once been a soldier, even a man of fashion as mine had been, until the day when he had shocked his stylish friends (and lost an inheritance) by entering the church. Helen, like her father, and like myself, was an odd mixture of rebel and idealist, bohemian and stylist. Above all she was very much a gentlewoman.

But Howard was the man I loved, rapidly becoming more important than Helen. He was living at that time with A. D. Peters, the literary agent, in a small flat above the Mirabelle Restaurant in Curzon Street. I remember the sitting-room, the open fire, the shelves on either side of the mantelpiece crowded with books; poetry, thrillers, bright coloured paperbacks, old thin classics, much read because he loved them, especially a little thin dirty copy of Plato, which I still possess.

There were two doors, leading to their bedrooms, and two armchairs, one for Howard, the other for Peters. In the beginning, before we became so anxious to be alone, I often joined them. The three of us drank cocktails, or whisky, or gin. I enjoyed the long conversations about books and politics and war. Howard was a fascinating talker, as Charles had been, but they would not have liked one another. Howard would have been too dignified for Charles, and Charles would have been too ribald for Howard.

On bad nights the noise of London made it difficult to talk.

There was always the barrage, the battery of huge guns in Hyde Park with different voices, booming and screeching and suddenly exploding, defending us from Hitler like an elderly collection of angry but toothless animals. We knew each of their voices and were comforted by them as by friends, even if they made no difference to Hitler. Perhaps they amused Hitler as they amused us. Between bombs, like an orchestra, they gave us a background of noise, a continuous booming and banging. Somehow it lessened the shock when a bomb fell in the next street.

Conversation, during an air-raid, became an art.

In the first stages of the battle we used to stop our talk. We waited for death and occasionally clung to one another. Later, when bombs became part of London life, we paused in the middle of a sentence, allowed time for booms and bangs, listened for the next crash, trembled, had another drink, then continued speaking, glass in hand as though nothing had happened.

To continue talking became a point of honour. We refused to be interrupted by Hitler.

When I was alone with Howard in the sitting-room he read me his favourite poems. Peters tactfully left us. I remember so well the spellbinding voice, like a musical instrument, like a cello, shaping the sentences, moulding and beautifying the words, creating something even more exciting than the poet had created.

His favourite poet was Ralph Hodgson and his favourite poem was *The Song of Honour*. I can hear his voice now, his wonderful voice, and those final hypnotizing words:

> I stood, I know not why
>   Without a wish, without a will
> I stood upon that silent hill
>   And stared into the sky until
> My eyes were blind with stars and still
>   I stared into the sky.

It was more like music than poetry and more like religion than music. It lifted us both. I really believed that he and I had reached the stars within our souls. There was no thought for the future. In those magic moments we were lost in the glory and wonder of two human beings, unexpectedly united, in a state of ecstasy, and caught, I suppose, like many another couple, by the war fever and the noise of bombs.

We were both Londoners. We told one another that Hitler was one of London's admirers. And yet London was finished, or so Hitler stated. After the British raid on Berlin he announced publicly that London was to be destroyed. On 4 September he declared:

'If they attack our cities we will simply erase theirs.'

That was why the people of London were bombed relentlessly for fifty-seven nights.

'I believe Hitler means it,' said Howard.

In the words of Winston Churchill: 'London was like some huge prehistoric animal, capable of enduring terrible injuries, mangled and bleeding from many wounds, and yet preserving its life and movement....'

I believe many Londoners felt like that about London. Nothing would induce us to leave our suffering city. At the same time, we were sick with fright.

While the bombs continued to fall my gentle companion sat by the fire and softly told me the story of his life, or bits of it, allowing me to fit the pieces together.

There was the Oxford bit.

As a young man his head and his body must have been godlike. I still have those youthful photographs. He was tall and strong and magnificent, a rugger blue, a Buddhist, a beautiful romantic young man with a soft voice and a burning sense of poetry.

His ambition then was to play rugger for England. This he never achieved. Instead he played for the Harlequins and captained them, I believe, in the end. His passion for rugger and cricket and poetry never left him. He remained with the Harlequins for twelve years.

I can see the shape of his heavy body resting in his armchair. I can see him lighting his pipe, reaching for another book of poems on the shelf. I have always hated the smell of a long-used pipe and yet so much in love was I that his old pipe appeared as clean and charming as the man himself.

He told me about his childhood. His father had been a London publisher, Percival Marshall, the man who had made and lost several fortunes. His father had endeared himself to thousands by organizing in London a yearly exhibition of model trains. His father still called Howard 'laddy', which Howard still hated.

There was the strange bit about the billiard table.

As a little boy with an evil genius he had decided to cut and rip the smooth green precious cloth of his father's billiard-table with a pair of pointed scissors. When the wicked deed was done, both thrilled and agonized, he had informed his parents in the third person.

'Howard,' he told them in a tone of pride, 'has ruined your billiard table.'

There was the bit about the BBC.

When he came down from Oxford University (rather suddenly, because his father had just lost another fortune) he had attempted, as I did later, to make a living in Fleet Street. He had rented a private office. Each morning he had made himself sit down to write articles and short stories. At first, like mine, they had all been returned.

Then his mother had suggested the BBC.

'You have such a nice voice. Why don't you use it?' his mother said. Soon after that he was engaged by Lord Reith at £5 a week as a news announcer.

Then he told me about his friendship with Dick Sheppard,

London's most famous priest, the vicar of St Martin-in-the-Fields, that beautiful church in Trafalgar Square. Howard and Dick Sheppard had worked together in London youth clubs. While the London we both loved was burning and smoking and suffering and smouldering I listened to Howard and he listened to me. We were two human beings of a different style. (That was what bothered Helen.) I can see myself, gay and excited. I can see Howard, solemn and gentle and melancholy. We spoke about love like amorous foreigners.

I believe Cammy and Renie would have liked and admired his self-made father. His mother would have baffled them, as she baffled me. His mother once said to me on the subject of death: 'I'm not afraid of it, dear. You see, I have nothing to reproach myself with.'

There never was a more respectable woman than Howard's prim little mother and I can see now that in some ways his character was moulded by her. Perhaps his shortage of humour came from her as well.

For example, the three of us were gathered in his flat and Howard was pouring out another drink. I remember this incident well. We all heard a knock. Before anyone could lift a finger to stop it happening a brass bedstead appeared at the door and was carried ceremoniously across the sitting-room into Howard's bedroom. It was a double bed. A few minutes later the single bed, no longer required, was removed by the two chambermaids, both smiling broadly at Howard and myself.

Even Peters was smiling. I was laughing out loud, as Helen would have laughed. It was difficult to be serious at such a moment and yet the arrival of a double bed, which everyone knew that Howard and I were intending to share for the first time, was in some mysterious way a blow at respectability.

For my dignified Howard it was a bad moment. It was no laughing matter. Everything about him was precious to me, including his dignity, but I could not help laughing at the expression of horror on his face when the brass bedstead made its dramatic appearance.

I had never met anyone like him. I had never loved anyone so much.

We Londoners understood what was happening. After the fall of France we were by ourselves in a war against Nazi Germany and Italy. If defeated by the German planes we should immediately be invaded by the German Navy across the Channel.

I suppose that was why we had the courage to behave as we

did in the summer of 1940. The Battle of Britain lasted officially from 8 August until 31 October. You might say we had three months of hell.

There was a bad day in London when Buckingham Palace was bombed. There was a thrilling day when the German Dornier crashed outside Victoria Station. Members of the German crew landed by parachute on Kennington Oval. The British pilot who had shot it down (and whose Hurricane went into an uncontrollable spin when the Dornier blew up beneath him) landed by parachute in Chelsea.

Of course the night raids gave us no rest.

The journalist in me insists on figures and facts. Let me record that during one night Hitler killed 12,581 men and women, injuring 16,965.

I remember so well the nervous noise of aeroplanes droning overhead. It was like the steady and maddening rhythm of a vacuum cleaner. In Portland Place it usually started at 9 p.m., soon after the sirens began screaming, and the noise continued until early morning.

I used to say, 'I wonder what will happen to us tonight?'

Helen used to say, 'We shall soon know, if we're still alive.'

One evening in the October blitz an alarming thing happened to Howard and myself. For a couple of hours there had been explosions and gunfire, but a lull came conveniently just at the moment when it was decided that Nerina would drive Howard to his flat in the Baby Austin belonging to Andy. We had dined with Helen and Andy at Portland Place. Since it was almost impossible to hire a taxi, the little car was offered by Andy, and Nerina, who was something of a bomb snob, insisted on driving it.

'I'm very good in the black-out,' I boasted. 'I've got eyes like a cat.'

As the sirens had sounded the all clear signal, there was no objection to this arrangement. We prided ourselves on ignoring the raids except when bombs were actually falling nearby.

'Well, do be careful,' said Helen. 'Driving in the black-out isn't as easy as you seem to think.'

'I'm afraid I can't offer to drive,' said Howard. 'I'm too big to get under the steering-wheel.'

So the trip started, and we trundled pleasantly down Portland Place to the BBC, turned right, then nervously crept into the darkness of Cavendish Square.

Howard said, 'Can you see?'

'Of course. I've got eyes like a cat.'

We arrived safely at Oxford Street, crossed slowly into Bond

Street, and then noticed in the middle of the road a pair of red
lanterns.

'By the way,' said Howard, 'I believe there's quite a big crater in
Bond Street. Do be careful.'

I managed to avoid the red lanterns, carefully keeping to the
left. I remember smiling in the darkness at my own cleverness.
The next moment I heard a curious crunching sound which came
unaccountably from the front of the car, like a grunt of pain, and
in two seconds, with no other warning, the Baby Austin was
perched like a sparrow on a huge pile of rocks and bricks and
lumps of concrete.

'Well,' said Howard, as the engine stalled, 'this must be the
crater I was telling you about.'

It was.

When I clambered out, tearing my silk stockings and scratching
my new shoes, I could see what had happened. The little car,
more like a golf-ball than a sparrow, was mounted on a vast slag
heap. A couple of yards beyond the car was the crater, ten feet
deep, and just big enough, as Howard pointed out, to accommo-
date the Baby Austin like a grave.

'What a good thing the engine stalled,' he said thoughtfully,
'otherwise we should both be sitting in the crater at this moment.
It would probably take days to dig us out.'

This made me laugh.

'I thought you had eyes like a cat,' he added unkindly. 'Cats
don't drive into craters.'

But the situation lost its humour when it was found that no
amount of struggling and swearing would induce the Baby
Austin to move off the slag heap. It stayed in its place, as firm as a
rock. Howard pushed and shoved, assisted by Nerina, both of us
cursing and swearing, until at last a warden appeared. He
ordered us to get a move on, saying that unless we wanted to be
caught in an air-raid (a sarcastic remark), we had better stop
playing about like children on a sand pile.

'I'll find a garage and get a rescue car,' said Howard, 'and we'll
tow this damned Baby Austin home.'

'What about *me*?' I said anxiously.

'You'd better stay here and look after the car,' said the warden,
'because *I'm* going home.'

'I'll be as quick as I can,' shouted Howard, as he ran up Bond
Street into Oxford Street. Both men disappeared into the
darkness, and at that moment it began to rain. I remember the
feeling of desperation. Knowing that Howard must be far away,
presumably running up Oxford Street, I then heard the
miserable sound of wailing sirens rising through the night.

Hitler was on his way.

As long as I live I shall never forget the loneliness of it. When the barrage began, the familiar gun voices, I climbed the rubbish heap and squeezed myself into the driving seat of Andy's little car, where I felt even less secure than I felt outside. I felt cold and cross. To die by myself on a slag heap was the final insult. I was caught like a rat in a trap. At any moment my life might be ended. To die beside Howard was something which could be endured, but to sit in the car by myself, waiting for Howard, waiting for death, was a nightmare.

How could these things be happening to Nerina, the Bond Street blonde? Was I really intended to die by myself in Andy's Baby Austin?

As I listened to the boom-bang-boom of the barrage, and became aware of occasional bombs diving like huge seagulls over Bond Street, another thought reduced me to pulp. I suddenly remembered that Hitler had dropped them night after night in the same places. I knew this was true. Quite often, in London, the same house or the same shop or the same crater would be bombed three or four times.

So then I knew that I and the Baby Austin were doomed.

Without hope I waited for the end, and as each bomb approached and whistled and passed overhead I believed it would stop and drop on the rubbish heap and me. Of course it would kill me. How could it possibly do anything else?

For twenty minutes I sat in that little car, perched on the rubble, and balanced with it like a nesting bird on the side of that crater, too frightened to move.

Howard said afterwards that the noise was no worse than usual. To me it seemed intolerable. Each bomb seemed nearer. Each gun seemed louder. Soon I reached a point of delirium and could see the pieces of my own body mixed with pieces of the little car as we lay together in the womb of the crater. I hated Hitler, I hated the Baby Austin, I hated Howard. No man had ever taken so long to find a garage. When a bomb whistled overhead it was Howard's fault as much as Hitler's. With all my heart I longed to be at home in bed, and not alone on a slag heap, unloved and unwanted.

When at last he returned I felt that Howard was not the type of man with whom a woman like myself could fall seriously in love, and when he said in his gentle voice: 'Wasn't I quick? I ran all the way and it only took me ten minutes!' I was tempted to hit him.

'I hope you weren't frightened, Nerina?'

'Not frightened! Absolutely terrified! Where the hell have you been?' I said furiously.

Later we were settled in his flat, as happy as ever, each with a deep glass of sherry, sitting as usual on either side of the fire while engines roared in the sky and bombs dropped and vast explosions shook the walls of the sitting-room.

There was always so much to say, so much to explain and try to understand. We continued all night, taking it in turns, listening to one another, sometimes stopping for the noise to die down, interrupted, forced to wait, with a shrug of irritation, before finishing a sentence. On noisy nights he pulled off his tie and jacket. It seemed wrong to be sitting sedately in a pin-striped suit while bombs rained and buildings tumbled.

I can see him now. He had changed into a blue shirt, a pair of grey flannel trousers, a soft grey sweater which he loved, he said, because he had worn it so often while standing in a trout stream in Wiltshire.

At first we talked with affection about Helen and Andy. We talked about the Baby Austin, which by now had been towed to the garage, and tomorrow would be repaired. Then we settled down to talk about ourselves. I can see his face, his eyes, his pipe. I can hear his emotional voice. 'Go on. Tell me more about Charles. Did you love him, Nerina?'

'Do you really want to know?'

'Yes, I do. Of course I do.'

On that night, inspired by the bombs, without bitterness, I tried so hard to describe what had happened, to explain the charms and vagaries of Charles, the disreputable one, to Howard, the respectable one. Both had been educated at Oxford. But Charles, as a medical student, had also spent a year or two in French and German universities. His rich father had allowed him to spend money like water. (Howard had done the same thing.) Charles had been given a wonderful sports car. This I remember telling Howard. He had driven his new car round Europe, and then, believe it or not, he had left his car, no longer wanted, on a roadside in France.

'But why?' said Howard.

'I don't know. He was a difficult person to understand.'

'He must have been a peculiar chap.'

'Yes, but he taught me a lot about life. Only Charles would have taken a girl like myself to that party in Chelsea.'

'Go on,' said my future husband, 'tell me what happened at that party.'

When the story came to an end he quietly said: 'Now tell me about your work. What happened when you met Lord Beaverbrook?'

I must explain that Lord Beaverbrook was now Minister of

Aircraft Production, a war-time hero, and Howard had met him more than once.

'Go on,' Howard kept saying, 'tell me what happened. Tell me what Beaverbrook said when you met him. I want to know everything.'

So that is how it was between us. During one of London's worst air-raids I told him the whole of my Beaverbrook story from beginning to end, about the thrill, and the agony of shyness, and the car to receive me at Leatherhead Station, and the long wait in a room with a white carpet and white furniture and blood-red cushions on a white sofa.

'Go on, Nerina. Tell me everything.'

At about three o'clock in the morning, stimulated by sherry and bombs and love, I even remembered to tell him that Beaverbrook was the first man to call me a beautiful woman.

'When we said good-bye he gave me a five pound note.'

'Why did he do that?'

'I don't know.'

'What did you do?'

'I thanked him.'

'How did you spend the money?'

'On a new pair of riding breeches.'

Howard smiled with pleasure.

'Go on, Nerina, tell me more. I want to know everything about you.'

This would have been the moment to tell him about my relationship with Helen and Andy, my love for Helen, my desire not to become a lesbian, my tendency to fall in love with women as well as with men. Did I have the courage to tell him? No, I did not.

By this time I knew enough about my future husband to realize that passionate friendships between women would have shocked him to death. He would have looked at me in horror. He would have forced himself to end our relationship. He would never have spoken to Helen and Andy again. Charles would have found a confession of this kind both amusing and charming, not in the least immoral, not even mistaken, or unwise. He would probably have laughed about it with Helen. But Charles and Howard were totally different in character. In any case, even today, there are not many normal men who can accept a bisexual woman as a possible wife. Passionate friendships are dangerous.

I can see now that Howard should have been told the whole truth and not just part of the truth. It was not fair to withhold something vital from him. And yet – and yet – how could I tell him the whole truth without disloyalty to Helen and Andy? How could I tell him the whole truth without losing his love forever?

At any rate, in the same situation, I believe I would do the same thing today. I would make the same mistakes. Rightly or wrongly, fairly or unfairly, I believe I would accept his love and pray that after the war, if we both survived the bombing of London, something or other could be arranged. He might return to his wife and family. I might continue to be his mistress. Who could say what would happen? After all, we might both be killed! So why worry about the future?

As usual during an air-raid the talk grew serious and turned sometimes to religion. Like others in the sitting-rooms and the basements and the shelters in every part of London, we found ourselves discussing the brave new world which was one day to rise out of Hitler's ruins. Is there a God? If so, why does he allow all these horrors to go on happening?

Howard believed strongly in God. His voice was thrilling. It was fiery, dreamy, spellbinding talk which he and I both loved and enjoyed, the talk of God and Socialism and the brave new world. When he talked he nearly always quoted poetry. Sometimes he stretched along the row of books on the mantelpiece for a little favourite book holding Yeats and Masefield and Chesterton and Sassoon, and several others who wrote, Howard said, as *he* would wish to write if only he could.

After poetry came love-making. We lived through a wonderful night. For the first time in my life I then had a genuine feeling of identity. I belonged to this man. I belonged to this war. I was lifted by love and fear into a world beyond and above the escapists I had known in the past.

In war-time you no longer wish to escape. You belong with joy and fear to the others who suffer with you. War is bigger than you are. Therefore you rise like a flame and burn through yourself into love and suffering and bliss. How can you try to escape? How can you wish to escape from these forces, these tall flames, so much bigger than you, your former self?

It is this sense of identity which is now so difficult to explain to post-war people. They can never understand it, the young ones who missed the war because they were not born or not old enough.

We who went through it know what we are talking about. There was suffering in it. There was magic in it too.

8   'People make such a fuss about sex'

If it had not been for Lord Beaverbrook and his brilliant work as Minister of Aircraft Production, we might never have won the Battle of Britain. In some ways it brought out the best in all of us. I would be happy to live through that wonderful time again.

> Bliss was it in that dawn to be alive,
> But to be young was very heaven!

Londoners did magnificent things without thinking twice. For Churchill we did the impossible. And Howard, my future husband, on D-Day, became a war hero. He did, I think, the bravest deed of his life.

For me the best and most exciting emotion was probably the pink sky at night and the blinding love for him and all of London as I listened in terror to the sound of explosions. I would like to feel that kind of fear and ecstasy again. I can feel some of it even now. I think we felt love and fear mixing together like a drug, a bit stronger and more potent than ever before or since. As I write about it I can see his face and hear that voice on the telephone:

'Are you all right?'

'Yes, what about you? '

'Very tired. No sleep at all.'

'Me too. Have you heard the news?'

'Yes, they nearly got St Paul's.'

'But it's still standing?'

'Yes.'

'Thank God for that.'

'Shall I see you tonight?'

'Of course.'

'Good-bye Nerina.'

'Good-bye Howard.'

As I put aside the telephone I can see Helen's laughing face and hear her mocking voice.

'Was that your boyfriend?'

'Yes. Who else?'

'Tell him to send you some more floral tributes.'

'He sent some yesterday.'

'What, no floral tributes today? Tell him we need some more roses!'

More than ever there was something motherly about Helen. She was always laughing, at the same time protective, afraid that Howard might hurt me. I can remember her indignation when a bomb made all her bottles of medicine jump off the shelf and smash themselves on the bathroom floor.

'Damn Hitler! Damn his impudence!'

In the background, trying her best to look after both of us, I can see little Andy, in a blue woollen dress, with a long full skirt and a zip up the front. I had one exactly like it. So had Helen. It was really quite an essential dress, for the act of leaping out of bed and zipping it up could be done in a flash. 'I want you and Helen both to wear them,' said Andy. 'It's important. Like a gas mask.'

She was the one who did our shopping. The ration books and clothes coupons were sometimes lost and nearly always found in Andy's bulging handbag.

I always think of Andy in her long blue dress. She was wearing it on the day she showed me her hands and pointed for the first time to the lump on one of her fingers. The lump had suddenly appeared. Andy had just left hospital (after performing a Caesarian operation) and none of us knew that the lump on her finger was the beginning of rheumatoid arthritis. The three of us were happy together. Andy had her boyfriend, a medical man with whom she sometimes spent the night, as did Helen with her fiancé (known as 'Tankie'), and I with Howard. It made no difference to our love for each other. Andy used to say: 'People make such a fuss about sex,' and Helen used to say: 'Friendship matters more than anything else.'

Poor Andy! She was wearing her nice blue dress on the day we called Black Wednesday. We had turned out the light in the sitting-room and opened the window. Helen was in the bathroom, having a bath. Andy said to me: 'We ought not to do this. It's dangerous!'

Standing side by side, we stared into the wide and silvery street. It lay beneath such a brilliant moon that no one could ever forget it. We looked over the black buildings and shadowy roof-tops into a gleaming sky, and from the great dangerous moon to the crazy loveliness of flames and streamers of light which were bursting from the clouds.

The German flares were dropping on London, falling slowly like flower petals.

I said, 'I wonder if they'll hit the BBC this time?'

'Shut up!' said Andy.

It was a fatuous remark. Immediately the words were out of my stupid mouth, a white flash of bomb lightning crossed the sky. A stuttering crash of glass and metal and falling buildings instantly followed. Hitler had replied to my idiotic question.

'See what you've done!' said Andy.

She and I, in one movement, swung round and threw ourselves flat on the floor. We could feel one another trembling. We could hear the singing, splintering sounds of glass flying into pieces and the strong familiar smashing sound of nearby houses, the bursting of windows and glass-topped front doors and mirrors and chandeliers and tumblers and wine glasses. We could hear all of them being destroyed in one fleeting second of smashing and singing and splintering.

'It's all right,' said Andy.

'What's all right?'

'What I mean is, we're not dead.'

'We found that Helen was still sitting in her bath with smashed bottles all round her.

'It's all right,' Andy said again.

'What's all right?'

'We're not dead, and neither are you. It's all right.'

'That's what *you* think,' said Helen.

Andy in those days was constantly saying, 'It's all right,' and somehow the words were comforting. I remember we moved our mattresses from the bedroom into the windowless hall which was now the most useful room in the flat. It was safer than the basement in the old house across the street, the house we loved.

That was Black Wednesday.

On Thursday morning we felt even more tired than usual. A bomb had fallen at the entrance of our building. A warden had been killed within a few yards of our front door. Helen was told a horrible story by a father living in a flat opposite. He said his baby was quite unhurt and unafraid. But the hand of a man had been found on the baby's quilt. It had been blown through the window when the bomb had fallen outside.

Some of it was indescribably tragic, and yet I was living with glory and friendship and courage. I was working as a Red Cross nurse and on Thursday morning, after a telephone call from the hospital, I found nearly two hundred casualties (most of them soldiers) waiting for treatment. They had blackened faces. They looked like miners up from the pit. The dirt and glass and small pieces of metal were deeply embedded in their skins.

I said to one of them, 'Does it hurt very much?'

'No, not a bit. I'm lucky to be alive.'

I am afraid I hated hospital work. It was mostly concerned with bedpans and scrubbing out lockers and fetching dinner trays. When Andy came on duty, I was invited to watch my friend, transformed into a surgeon, operating on her patients. This made me feel sick and faint.

Afterwards the professional nurses said kindly, smiling at me, 'Well, did you enjoy seeing that?' Out of courtesy I replied, 'Yes, thank you. It was wonderful.' And then they would say, as though offering me a five pound note, 'I'm going to do an interesting dressing. Would you like to help me?'

There was no way to escape and so now I had to stare at a gaping wound and share the distress of a miserable patient.

'Well, did you enjoy that?'

'Not much,' I said.

'Would you like to be a professional nurse?'

'Well, no.'

'Why not?'

'I'm not unselfish enough.'

Yes, I hated hospital work. I longed to be at home with Helen and Andy, or better still, at home with Howard. I knew that Helen was beginning to feel jealous of Howard. 'I like him very much as a man,' she used to say, 'but Nerina, you are bound to get hurt. Has he told his wife about you?'

'No, of course not.'

'How will you feel when he returns to his wife?'

'I only know that I love him.'

I felt safe with Howard. He felt safe with me. My gentle companion, my Labrador, was guarding me, owning me, defending me. What is more he was managing to give me a sense of purpose and a sense of God. Even now I can hear him saying, 'How can anyone doubt the existence of God? I believe,' he used to say, 'in the future. I believe we are going to rebuild Britain and create a worthwhile place for our children to live in. Do you believe in God, Nerina?'

'Yes, but I seldom go to church.'

'Do you pray?'

'Of course I pray.'

'What do you pray for?'

'Guidance.'

'You want to be shown what to do?'

'Very much indeed.'

'You're like me. I seldom go to church. Dick Sheppard used to call me a blue domer.'

'Am I a blue domer too?'

'I believe you are.'

October ended. All of us were comforted by Churchill, our magnificent leader. The bombing of London became more spasmodic. The next phase was a cloud of incendiary bombs, which Londoners pursued like football players, and controlled, and sometimes put out, with a touch of enjoyment. (I never had the luck to get one myself, but Howard did, on the roof of his block of flats. I remember feeling envious.)

At this stage everyone began to feel better, even cheerful. Churchill gave us confidence. He made us believe in ourselves as a nation of giants. Each of us could see that we were fighting in a heroic war.

I began to feel carefree, light-hearted, happy, in spite of Helen's motherly warnings. Somehow Howard had liberated me from the past. I belonged to Howard as I belonged to London. I had found my identity at last. Both Helen and Howard were passionate friends but the one I loved most was Howard.

By now I was working on a book called *We Mixed Our Drinks*. It was about myself and my friends in pre-war London. Since then we had escaped, all of us, from the bad and greedy years, the time of cocktail parties and publicity stunts, hunger marches and unemployment. We had stopped being escapists. There was nothing to escape from, except Hitler, and who wanted to escape from Hitler in time of war?

Howard continued to read poetry aloud, thrilling me with the music and emotion of his deep and velvety voice. The words of D. H. Lawrence held for us both a new and exciting message.

Not I, not I, but the wind that blows through me
A fine wind is blowing the new direction of Time.

When he read these words in his musical voice I began to understand the man I loved. I admired my solemn Howard more than anyone I had ever known, and yet, in some ways, the new love was strangely restricted.

The Mirabelle Restaurant, beneath his block of flats, was always our meeting place in the evenings. There we dined at a corner table. We were becoming well known to all the waiters and it was soon understood that if a celebrity entered, or someone who recognized Howard, we quietly disappeared upstairs. The outside world knew nothing about us. Here was a war-time love affair and the waiters protected us from gossip and embarrassment.

Howard made me see that subterfuge was necessary. We might be dancing together. The band might be playing our favourite music. And then would come a movement of people at the entrance, a sudden tension, a frown from Howard, a quick decision to stop dancing and hide ourselves from intruders.

Howard would say, 'I know that man. Do you mind if we go upstairs?'

'Do you think it really is necessary?'

'I am afraid it is.'

'I was enjoying myself.'

'I am sorry, Nerina.'

I began to understand that Howard must not be seen with me in public. It had something to do with Howard's respectability. Of course I knew he was right, and yet it really was a new and unpleasant sensation to be hurried out of a restaurant when someone special arrived, someone from the Saville Club perhaps, or the BBC, or one of the Ministries, someone like Julian Huxley, or Stephen Potter, or Francis Meynell, or C. P. Snow, or Compton McKenzie.

'I am so sorry,' he would say. 'You don't mind, do you?'

I minded very much.

'No,' I said, 'I don't mind.'

I told myself I was lucky to have such a well known admirer. Everything about him delighted me. I was pleased by his thick smooth hair with a slanted parting on the right, not the left side of his head. I was charmed by his straight nose, rather short, and his large eyes, and his full lips. Most of all I was fascinated by his voice and by his thoughts. This big man, so gentle and serious, so different in many ways from Charles, had the emotions and intuitions of a woman.

Why should he find in me what he needed? Was it sex? Was it soul?

Helen said: 'It's sex, Nerina. Don't take it too seriously. I don't want you to be hurt.'

Even now I find it difficult to write about Howard. I was blinded by him. When I think of him, and try to describe him, I see that gentle Labrador, guarding me from others. Unlike Charles, he was extremely possessive. It seemed to me that he and Charles were two sides of the coin. One was a winner and the other was a loser. One was good and the other was bad. He used to say: 'Why do you love dancing?'

'I don't know. I've always loved it.'

'All right, let's dance. I'm afraid I'm not very good.'

He had seldom danced, and yet he was full of rhythm. I love to remember those evenings when the floor was almost empty and we danced like one person to a heartbreaking little tune called *Begin The Beguine*. At that time, dancing at the Mirabelle, we even made plans to have lessons in dancing. We would always dance together, never with anyone else. We would learn to dance like professionals. In those moments he and I were deeply happy, and then, like a cold wind, would come the sudden arrival of someone he knew, and the expected words, 'I'm sorry, Nerina, do you mind if we go upstairs?'

I tried so hard to understand him. I used to say, 'What makes you so different from other people?'

'Am I so different?'

'Sometimes I think you must be unique.'

'Why?'

'Your attitude to women.'

'What do you mean?'

'In some ways you're almost a Puritan.'

'Are Puritans unique?'

'I suppose they exist. You don't find them in London.'

Until we met there had never been a woman in his life other than the beautiful girl he had married. (What would Charles have said about this?) The honeymoon had left him disappointed and puzzled. He knew he was not very skilful as a lover. Later they became parents, and he, my charming Howard, became a celebrated man whose voice, once a week, telling them about his home and his children, could be recognized by thousands of people in Canada and Australia and the Commonwealth countries as well as in the United Kingdom. Howard had become a symbol of the good life. He was 'The Voice of England'. All over the world his fans knew the names of his sons, and his wife's name, and even his dog's name. He was a symbol of home and family. No wonder my admirer was respectable. No wonder he made me feel safe and protected.

But his listeners had no idea what was now happening to Howard. With his loved ones in America, he was still giving weekly broadcasts about England. He talked constantly about country fields and rivers and fishing, and London air-raids. What he told them had nothing to do with Nerina, with his passionate friendship, and certainly not with dancing night after night at the Mirabelle.

'I feel a bit of a cheat. I've never done this before.'

'Perhaps your listeners would understand.'

'I don't think they would.'

In a way (as the world of a small fish is like the world of a bigger fish) his problems and plans were those which had faced the Duke of Windsor when he met Mrs Simpson. Howard was not on the side of the Duke. Yet Howard was caught in the same trap. We had both been caught. That was why the waiters in the Mirabelle smiled at us and helped us to keep our secret. No one at the BBC must hear about this.

I continued to ask him difficult questions. Why had he possessed only one other woman? How could such a man with a fine strong body confine himself to a single experience until he met me?

Howard told me that fidelity mattered as much as love. Should a woman be unfaithful to him he would never look at her again. He expected fidelity, and he gave it. Nothing else would do.

'You are the second woman in my life. I shall never be unfaithful to you, Nerina.'

'What would happen if I were unfaithful? Supposing I fell in love with another man?' (I dared not say, 'Supposing I fell in love with another woman?')

'If you were unfaithful I should leave you.'

'I believe you would. That's what I mean when I call you a Puritan.'

'All right, I'm a Puritan.'

'Charles used to say that any experience is better than none.'

'I'm not Charles.'

But I could not help wondering what Charles would have replied. My first lover had known and seduced so many grateful young women, and I wanted to know what was wrong with romantic promiscuity, the love-and-let-love style of living I had learned from Charles.

'Well, you see, it *debases the coinage,*' Howard told me.

Howard, my solemn Howard. I think it impressed me more than anything he ever said. So there we sat in the two armchairs in the flat above the Mirabelle, air-raids outside, love and fascination within, questioning one another about the past.

'Do you regret the past, Nerina?'

'No, I don't think so. I learnt a great deal from Charles.'

'There were others?'

'Yes, there were others.'

'Not important?'

'No, not important.'

How could I make him understand that when you are young and rebellious there comes a vital need to kick over the traces?

Until he met me Howard had never talked to an escapist. He belonged within his English background like an oak tree. He was a man of integrity. Now he was listening and learning from Nerina, who was listening and learning from Howard. Talk was important to both of us, and so, as Helen pointed out, was sex.

* * *

During the October blitz, and the winter which followed, I listened in wonder to the spellbinding voice. He was telling me about God, about poetry, about love. I told Helen that I belonged to this man. I began to see the brave new world which he and I were helping to build, entering it without loneliness, lovers and companions. I began to believe in the future, as he did, knowing that after the defeat of Hitler the pattern of living, in England, for each of us, would be more serious, more rewarding, more hopeful.

We had found happiness. We had been given a sense of purpose. Perhaps it was part of the war fever. I only know that it brought out the best in all of us and I would be happy to live through that wonderful time again.

To be young was very heaven.

It has been said before but let me say it again. We survived in London because of a handful of fighter pilots had the courage to prevent Hitler from gaining control of the air over the Channel. Hitler found this could not be done. So the German admirals refused to attempt an invasion. I am proud of it still. Today, for fear of boring the young, we never speak of the war with Hitler. I think this is wrong.

The story is one of incredible courage.

The British were fighting Hitler on behalf of our friends from 10 May 1940 until 22 June 1941. We were unprepared. During that awful time it never occurred to Churchill or anyone who loved him that we might not succeed in winning the war. For this reason, out of courage and conceit, we stood alone against more than two hundred German divisions and the massed Luftwaffe. We also had a war on our hands against the Italians in North Africa. What Churchill made us feel was a sense of exhilaration. We were afraid to show that we were afraid.

For me it was a time of starting and startling happiness. I no longer felt lonely. I belonged in London, with Helen and Andy, who were now my family, and with Howard, my lover.

Where was Aimée Stuart and where was my mother?

My beloved Aimée, having left London for Scotland, was now settled in her new flat (opposite Harrods), living in comfort with a sister and an aunt, supporting them both out of royalties. Her husband, Phillip, had been an alcoholic, and had died before the outbreak of war. Aimée had spent a few months in Vienna in order to recover from the shock. At the time when I left Wentworth Day, she had given me a bed (as she always did when her friends were between husbands) and had listened endlessly to my problems.

Now, on a quiet afternoon, wanting to tell her about Howard, I went to her flat for a cup of tea.

'Why don't we meet more often, dear? Are you in love with someone?'

'Yes.'

'Is it a man or a woman?'

'It's a man.'

'I thought so. Is he married?' said Aimée, coming straight to the point.

'I'm afraid he is.'

'Where is his wife?'

'In America.'

'What is she doing in America?'

'Looking after two sons.'

'Does she know about you?'

'No, not yet.'

'Is he going to tell her?'

'I believe he is.'

'She will probably forgive him, but when she comes home,' said Aimée, 'she will claim her husband and you will lose him.'

'I know, I know.'

'Poor poppet! You learn about life the hard way, don't you?'

Aimée was then writing a play called *Jeanie*, a comedy based on her holiday in Vienna (later to be filmed). I found it easier to tell Aimée about my problems with Howard than to tell my mother. Renie was already looking round for her next husband. From Rottingdean she had moved to a small house near a good riding stable between Patcham and Hove.

'I have bought a very good mare. She jumps beautifully. Would you like to try her, dear?' said Renie on the telephone.

'I'd love to try her.'

'Then come and spend a week-end in my new house. It's time we had a talk.'

'What about?'

'Marriage.'

'I don't want to talk about marriage.'

'All right. Let's talk about horses.'

'That's a good idea. I prefer horses,' I said, 'to marriage.'

In fact Helen and Andy and Howard were the people in my life who loved and helped me more than anyone else. Helen kept saying: 'Nerina, I don't want you to be hurt.' Andy kept saying: 'This infatuation won't last.' Apparently I was loved very much by all three, especially by Howard and Helen.

Howard was still with Lord Woolton at the Ministry of Food. He was longing to be in uniform. This he finally achieved, in spite of his age, for which Helen and Andy admired him. He became, to his delight, chief war correspondent for the BBC, eventually served in North Africa and wrote a book called *Over To Tunis*. It was published in 1945 and it sold 10,000 copies. His act of courage on D-Day is something I can never forget.

As I write I am remembering a summer holiday in 1941, before the excitements of D-Day (which was June 1944), when the Germans were invading Russia and the Atlantic Charter was being signed by Winston Churchill and President Roosevelt.

We went to a village in Wiltshire. We stayed for a time at Rose Cottage, near a trout stream, a place we both loved, pretending to be husband and wife. This made us both feel a fraud. All the same, it was fun. One morning I found myself in a valley of mud and juicy grass where amiable cows stood knee-deep in sweet-smelling slush. They looked at me with quiet disapproval.

Howard said tactfully, 'I'll leave you by yourself to practise.'

'I'm no good at fishing.'

'Never mind, you'll soon learn.'

'I haven't got the patience.'

'You can do anything you want to do.'

'Can I?'

'Of course you can. You're that kind of person.'

I can see him now, with his fishing-rod, as he walked up the river-bank, a broad country figure in a tweed jacket. He moved slowly in enormous rubber boots, puffing at his awful old pipe which I was not quite able to love, and it, the pipe, could just be seen when he turned his head to watch the scuffle of a moorhen, rushing and swishing in the clean clear water.

I was very much in love.

I stood on my bit of the river-bank, hoping to please Howard by catching a fish. I did. I caught a grayling. It rose to my fly and I managed to bring it to the bank. But Howard had taken the landing net. To land my fish was impossible owing to a barbed-wire fence between me and my squirming victim. In my efforts to do the impossible I broke Howard's delicate rod.

Now this may seem a small mishap. To a fisherman it is almost unforgivable. It is worse than laming his horse, or stealing his money, or smashing his car, or burning down his home.

When I found Howard he was fishing imperturbably, pipe in mouth, a couple of fine trout in the grass beside him. I was almost in tears. I shouted at him furiously. 'You took the landing net! And now I've broken your beastly rod!'

'What? You don't mean you've *broken* it?' We both knew it was his favourite fishing-rod, owned by him since childhood.

'It was your fault! You took the landing net!'

'Oh well, never mind,' he said sadly.

'I hate fishing! I hate it! I hate it!'

Because I loved him I tried again, and caught the smallest trout either of us had ever seen. I threw it back in the river.

'It's no good, Howard.'

'What's no good?'

'I shall never like fishing. It's not my cup of tea.'

'Don't give it up. It might grow on you.'

'I don't want it to grow on me. I haven't got the patience.'

'Why don't you like it?'

'I find it so *boring*.'

Fishermen's wives have much to suffer because most of them dislike fishing as I do. In a moment of confidence one of them once said to me, 'When you fail to catch a fish it's like failing to have an orgasm. Do you know what I mean?'

At any rate, I decided not to spoil the holiday by allowing Howard to teach me to fish. He did the fishing. I did a lot of reading. At night, by the cottage fire, when the little cold room was warmed by flickering logs, we tried to make plans for the future. We pretended the war was over. We talked about socialism.

Howard used to say, 'I love these talks. I'm thinking aloud.'

'Me too.'

'Do you really believe in socialism?'

'Of course I do.' (Today, of course, I believe in Margaret Thatcher.)

I can remember the thrill of socialism. In our brave new world the banks and insurance companies and building societies and railways and mines and hospitals would all be controlled by the Government. After the war everything would be different. Private enterprise might still exist on a small scale. The new system of living would be based on the ideal of service. Every boy and girl in Britain would be expected to give two years of service to the state, one year of military training and one year of citizen training.

How wonderful it all seemed!

Better still, I remember returning to London with a feeling of relief and delight because now the decision had been made. It was wrong to deceive his wife. Somehow he would manage a visit to America in order to see her and tell her the truth.

Back in my London room, nearly filled by three bookcases and two chests of drawers, stacked with reference books and paperbacks and biographies from the London Library, I worked much harder than before. I was finishing something. It was the story called *We Mixed Our Drinks*. I was struggling to set on paper the tale of a 19-year-old girl who became a film critic, myself and Charles, cocktail parties, marriage.

It was a true book like the one I am writing now, but not nearly so frank about women who fall in love with women. It was a picture of pre-war London. I felt happy to write about the past because I believed so firmly in the future.

That winter (1941–42) everyone became more hopeful.

When Japan attacked the U. S. fleet in Pearl Harbor the picture changed. It was a world war. The Allies were now supported by the United States and Russia against the forces of Germany, Italy and Japan.

On Christmas Day Howard gave a magnificent broadcast.

I remember listening to it, filled with pride, loving the emotional voice, the tone of reassurance. The one who managed to describe it was Andy. She called it a 'double-bedded voice'. Even Howard laughed when Helen told him this.

'I wish *I* had said it,' said Helen, speaking as the wit of the family.

'You will, dear,' said Andy, 'you will.'

When the broadcast was over I walked with him round and round Regent's Park, in a biting wind, living through every word of it, repeating and remembering it, reviving the lifeless Howard with praise and sympathy.

'Was I all right?' he kept saying.

'You were marvellous.'

'Do you mean that? What did you really think of it? Tell me about it.'

He was a true artist. When a broadcast was out of him he needed help. I felt like a doctor as we marched in that icy wind round and round Regent's Park. I felt needed more than ever before in my life.

Howard kept his promise about visiting America. I forget how this was arranged, and it must have been difficult. His wife was informed about me. She was told what many war wives must have been told. She decided to return to London.

I remember those enormous fat letters from America. I can almost feel them between my fingers. I received those love-letters by every post. I read them in the house at Quainton, a week-end house, with a garden, an orchard and a field for our horses. It belonged, of course, to Helen and Andy. I remember telling them that Howard's wife had agreed to come home. I had offered not to see him for three months. If he and she could

manage to put their marriage together I would never see
Howard again.

'Do you really mean that?' said Helen suspiciously.

'I do.'

'Are you absolutely certain?'

'Yes, I am.'

'Good girl!' said Helen in her motherly voice. 'Give the poor
man a chance to settle down with his wife.'

Indeed I meant it. I was waiting to be told my destiny. As a
nation we were all waiting for a decision about D-Day, and I,
Nerina, was waiting for a decision about Howard.

In London we still had occasional air-raids. By now we
understood them. They were part of our lives. Many people
continued to sleep on the platforms of the Underground
stations. The trains whistled by their beds and blankets and
bodies as if they had no importance. We were waiting for
Churchill to tell us what to do. It is strange how confident we all
felt about the future.

In the summer of 1942 I was working for British Overseas
Airways. Each morning and evening I rode through the London
traffic on a bicycle. On wet days I wore a bright yellow
mackintosh cape, like an errand boy. At the office I changed into
a smart tailor-made suit which was carried in the basket on my
handlebars.

These bicycle rides were exciting.

At the week-ends I worked with Helen in the garden at
Quainton. We galloped our horses round the field. My country
bedroom was very small, overlooking the orchard. From my
window I could see a green round hill with a crown of elm trees
leaning away from the wind and supported, it seemed, by the
sky. In this room I read his letters until I knew them by heart. It
was a good life even when Howard was away. My generous
mother had decided to give me Kitty, her well-mannered mare,
a wonderful present, and now she sent us a second horse on
trial. He was huge and magnificent, a dapple-grey with a long
mane and tail, suitable for Helen. But my mother said he was
untrained. Andy, a bad rider, decided with great courage to try
him when no one was looking.

I remember so well what happened.

We came out of the greenhouse, Helen and I, having left poor
Andy in the kitchen. She had managed to saddle him, mounted
in the field (a stupid thing to do) and had instantly been thrown
by the indignant horse.

She came to meet us with a guilty expression.

'I ought not to have done it.'

'Done what?' said Helen.

'I ought not to have annoyed him.'

'Who?'

'Nerina's new horse.'

'Do you mean he bucked you off?'

'Yes, but it's all right.'

'What's all right?'

'It might have been worse. I've broken my arm, that's all.'

'Are you out of your mind?' said Helen. 'Have you lost your reason?'

'No,' said Andy, 'it's quite all right. Don't be angry.'

'Does it hurt?'

'Not at all. It's only a broken arm.'

In the end Helen began to laugh, so did poor Andy, so did I, and so, perhaps, did the horse. We bandaged her up and put her arm in a sling. The big grey indignant horse was returned to my mother, my intrepid mother, who rode him on the Brighton Downs, as gallant as ever, and then sensibly sold him to someone who unwisely bought him.

While I was in Quainton, dreaming of Howard, my mother, in her Sussex village, was already dreaming of Noel. Did he know it? She had decided to make him my next and most youthful stepfather. I suppose you could call my mother a compulsive marrier. She kept on doing it because it always seemed right. And Noel, a bachelor, twenty-two years younger, unsuitable in every way, finally turned out to be the one she loved best and needed most. (He was to become Number Six.)

But I was not a compulsive marrier.

I read again and again the long fat letters from America and promised Helen to prevent myself from hurting Howard's wife and family if that were possible. I used to read those letters at my window overlooking the orchard. That is why I remember so clearly every detail of the garden; the croquet lawn, the sundial, the little pond with goldfish and waterlilies on it, and especially the orchard and the green round hill and the elm trees leaning on the skyline.

It was difficult to think of anything but Howard, and yet I seldom mentioned my secret problems and doubts. To Helen and Andy it was just a war-time romance. They wanted me to be happy and not to make others unhappy. When his family returned from America, Howard would settle down like everyone else to the joys of married life. Nerina would then have to forget him, whether she liked it or not.

'And about time too,' said Helen with her usual grin. 'Howard is not like us. He's far too respectable for a girl like you.'

Andy said: 'For goodness sake, put him out of your mind.'
'How?'
'I don't know. Write another book, or something.'
Meanwhile I grew tense and nervous. It was a long summer
for all of us. We were waiting for news. What about D-Day?
What about the shortage of ships? What about Howard? What
about Nerina?

He came home, as arranged, followed a little later by his
family, and we promised one another to play fair, not to write,
not to telephone, not to meet. At the end of three months we
would know the answer. In my heart I knew that Helen and
Andy were right. All I had now was a bundle of letters from
America and these I continued to read. They were comforting. If
he loved me so much, how could he leave me? To be parted
from Howard seemed unreal. It could not be the truth.

What I remember now is a guilty feeling followed by joy and
surprise and relief and a sense of hungry delight when I met
him by accident. I believe it took place in Park Lane. I was riding
my bicycle, perhaps on my way from work, and was greeted
suddenly by a man, the most familiar man in the world, who
raised his hat and smiled as though nothing had been changed. I
stopped and we talked.

We were breaking the rules, for we had not been parted for
three months, as promised, only for two. I suppose he must
have been waiting in Park Lane, or wherever it was, for he knew
my bicycling habits. I remember the expression on his face.

'I can't stand it much longer, Nerina.'

As I leaned on my bicycle, hiding my emotion, he told me he
had made up his mind what to do. It was not, he said, to live
with his wife and family.

9 D-Day

His uniform was a great success. His huge figure seemed even more enormous in khaki battledress and the general effect was masculine magnificence, even though I never quite liked the beret. His thick hair was concealed by it and somehow his head looked too big for it.

'You're not the type for a beret,' I said.

'Why not?'

'You're too dignified.'

'I don't want to look dignified. I want to look like a war correspondent.'

'You mean you want to look like everyone else.'

'Yes, I do. I want to be part of this war.'

I knew exactly what he meant. London was full of young men in blue and khaki uniform, and now, in spite of his age, Howard was one of our defenders.

His new job suited him. He was chief war correspondent for the BBC. Part of his job was to work out a training course for himself and his team. He was the leader. Among them were some famous names: Richard Dimbleby, Wynford Vaughan Thomas, Chester Wilmot and several others, but Howard was indisputably the boss. Before they all went to North Africa his team of young men were training like rugger players, running and jumping and leaping over walls. He enjoyed every minute of it. He had not been captain of the Harlequins for nothing.

I knew he was longing for this experience, and of course I was proud of him. So when they departed, and when I heard his voice on the radio, telling us about the Eighth Army and General Montgomery (already known as 'Monty') I felt honoured as well as excited. In London the radio became much more important to all of us. To me it became a lover. I listened to the six o'clock news, the nine o'clock news, the final news, the early morning news.

'Can't we turn off that bloody radio for five minutes?' Helen enquired.

'No, I might miss Howard.'

'That's all very well. Andy and I know everything Howard ever said. We know it by heart.'

'It's the sound of his voice that matters. Not what he says.'

'Cor love a duck,' said Helen. 'Why do Andy and I have to suffer?'

'After all, he's my husband.'

'No, he isn't. Not yet.'

'In the eyes of God he is.'

'Not in my eyes,' said Helen.

In May 1943 the German armies in North Africa surrendered. Soon after that Howard returned home. Reluctantly he changed from his uniform into a dark pin-stripe suit and resumed his work with Lord Woolton at the Ministry of Food. But he was still employed by the BBC, and at any moment he might be ordered abroad.

Howard and I were wildly happy.

The Battle of the Atlantic had been won. The fall of Mussolini came in July. Hitler's nightmare was said to be a war on two fronts. We all knew it was coming. We were talking of the Second Front as people now talk of Ascot or the Derby or the Grand National.

But the time had not arrived.

What I remember most clearly is the sense of rising happiness, the delight when we found a small furnished flat in Basildon Court, not far from the BBC. At last we had a bedroom, bathroom, sitting-room and kitchen entirely to ourselves, and it seemed too good to be true. It cost eight guineas a week, which then seemed a lot of money. The little rooms looked south over Devonshire Place, catching all the sunlight. I loved it, and so did Howard. It was the nearest thing to paradise.

Something else comes to mind.

He had not long been with me and both of us were still in a state of fine careless rapture; exuberant, youthful, possessive, inexperienced in the sudden joy of this close and overwhelming love. We were vulnerable. Neither of us quite understood what was happening to the other one. In a way we were still strangers.

As usual I see things in pictures. I remember walking along Devonshire Place in the summer sunshine. I looked up. I saw him in a white shirt, open at the neck, his elbows resting on the window-sill, his face changed by something inside him, dark with anger, as though waiting for me in a state of anguish. What had I done to annoy him? I was returning home a little later than promised. At that moment I suddenly felt like running away.

But when I caught his eye, and waved and smiled, the

expression on his face disappeared. I remember feeling alarmed. Somehow that angry frown was a signal, a cloud no bigger than a man's hand.

At that time each day was an experience in love. We were learning fast. After a few weeks of bliss in the furnished flat we found an unfurnished flat in the same building. The rent, I believe, was two pounds a week. Our new home faced a public house in Marylebone High Street. The kitchen was the size of a cupboard. Never mind, we loved it. We both knew it was not beautiful, or comfortable. For two large people who immediately acquired a dog, it was more like a box.

'We've got to economize,' I said.

'That's what my mother used to say to my father.'

'Well, she was right.'

'I'm like my father. I can make money but I can't seem to keep it.'

'Why not?'

'Well, you see, I never know what happens to it,' said Howard.

I soon discovered that although he was earning and had usually earned a large salary he was, and had usually been, on the verge of bankruptcy. With him it was an occupational disease, a financial ulcer. It seemed to have no understandable cause, and yet it was never far away. My mother had suffered all her life from the same disease. I knew the symptoms. There were terrible interviews with the bank manager. When these failed, there were terrible interviews with Graham Maw, the solicitor. Howard's financial ulcer was giving him a lot of trouble.

Someone suggested that I was the one to sort things out.

Remembering the sufferings of my mother, I agreed to become his manager. It was just as I feared. We had arguments about money. Had I not seen men and women attempting to manage my mother?

I was thankful when Graham Maw took over my job. He arranged Howard's life very well. The rent and all the enormous accumulated debts were paid monthly by him who worked out the budget, and each week a registered envelope containing £8 was received by us.

This tiny amount was Howard's allowance for personal expenses and housekeeping and entertaining.

'It's ridiculous! How can two human beings manage on £8 a week?'

'It's got to be done,' I said.

'For one thing, we shall starve.'

'Don't forget my salary. I'm earning £8 a week as well as you.'

'But I earned more than £8 a week when I was a boy.'

'You're not a boy now. We've got to economize or go bankrupt.'

'You sound like my mother.'

'I can't help it. I don't like it any better than you do.'

Sometimes it made him angry. I was beginning to know his faults. But my dear extravagant companion agreed to this unpleasant weekly budget for twelve months, and by then, Graham Maw told him, our problems would be over. The situation was comic. No one understood, except my mother, how it came about.

His friends thought of him as rich and successful, at the top of his profession, a man to be envied. Howard was all these things. But, like my mother, he suffered from a chronic hardupness and overdrawnness, a condition of chequebookitis. These troubles were coupled with a total inability to understand, as James Thurber sympathetically put it, that the jaws of the Sea Puss get you in the end.

Now most of us possess a cheque-book. Through the years we form the habit of writing cheques, and filling in the stubs. Howard was different. He loved writing cheques. To my knowledge he had never in all his life filled in the stubs of any cheque-book. For this reason he never had the slightest idea whether or not he was solvent.

'What difference does it make?'

'It makes a great deal of difference,' I said.

'I don't believe it.'

He might have spent ten, twenty, thirty, even a hundred pounds on something he needed, or fancied, but when, where, why, how much, or what for, no one could ever remember, least of all Howard. When I told my mother about this little trouble she understood at once. He said he had always been like it, and could not bring himself to change. My mother said neither could she.

Unfortunately it was the only thing they had in common. At their first meeting they seemed to get along very well, and then, I think, he took fright. He had never met a woman with five husbands behind her, and another one looming up in front. To make matters worse, the new one was a man of his own age.

Howard had never been a ladies' man. He distrusted women. In self-defence he brought out his pipe and puffed at it, which sometimes drove them away. Notwithstanding Howard's pipe, my mother was at her best, gay, light-hearted, happy, determined to help and encourage. She was touched by our poverty. She offered at once to give us a small sofa and two armchairs.

Charmingly she said she had more than she needed, having just sold a house. Would we please accept a few curtains and cushions? What about a nice mahogany table?

I thanked her from the bottom of my heart.

She was then living in her third or fourth country house. In the next ten years she was to buy and sell and live in thirty houses. Sussex, her favourite county, is still stuffed like a cake with my mother's beloved houses, large, small, beautiful, hideous, little ones in need of help, villas, cottages, mansions. To her they were like unwanted animals, or handicapped children. She rescued them. She gave them new life.

Her latest house was so small we could hardly sit down. We went there to see the sofa and the two armchairs.

'I hated selling this little one. But I've found something so nice in Crowborough. Would you like me to give you a carpet, dear?'

Nearly everything in our Marylebone flat was provided in this light-hearted way. It was impossible to refuse. All the same our two rooms were far too small. I wondered what would happen when the dog arrived?

I need not have worried.

A corgi puppy, three months old, he sat by my desk when I was writing. He partly destroyed my favourite book on architecture. He pulled our new sofa to pieces, the one presented by my mother. But he came with us on bicycle rides, carried by one of us in a basket, strapped to the handlebars, and we both adored him.

'He loves you more than me,' Howard said.

'Oh no, he loves us both.'

'Anyway, he's your dog. I've given him to you.'

'Thank you,' I said. 'He belongs to us both.'

We named him after Clement Attlee. He was called Clem. He became the most important member of the household. One day, to our horror, he swallowed a stone, thrown for him by a child in the Park. After that Clem had a major operation, and we both suffered agonies. In the end, we nursed him back to health.

Howard was now writing *Over To Tunis*, which sold 10,000 copies, and my own book, which later sold out in three weeks, was being criticized and refused by one publisher after another.

Even this I did not mind.

As an act of love I was learning to cook, which I hated. Until then I had never learned, on the theory that no one can force you to do what no one has taught you to do. But cooking is like death. It comes to us all.

I was so happy that I hardly noticed the war. Howard kept telling me about it. In August Sicily was captured by the Allies. In September Italy was invaded. In spite of all the victories, London was in for a nasty shock. We were not expecting it. It hit us in the summer of 1944 when Howard was in France. The rockets and flying bombs brought us back to a sickening sense of fear, followed by panic, that awful thing in our stomachs, a new knowledge, a new terror, described by Churchill as 'blood, sweat, and tears'.

I had almost forgotten how frightened you could be when those raids started. Londoners called them 'buzz bombs'. You heard each one of them zooming overhead like a huge bee until the buzzing suddenly ceased and you waited during two or three minutes of tense silence for the monster to travel serenely and soundlessly, and then, with terrible violence, to vomit and explode in the next street.

The most awful part was the silence.

How far, you wondered, would the monster travel in those empty minutes? Would it fall in the next street? Would it fall in your own street? Would it fall on you?

It became known, and hated, and reported in the newspapers as 'Hitler's secret weapon'. To us, in London, it was the worst ordeal of the lot.

I was still working for British Overseas Airways, which was close to Victoria Station and therefore a target. We worked in a modern office lighted by huge windows. When we heard the sirens, and then, almost immediately, the first of the buzz bombs, we jumped to our feet and rushed into the windowless passage because there was no time to get downstairs. I can still see the face of a young man in my office which truly turned green with fright.

Once it came very close indeed. I remember that young man's face and my own, probably, was as green as his. When I answered the office telephone, a few minutes later, I heard Helen's voice saying: 'Are you all right, Nerina?'

'Yes, but what about you and Andy?'

'We're all right. What time will you be home? Would you like me to come and collect you?'

In Howard's absence I always returned to Helen and Andy for love and protection. Clem, my dog, enjoyed living with them as much as I did because they still kept two or three dachshunds, all of them bitches, which appealed to Clem very much. While this was going on, buzz bombs and green faces, I am glad to say my place of work was changed. Instead of helping in the publicity department of BOA (for which I was paid £8 a week) I found myself in a much nicer job as Appeals Organizer for the Girl Guides International Service. My salary was considered enormous by the Guides. It was £4 a week.

I remember being interviewed by Lord Burnham, and then by Lady Burnham, one of the commissioners. I was asked to raise a hundred thousand pounds within a year for refugee work overseas.

'I know nothing about it,' I said. 'I'm sorry to say that I've never even been a Girl Guide.'

I did not tell them I was a divorced woman, not quite married (as they thought) to Howard. I wanted to tell them I was living happily in sin whenever Howard was not in France or North Africa. But the Girl Guide movement was a bit too respectable for cheerful concubines like me.

I enjoyed my work. In their friendly way they asked me to criticize them in one of those open-air talks to leaders and organizers and I remember saying: 'We all know you are good women, but there is no need to *look* like good women.'

This little piece of wit made everyone laugh. It might even have done something to improve the appearance of the Guiders, who then wore a horrible blue cotton uniform so that dowagers looked like scullery-maids. Afterwards they changed it.

My kind employers liked Howard as much as they liked Helen and Andy. When Howard was in France they were always saying: 'How is your husband?' At one point, in France, out of zest and enthusiasm, he was is serious trouble with the army for being in a forbidden place at a dangerous time. He received a cable from the BBC and I still remember the laconic words: 'Please stay put.'

When we read in the daily press about Howard's problems with the army, I had a sympathetic smile from my employers.

'Is your husband in prison?' they said.

Perhaps they guessed we were not so married as we tried to appear. I wonder? At any rate, our marriage took place in Marylebone, in the Registry Office, not far from Portland Place and the BBC, when Howard was home on leave. There was no publicity. Nobody noticed a paragraph in one of the evening papers and for this we were thankful.

Each of us had been divorced, and now we were hurriedly and secretly married. The reception was given for us by Helen and Andy in the sitting-room of their flat and I seem to remember that Helen made a speech. My mother, dressed in sky blue, thought it was wonderful. I was glad she did not hear Andy's remark, spoken without a smile, with no sign of criticism, as only a Yorkshire woman could have spoken, 'Well, Nerina, I give your marriage six years.'

At this I laughed, even though I felt hurt. I think I reminded Andy of the day when her arm had been broken after riding the big grey horse against my advice. We all do things we are told not to do. In the end, it comes out in the wash.

After the wedding reception my two devoted women friends wished me luck, and kissed me good-bye. Helen joined me in the bedroom, helped me to put on my coat, and my pretty hat, then took me in her arms for a final hug and cuddle. 'I shall miss you very much, Nerina.'

'I shall miss you and Andy more than I can say.'

'I like Howard but I am afraid you are both going to be hurt.'

'Why?'

'Husbands come and go,' said Helen, 'but friendship lasts forever. You can always return to us. Don't forget that.'

A few tears were shed and then, with smiles on our faces, we returned to the sitting-room and joined the others, including my radiant mother, who seemed even more delighted than was necessary. Her turn was coming with Noel. I did not know it but she did. She would soon be a bride for the sixth time. She could hardly wait.

'I am so glad you are happy. I'm happy too,' she said.

Helen said, with tears in her eyes, 'Good-bye, old girl. Take care of yourself,' and then turned away, looking for another drink.

Andy said, 'We shall miss you. Good-bye, Nerina.'

And that was that. I have even forgotten the date of my wedding. For me it was not a landmark in life because I had lived and felt as a married woman during the past four years, since the 1940 blitz, and the legal side of it, the signing of a paper, meant nothing at all.

The bit in the registry office was more like a dream.

But my mother's happy face, Andy's strange remark, and Helen's anxious farewell, were important and lasting, like the gold wedding-ring which I wear to this day.

Another excitement, in some ways more rewarding, was the publication of both our books. Authors were doing well at that time. Few of us went out at night (owing to the blackout regulations), and no one yet had a television set.

'Have you read a good book lately?' we said to one another.

I never hear that question now.

Howard's book was an immediate success. My own book, about permissive pre-war London, was considered shocking. My employers were disappointed in me. When I asked her what she thought of it, Lady Burnham just said: 'Oh, dear!'

Apparently words failed her. I was glad to find that my mother took it in her stride but Howard's mother was horrified.

Howard said: 'She may get over it in time.'

'I don't think she will.'

'Neither do I,' said Howard.

'Is it really such a shocking book?'

'I suppose it is, but I like it,' said Howard, 'because it's honest.' Today, of course, it seems a very harmless book. There is nothing shocking about it.

'Oh well,' I said, 'perhaps your mother will get over it.' (I wonder if Howard would like the book I am writing now? I hope he would.) At any rate, we both knew his mother would never get over that war-time book, and this made for a difficult relationship even when we all did our best to like one another. It was lucky for all of us that Howard's mother never met my own much-married mother. Two more opposite women could not be described or imagined. At our first meeting Howard's mother scarcely spoke, and when at last she managed it she only said, 'Can you cook?'

'I'm afraid I can't.'

'What a pity,' she said, and never spoke again.

However, she adored her son. I knew how she felt on D-Day. When this great day arrived in June 1944 she listened to the radio and waited impatiently for the news which thrilled and astonished the Western world. When it came, told for the first time in the voice of my husband, she felt as proud of him as I did. She said afterwards: 'The tears were running down my face.'

In London we discussed it for weeks in advance. We knew so little, and yet the importance of it made everyone air his or her views. When would we strike? Had we enough ships to do it? What about the air force? Would we dare to do it in bad weather?

No war secret had ever been kept so well.

On the first day of June we were still waiting. We had enjoyed a whole month of halcyon weather. Soldiers and civilians on both sides were expecting the terrific attempt. We knew that the act of invasion would make us, or break us.

But nothing happened.

The assault troops had been sealed off in their camps. They had seen air photographs of the area of coast on which they were to land. These unfortunate men had been cut off from the outside world. They were told what they had to do. The rest of us were told nothing.

The waiting period went on and on. Everyone talked about

the weather. We knew that low clouds would make it impossible for the air force to carry out their job of battering gun positions and dropping forces by parachute and glider. They needed moonlight. Storms and rough seas would put an end to the naval operations.

We did not understand about the tide. We talked about it stupidly. We were told afterwards that the enemy had placed their beach obstacles in such a way that they would be covered by high tide. For this reason it was decided to land three hours in advance. The engineers would have time to clear away the obstacles before the sea covered them. It was an excellent plan. But to get the tide right, and the moon right, and the weather right, was almost impossible. That was why it took so long to happen. D-Day was set for the fifth day in June, and then the weather changed. It became so bad that the Germans thought they had nothing to fear for at least a fortnight. We thought so too.

I remember this part vividly because I said good-bye to Howard no less than three times. Each farewell was agony. It was like something on the stage. At the same time it was so real, and so unreal.

Howard said: 'I may never see you again.'

'Don't say that.'

'I can't help it. You know it's true.'

'Please don't say that.'

'I'm as nervous as hell.'

'I know you are. So am I.'

'Do you understand?'

'Of course I understand.'

He was supposed to be in camp, sealed off from the others, and yet he was not a soldier. No one had any idea what his duties would be on D-Day. He was treated as someone special. I only knew he was unarmed, unprepared for war, an innocent abroad. He was tingling with nerves, enduring it, facing up to it; an untrained man, a middle-aged man, standing up in a soldier's uniform to face the enemy without a gun, not knowing the rules, not wishing to be killed.

Of course he was nervous. I have never been so sorry for anyone, nor so full of admiration. I understood why he came back three times to see me, and said good-bye three times. It was painful for both of us because Howard was quite sure he was going to be killed.

At a third farewell, which took place in the country, in the garden at Quainton where I was spending the week-end with my long-suffering women friends, Helen grew impatient.

'Look here, how many times is he going to say good-bye?'
'I don't know.'
'Tell him not to do it any more. Enough is enough. Both of you look like death.'
'I can't tell him that. I may never see him again.'
Had he been a real soldier they would have kept him in camp like the others. It might have been better for both of us. These repeated farewells were a form of self-imposed punishment. But the plan to invade was cancelled once again because of the storms at sea. Twenty-four hours later there was not much improvement. We waited. We went on waiting. When would something happen?
No one thought we would do it.
How could we possibly do it?
We did it.
In spite of everything the decision was suddenly taken. Five hundred warships with over 3,000 landing craft assembled in the mineswept area south of the Isle of Wight, which our men called Piccadilly Circus. Howard was among the soldiers.
He told me afterwards how bewildering it was.
The great fleet appeared to be headed for the Straits of Dover. At sunset you could see the ships moving. As darkness fell they separated and headed for Normandy. What was happening? What if the German radar picked up the change of direction?
Somehow we deceived the enemy.
It still seems incredible.
A fleet of small craft, each little boat towing a balloon, set out for Calais and Boulogne. On German radar they appeared to be a fleet of large warships and transports. To complete the deception our bogus fleet was accompanied by an escort of bombers.
Meanwhile the Allies landed in Normandy!
Howard said it was almost a miracle because the weather made the landing so difficult. On all the Normandy beaches the tide was half an hour ahead of the usual time. So the landing craft were swept into the mines and spikes set up by the enemy.
All this and a great deal more he told us on the radio a few hours after the operation took place. In London we were still waiting for something to happen. I remember feeling wildly excited as I sat in my usual place beside the radio. And then, to my amazement, I heard Howard's voice.
I have been in the sea three times. I am soaked to the skin.
Howard's story was described later in the *World's Press News*. It was recognized as a 'world scoop'. What greater tribute can a reporter be paid? I can only remember that he told us with

emotion about the raging seas, the wrecked boats, the German mines, the gunfire, and the British soldiers, singing songs before they landed.

I wish his broadcast had been scripted. I wish I had a better memory. But I still have that feeling of pride and joy and relief and admiration as I listened to him, in his wet clothes, telling us Londoners about the invasion of Normandy.

This was not a soldier. This was a middle-aged man untrained for war. This was a man with a brave heart.

And this was my husband.

10 'The years of anticlimax'

I must say more about the buzz bombs.

They were jet-propelled pilotless planes and they were known as buzz bombs, flying bombs, doodlebugs or V-1s. They came to London just after D-Day, when Howard was in France, and by the end of June no less than 2,000 of them had been launched; half of these were for Londoners, although many fell in Sussex and Kent.

The V-2 was Hitler's other surprise.

It was considered more deadly and yet most of us preferred it to the V-1. It was a 15-ton rocket with a speed faster than sound. During the winter over 1,000 V-2s landed in England, most of them in London.

I think we accepted them with less hatred than the others because we could not hear them coming. We all felt it was better to die without thinking about it. But the doodlebugs or buzz bombs rained down on our homes and the fear they inspired must have satisfied the enemy. They seemed to get worse as time went on. Alarm increased.

It was Hitler's attack on us, the civilians.

Soldiers coming home on leave were taken by surprise. They had not expected this new attack on their wives and children. The defenders were having a better time than their loved ones.

In London no one could tell when or where to expect these horrible things until the buzzing started, and then, within a few minutes, while we were waiting for it in the sudden silence, came death.

Somehow a jet-propelled pilotless plane was much worse than a German bomber with a pilot. We were being attacked by monsters, not by men. In one of the newspapers a cartoon was published. It showed a number of men and women crowded together in a London street. They were obviously listening for a buzz bomb because each character had developed a huge ear, like the horn of a trumpet, on one side of his or her head. This cartoon seemed to us Londoners extremely funny. Churchill told us we were sharing the sufferings of our soldiers. Again he made us feel like heroes. Churchill helped us to continue living with buzz bombs, and so, of course, did that silly cartoon!

Some people said the V-2 danger would compel the government departments to move out of town. Of course they did nothing of the kind. Londoners went on working and listening, ears growing big, faces turning green. Few of us left, or wanted to leave, our beloved city.

When Howard came home from Normandy, which he managed to do at intervals between battles and broadcasts, we were able to spend a week-end or a night together, brief and exciting, making us feel once more like unmarried lovers.

I tried to explain my fear of the doodlebugs.

'They're not like anything we've ever had before. They're much more frightening than ordinary bombs.'

'Are you really so frightened?'

'Everyone is. Not just me. Only they don't tell you about it.'

'Perhaps you ought to leave London.'

'No, no, I don't want to leave London. I'm part of London.'

'Well,' said Howard, 'I know how you feel about that.'

One night he heard them for himself. We were lying separately in our twin beds at Basildon Court and suddenly, within my deep sleep, came the nauseating sound. I woke up and began to tremble. It came nearer and nearer. The buzzing and zooming ended sharply, like a musical pause, and then, like a discord, came the crash in the next street.

We both listened while a second thing came buzzing and zooming. At the sound of another nearby crash Howard lifted his head enquiringly.

'There's bound to be a third one,' I said. 'This time it will kill us.'

'What?'

'It will kill us.'

Indeed there was a third one, so close that our building shuddered.

'Good God, what's happening?' said Howard.

'Now do you see what I mean?'

'Is it one of your doodlebugs?'

'Of course it is.'

'What a horrible thing!' said Howard in the darkness.

'It's the third one. I thought it was bound to hit Basildon Court. Didn't you?'

'Well,' said Howard, 'I do see what you mean.'

He was very tired and soon fell asleep. I was left staring at the ceiling and listening. Howard could never stay with me for more than a few nights, which meant a quick return to Helen and Andy. It was impossible to stay by myself during an air-raid.

Helen continued to say: 'You've always got us. Husbands come and husbands go, but friendship lasts forever!'
'Friendship is love without his wings,' I replied.
'Who said that? Did I say that?'
'No, Lord Byron said it.'
Helen sighed. 'I wish I had said that.'
'You will,' murmured Andy, 'you will.'
Day after day I found myself waiting for Howard's voice on the radio. I was always listening and waiting and longing to hear him. I can see now that Normandy meant a great deal to Howard. It was like his last game of rugger. It was the end of his youth and the time of his strength.
Years later he took me to see the town of Caen. He showed me the scene of those bloody and stubborn battles. The old town was full of memories for him, as thrilling as the fall of Paris. The glory of it was in him for the rest of his life. For this I loved him. I knew that his age had been a handicap. Until it was all over no one realized how much the war effort had cost him in health and vitality and courage.
When he did all those life-risking things in North Africa and Normandy he was a man in his middle forties. I can see now there was no need for Howard to do what he did. His job in London as PRO for Lord Woolton's Ministry of Food was interesting and important and better paid than his job as war correspondent for the BBC. He could easily have stayed at home with me.
This is something I have never understood. There was no reward for the man who did such wonderful things, no recognition of his bravery, and yet this middle-aged man gave us the first report of the D-Day invasion, for which the whole Western world was waiting, and then the Normandy reports, and the story of the fall of Paris.
What Howard did for his country was quickly forgotten in the post-war period when it ought to have been remembered. Of course I know he was only doing his job. But I can see now what a remarkable job he did.
Back to the doodlebugs in London.
Back to Helen and Andy, who bought and moved into a red brick house in New Cavendish Street. It had, and still has, a distinguished neo-Georgian entrance and at that time it had a bright green front door. Helen chose this colour because it matched the dental chair and the X-ray unit in her surgery.
I remember opening that front door on a beautiful morning in July. The bell rang very early, about 8 a.m., and my hair was looking hideous, full of hairpins, because Helen said the door

must be answered immediately. There on the doorstep was a
young officer in khaki uniform, smiling broadly, a brown paper
parcel in his hand.

'This,' he said, 'is from Normandy.'

I thanked him, and wished I had done my hair before meeting
him, and opened the brown paper parcel with a feeling of joy. It
was a Camembert cheese, a present from Howard.

How we enjoyed that cheese!

I can remember Helen saying: 'It smells wonderful. It smells
better to me than a rose.'

We were not exactly hungry with Andy as our provider, and
yet we were thankful for good food. The value of the meat ration
per week was something between 1 and 2 shillings per head.
The bacon ration varied from a quarter to half a pound per
person, and the tea ration from two to four ounces. Everything
else was subject to a 'points' system, giving each of us sixteen to
twenty points a month. For example, sixteen points would have
given Andy one tin of condensed milk, a pound of sweet
biscuits and one tin of Irish stew.

No wonder Howard's present was received with delight. That
particular Camembert cheese has been remembered in detail for
more than forty years. My two devoted friends liked it as much
as I did. I enjoyed being with them when Howard was away. In
Andy I noticed a change. This was the beginning of her
rheumatoid arthritis.

It showed first in a small lump on one finger. The lump was
removed by surgery. Another lump appeared. The fingers began
to swell. I was the one who suggested a starvation cure at the
famous clinic near Tring, called Champney's. After fasting for
two weeks she came home to New Cavendish Street, her
swollen fingers cured, or nearly cured, and Helen gave a party
at Claridge's.

'Let's have a celebration. It's time we enjoyed ourselves.'

Helen had suffered more than any of us because Tankie, her
special man friend, had been killed in North Africa, and now
Andy was starting an incurable illness. No one would dream of
complaining. Gaiety was the rule of life. Everyone tried to keep
pace with Helen and Andy, who were never defeated.

I remember that party. The men were all away from London
but among Helen's women friends were some of the top people
in the ATS, Bertine (the late Dame Albertine) Winner, the late
Pamela Frankau (a famous novelist), the late Lady Katherine
Cairns, and the late Moie Charles, a close friend of mine
(introduced by Aimée Stuart) because she had written the script
of a documentary film about the ATS.

Cammy, or Major Cameron
Shute, my Edwardian father,
good-looking until the end of
his life

One of the last pictures of my
intrepid mother, Renie, six
times married

Nerina Shute in 1934, the Fleet Street journalist who despised
pretty clothes and was known by her large black hat

Nerina and her favourite companion, a corgi called Clem, 1950

Mrs Howard Marshall, happily married and living in Mayfair, 1950

Howard Marshall, my brilliant husband, who became chief war correspondent for the BBC and gave us the first news of the Allied landing in Normandy. 'I have no notes,' he said. 'I have been in the sea three times. I am soaked to the skin.'

Noel Sparrow, my final
stepfather

below: Howard Marshall, BBC
broadcaster, at the beginning of
World War II

Phyllis Haylor, doyenne of ballroom dancing for over fifty years, as she was when I first knew her, 1959

Phyllis and myself on holiday in Cornwall during the happiest days of my life

Phyllis Haylor, my dearest friend for twenty-two years

Phyllis Haylor receiving the Carl Allen Award for outstanding services to the Ballroom Dancing Profession from HRH Princess Anne

By this time we had given up dancing. In London the restaurants were almost empty and theatres also.

Aimée Stuart had finished her latest comedy, the one called *Jeanie*, about a Glasgow girl in Vienna, starring the late Barbara Mullen, who was then almost unknown. Even this had only a short run in the West End. I believe it would have made a fortune in peacetime.

Aimée said, 'I'm a bit disappointed. I think it's my best comedy.'

'People are too frightened to go to the theatre.'

'Never mind. I'm glad I wrote it.'

'Anyway, you discovered Barbara Mullen!'

Aimée was already trying to write something else. No one felt bored. No one felt lonely. If they did, no one complained.

All around us life was highly coloured. It was tinted by love and fear and happiness and disaster and victory and defeat; so that London buses looked redder, the trees in the park much greener, and the dome of St Paul's Cathedral bigger and more beautiful than ever before or since. We belonged to the war generation. We could see the colours and feel the textures and shapes and patterns in our changing world. It was truly exciting. It was stimulating. It was romantic.

At about this time my mother wrote me a long letter about Noel. Did I think I would mind another stepfather? Would I care to meet him?

I had seen him once, only for a few minutes, and did not immediately realize that he was to be the next one. He was, as I have said, twenty-two years younger than my mother.

She now told me that Noel's other name was Sparrow, and I said yes, I would like to meet him before she married him. Could she put it off a little longer, please? In my letters to Howard I said nothing about a new stepfather. I knew he would disapprove. Perhaps Renie would get over it.

Howard's name was much in the news. On the radio I heard his voice every week, sometimes every day. Because I was living with Helen and Andy, they had to listen too.

'I really am getting tired of his beautiful voice,' said Helen.

'So am I,' said Andy.

'Never mind. You've *got* to listen!'

At last came the great news for which we were anxiously waiting. I remember the excitement in Howard's voice. He described in detail the welcome of Paris to the Allied soldiers on the day of liberation. I wish I could remember his words.

For us Londoners the fall of Paris was so vivid. We all felt like soldiers, I believe. We could all feel the delight of the French girls. We might have been in the boots of the young men who returned their kisses and gave them cigarettes and received presents from them of biscuits and wine and cheese. We were part of it, heart and soul on the side of free France, sharing with joy the noise and thrill, laughing and weeping and belonging, like brothers and sisters, to the delirium in Paris.

When Howard came home at long last I heard all those wonderful stories. I never grew tired of listening. He told me about it in the peaceful garden at Quainton. Invited by Helen and Andy, we spent a wonderful week-end together. The flower-beds were filled with antirrhinums and asters, pinks and yellow roses. That year the gold fishpond was almost encircled with marigolds and nasturtiums, a blaze of yellow and gold. I remember showing them to Howard. He towered above the little pond in his khaki battledress, tall and thick, an enormous figure of strength, like the trunk of an oak. In that garden, still warm and scented with summer flowers, we made our plans for the future.

It was our war and we meant to win it. It was our world and we meant to reform it. Nothing, we felt, would ever be the same again.

We lay side by side in the garden, sprawled on a green bank by the croquet lawn and sat with our backs against an apple tree, endlessly discussing the changes and charms of our beautiful brave new world.

'Are you happy?' said Howard.

'Happier than I have ever been in my life.'

'Do you think we shall be all right?'

'Of course.'

'I think so too.'

The trees in the orchard were heavy with apples and we lay on the grass, in the sunlight, beneath the green wooded hills. It was like a golden dream. During this time of tenderness and joy and confidence and love I was quite sure that my husband would not be killed, that Hitler would be defeated, and that Andy would be given her health.

To the war generation nothing seemed impossible.

Nothing even seemed difficult.

When Howard came back on his next visit he found we had all become members of an organization called Common Wealth. It was only another name for socialism. Howard became a member too.

Hitler committed suicide on 30 April 1945. Eva Braun, married to him the day before, died with him. She killed herself for Hitler's sake and so did his propaganda minister, Goebbels, whose wife and children died in the same way.

So far as we Londoners were concerned it was all over. No more bombs on London. No more doodlebugs. Nobody sleeping on the platforms of Underground stations.

Of course it was not quite finished. We thought Churchill would continue as Prime Minister at least until the defeat of Japan. He surprised us by calling a general election.

Poor Churchill! I remember him clearly. On election day, in the summer sunshine, sitting in the back of an open car, his pink and cherubic face turned on the Chelsea crowds with a frown of reproach, he passed us by like an angry parent.

We Londoners gave him a gentle cheer because we loved him, but we were there to get rid of him and later he knew it. In 1945, at the end of July, we heard the results of the General Election. The Labour party had won 395 seats, the Conservatives 213, and the Liberals 12. It truly was a dusty answer for the old man who had given us victory. He was rejected. It came to him as a complete surprise.

The truth was that Churchill was no longer needed by his people. We had turned socialist. It was Henry Wallace who told us that the war had introduced a new era, and called it 'the Century of the Common Man'. We liked this idea. We wanted more of it. We wanted a classless society, without privilege; a world of well-trained men and women with social and economic equality.

It was not a hopeless ideal.

During the war the whole system of rationing and conscription and social welfare had been based on it. We remembered the pre-war period of poverty and unemployment. We wanted our children to continue to be properly fed.

And yet Churchill, our beloved Churchill, had not seen the change of heart. He feared communism. He seemed to be losing his touch. Everything he said during the election campaign was out of tune with the mood of the people.

Said Churchill:

> On with the forward march! Leave these socialist dreamers to their utopias or nightmares! Let us be content to do the heavy job that is right on top of us. And let us make sure that the cottage home to which the warrior will return is blessed with modest but solid prosperity, well-fenced and guarded against misfortune, and that Britons may remain free to plan their lives for themselves and those they love.

To us it sounded terrible. Warriors and cottage homes were a thing of the past. How could Churchill be so blind?

So that was why we stood in the King's Road, Chelsea, and cheered the old man and noticed his frown of reproach and continued to admire him deeply, and then, with love in our unfaithful hearts, voted against him.

Even Helen, a typical Tory, was converted to socialism, following the lead of myself and Howard.

'I don't like it, but I can't stop it. I might as well accept it,' said Helen, 'like having my teeth out.'

'But you haven't had your teeth out.'

'My time will come,' said Helen with a laugh, 'and so will yours!'

In Chelsea we were all fighting the Conservatives. Andy was the candidate for the new party called Common Wealth. (After the election it was never heard of again.) Howard helped her. So did I.

But when the excitement was over we all had a feeling of anticlimax. We had done our job. We had won the war. We were unprepared for the long littleness of life.

Howard and I were blissfully happy at first. I have often wondered what became of all those other couples who found one another as we did, not young, not old, the war generation, the men and women who fell in love and married in a time of terror. Did they encounter boredom? Did they discover how hard it is when your war is ended to find a personal peace in your own soul?

I remember how lost and puzzled the two of us felt when at last the fighting was over.

I said to Howard: 'Where do we go from here?'

'I don't know. Give me time.'

'I expect it will be all right in the end.'

'Of course it will,' said Howard.

Both of us were unemployed. The two-roomed flat began to seem unattractive and poky. I suppose we felt lost because we were out of work, unwanted, adrift in time, without a controlling discipline, suddenly lacking a sense of purpose. After breakfast we kissed one another good-bye and there was, for the first time, nothing important for either of us to do.

'What time will you be home?' I said.

'About six. What about you?'

'I'll be waiting for you.'

'Good. I might have some news about a job.'

'What would you like for supper?'

'Let's have fish pie.'

'All right. Fish pie.'

Sometimes I walked with him down the passage to be with

him a few minutes longer. Each day Howard went to the Savile
Club. He read every newspaper from cover to cover and then
lunched and talked with Stephen Potter, or Compton Mackenzie
(Monty) or Francis Meynell, or Julian Huxley or Val Gielgud.
What he did in the long dull afternoons I never knew. When his
friends had departed I believe he slept, or wrote letters. Each day
was a period of boredom. At the end of it we were anxious to find
one another, longing to exchange ideas; and yet, like Howard, I
felt the need to go somewhere else, to leave home each morning,
to take part in the clatter and movement of the world outside.

He used to say: 'Where are you going today? What are you
going to do?'

'Nothing in particular.'

'Are you writing something?'

'Yes.'

'Where is your typewriter?'

'Helen and Andy are keeping it for me at New Cavendish
Street.'

'Why don't you work here?'

'I can't work here. Don't ask me why.'

For some reason the questions made me feel guilty. The truth
was that I worked at the top of their house in a dusty storeroom
where Helen and Andy kept boxes and trunks and unwanted
furniture. Clem was my only companion. He slept by my feet
while I worked.

It was my first historical novel. The subject was Fanny Burney.

'I wonder why you can't work at home?' Howard used to say.

'I don't know. I just can't.'

Probably I went to my dusty storeroom for the same reason he
went to the Savile Club. I needed somewhere to go. We were both
driven by boredom. We both had to move from one place to
another by force of habit.

Howard said something I have always remembered.

'You're still on the tram-lines, Nerina.'

'Yes, I see what you mean.'

'We must all try to get off the tram-lines,' said Howard.

Perhaps I felt redundant. Of course I did. After learning to
conduct your life in a London office from nine till six, and twice
daily to cross the London streets by bicycle, happy and useful,
every moment of your time filled by excitement and action and
wartime danger, it was hard, suddenly, to face those empty days
presented by peace and victory. When the twin beds had been
made and the dishes washed, I became frustrated. How many
war wives felt as I did?

Sometimes I tried to settle at my desk in the window and then, as I expected, the little black words eluded me, and the vision of Fanny Burney disappeared, and the piles of virgin pages beside my typewriter began to dazzle me with their untouched whiteness.

At this point of confusion the charwoman arrived.

With Mrs Thing in the flat, banging and sweeping and breaking and grumbling, the effort to write about Fanny Burney was greater than ever before. And yet, in the crowded storeroom, where I now went each day, with Clem sitting beneath the table while I typed, the pages were quickly covered by precious little black words. Fanny Burney came at once, as soon as the door closed, and I worked contentedly until evening, knowing that Helen was downstairs in her surgery, and Andy was at the hospital, operating on one of her patients.

On the way home I did the household shopping, a couple of chops, or best end of neck, or something to make a fish pie. Peeling potatoes was torture. Handling raw meat gave me the shudders. The smell of uncooked fish tingled in my nose. Worst of all was the next-morning smell of bacon and eggs, the spitting fat, the burnt toast and the look of resignation in Howard's eyes when I handed him his plate of breakfast. He was patient and kind. He was accustomed to women like his mother who were able to produce an exquisite meal without personal suffering.

'Take it easy,' he used to say. 'Don't look so worried.'

'I'm afraid I'm a terrible housewife.'

'I don't think so.'

'Your mother does.'

'Never mind. I like what you cook. Your fish pie is wonderful.'

But his mother had no patience with me.

'What? Can't you make an apple tart? Or a steak and kidney pudding? What does Howard eat?'

'He eats at his club,' I said.

'What does he have at home?'

'Fish pie,' I said.

Cooking was like an enemy. I thought I should never win the battle against a husband's hunger which attacks the housewife every evening.

What should I have done without Fanny Burney? Grateful to Fanny, dear Fanny, whose face I still love and whose portrait I still possess, I escaped from the tortures and smells of cooking into the world of Mrs Thrale and Doctor Johnson, the court life of George III at Windsor Castle. Life in the eighteenth century was more congenial than post-war London.

The brave new world we had both visualized while bombs were falling was now something which stood before us and between us, baleful and threatening, like the ugly and sudden appearance of a skyscraper.

As two people we had not changed in any way whatsoever and yet the greatness in us began to diminish.

And then, after weeks of unemployment, he told me it was all going to be different and he, Howard, on that happy day, had been offered a job, not an ordinary job but one with a princely salary. At first neither of us could believe it. Howard was to become an industrialist. Howard was to work in the steel industry as a director of public relations.

'Come on,' I said, in Helen's voice, 'let's go out and celebrate.'

'What do you mean?'

'Let's have a pub crawl.'

'What's that?'

'A drinking session. You go from pub to pub and make friends and talk and laugh.'

'I've never done that in my life.'

'Why not?'

'To me it's a new idea.'

'What's new about it?'

'Well, I've never been out drinking in pubs with a woman.'

'It's time you did,' I said.

The art of the pub crawl was something I had learnt reverently, like a sonnet, from Charles. In Marylebone the pubs were numerous and friendly and full of history.

'Come on, let's have our first pub crawl,' I said.

And Howard, who had never done such a foolish thing in his life doubtfully said, 'All right.'

The one facing our flat was ugly, in the late Victorian way, and the couple who managed it were in love like ourselves. Although such an old-fashioned word must not, even now, be used, the pretty wife was 'a lady'. She had married a publican against the wishes of her parents.

I can still see that anxious well-bred face behind the bar, the quick smile, the glance at her heavy handsome partner for reassurance, the beginnings of a sadness.

Once a week Howard now came with me to this pleasant pub. When I drank a pint of bitter I watched every movement as the woman polished the glasses, and I entered her inner life and shared the disappointment of it, without her knowledge.

'You ought not to stare,' Howard used to say.

'When I was a child the same thing was said by my mother and my nurse. I can't help staring.'

'Why do you do it?'

'Because I like other people. I get involved.'

'There's no need to stare.'

'Don't you see, it's like reading a book. If you can't read it from cover to cover, you turn the pages. You enjoy the dialogue, or the style.'

'It makes me feel uncomfortable,' said Howard.

To please him I tried not to stare. I tried to concentrate all my attention on Howard's presence, his face, his eyes, his hair, his large body, his fingers, short and pointed, unexpectedly feminine. I knew and loved every detail about him. I was stimulated by his conversation. And yet, to his concern, I was compelled to stare at men and women in pubs and restaurants, waiters, publicans, total strangers, memorizing their faces, longing to speak to some of them.

'I can't understand why you do it,' said Howard.

'I really can't help it.'

'You must try to stop it.'

'People are like books. I love watching them.'

'It's a bad habit,' said Howard.

'I don't mean to be rude,' I said.

In my imagination I managed to enter the lives and dreams of the people and wiped their tears and picked up their burdens, enjoyed their company and shared their laughter. Once, in a moment of anger, I said to him: 'You always want to be alone with me. You don't know the meaning of gaiety. You're not like Charles.'

The gentle Labrador was hurt.

'I am not a gay person,' said Howard.

The truth was that gaiety might be a threat to our guarded happiness. I belonged to the outside world of bright lights and dancing. It might become dangerous. It might become an enemy.

Howard had no wish to go out. 'I want you to give up your Fleet Street friends, I want us to start a new life,' he said. But he continued to come with me to watch human beings, like shadows on the wall, the expressions on faces, the movements of hands and feet, and we sat in many pubs drinking beer. The Dover Castle was a dear little pub. I used to sit and stare at Mooney, behind the bar, longing to make friends with her. Howard refused, but later, with Helen, I managed it. I discovered that Mooney's father had been butler to the Duke of Marlborough. She had a wonderful story about Queen Alexandra at Balmoral.

Mooney's father, as the Duke's butler, was standing at the foot of the great staircase. Near him stood King Edward. Guests were waiting in one of the drawing-rooms, and the Queen, as usual, was behind time.

Her Majesty appeared at last at the top of the staircase, small and exquisite, a Dresden china shepherdess. She descended gracefully to her fuming husband.

The King said, 'Madame, you are late.'

Alexandra whipped out the most enormous fan that had ever been seen, and replied, with a fine show of dignity, like a cat with arched back, 'Do not forget, I am ze Queen.'

As I write of these pleasing things, and remember Mooney, outlined by the red and gold glitter of bottles, I am thinking of the time when I sat in her bar beside Howard. She never spoke to us. She talked to all the others. I was guarded from her by Howard.

I can hear him saying, 'You ought not to stare. It's rude to stare.'

'I'm so sorry. I just can't help it.'

'Why do you keep on doing it?'

'People are so interesting.'

I was flattered by his need to separate me from the rest of the world even though I hated it. We were like two swans on a lake. Marriage was to be the best experience of all.

'I'm so glad we're married,' I said.

'So am I. It's wonderful.'

At that time marriage was in the air. We were filled with hope and a starry-eyed faith in the future. It was the dawn. It was the morning at seven. We felt we deserved a long spell of peace and prosperity, and now, at the beginning of things, we were hungry for happiness.

My mother had married Noel on 30 June 1945. But then, of course, my mother was always doing it, and Howard said in a gloomy voice: 'I don't approve of your mother's marriage.'

'Why not?'

'It will end in tragedy.'

'How do you know?'

'I feel certain it will. Because it's wrong.'

'Yes, I suppose it is.'

At the age of sixty-six, how could my mother expect to start life all over again with a man of forty-four, who, in her own words, 'lifted his elbow'?

'We must have nothing to do with it,' said Howard.

Of course I was longing to go to my mother's wedding but this was not allowed. 'I am sorry,' said Howard, 'I don't wish you to go.'

For a time I was nervously happy with my work as a writer and deeply happy with my husband. He quickly became a success. He was soon earning an enormous salary as a director of public relations for Richard Thomas and Baldwin. This carried with it an expense allowance and the use of a magnificent car.

So our pub crawls were ended. We became too grand for that

kind of thing. In a very short time we moved from the tiny flat in Marylebone to a large and expensive one in Mayfair. We found ourselves living in comfort, with windows overlooking plane trees and sweet rich grass and a church spire against the sky, and in the distance, beyond a pretty, small house which I learned to love, we could see the flash and colour from the red buses which used to rumble up and down Park Lane.

It was all very surprising. He earned a great deal of money, and yet somehow we never had enough to pay for a few more bath towels. As for me, I had no dress allowance and very few clothes.

'I'm not very good with money,' said Howard.

'But you earn such a lot.'

'I know I do.'

'What happens to it?'

'I don't know.'

The only bit I understood was about his broadcasting fees. Supposing he was paid fifty guineas for a broadcast. The following year he would be informed by the Inland Revenue that in reality he had earned only fifty sixpences and by then, of course, all the money had been spent.

Meanwhile, we decided to employ a French housekeeper because Nerina was such a bad cook.

'Is she pretty?' said Helen.

'Very pretty,' I said.

'Then you'd better be careful,' Helen said.

I can see now that my life was changed by that pretty French girl. Nothing would ever be the same. I can see now that I was missing all my Fleet Street friends, the sound of Helen's laughter, the sight of Mooney behind the glittering bar, even the excitement of the bombs and explosions. The post-war years were so dull I can see now that the war was like a gigantic party followed by an international hangover. For me, for Howard, for the war generation, it was the morning after the night before.

I think of them as the years of anticlimax.

Sometimes I still wonder how it all happened.

11 *Loneliness*

In my comfortable Mayfair study I sometimes felt like a prisoner.
It was the first study I had ever had, with a fitted table at the
window, where I typed, and against the wall a divan bed
piled with cushions, where I rested and slept and did my
thinking and filled my copybooks with notes about the
eighteenth century, and Fanny Burney, and later Shelley.
To me, a prisoner, suffering from boredom, the past was more
pleasing than the present. I seldom went out. London was dull
and depressing. I no longer felt like a Londoner.
Fanny Burney and all her friends came to me in this little
thoughtful room. The book about her was soon published. It
was called *Georgian Lady*. It was given a good review by Richard
Church, another by Elizabeth Bowen. To my amazement it was
well received. Howard was delighted.
So then I sat by my window, in a state of boredom, thinking
about my pre-war adventures. What had happened to Renie's
daughter, the person called Nerina Shute, the ambitious
journalist, the girl of nineteen who once interviewd the great
Pavlova? I remembered the girl in the black hat who had waited,
trembling, in the dancer's dressing-room. It was a matinée. At
the end of her performance Pavlova entered, wrapped herself in
a dressing-gown and began, just like a journalist, to ask me
questions.
'Why do you want to interview me?'
'Because I admire you.'
'Yes, but why are you a writer?'
'Because I want to tell the truth.'
'Do you write books, or just interviews?'
'I want to write books. I'm writing one now.'
'How old are you?'
'Nineteen.'
'What is the title of your book?'
'It's a novel. It's called *Another Man's Poison*.'
'Why call it that? What is the theme?'
'What's right for one person is wrong for another. That's the

theme. For example, stealing or telling lies or being a homosexual. It might be wrong for you and right for me.'

'Or the other way round,' said Pavlova.

'Yes, that's exactly what I mean. One man's meat is another man's poison.' (This little piece of childish philosophy has stayed with me all my life.)

'What makes you do it?' said Pavlova. 'What makes a writer write?'

'I don't know. It's just a longing to tell the truth about something and make other people see what you mean. For example, homosexuality.'

'Thank you for telling me about it. I like you,' said Pavlova.

And then she dismissed me because she had no more time.

'Come back tonight. You can watch me dance. Afterwards you can come to my dressing-room and ask me questions.'

But that night, as I sat in the spellbound audience, watching an effervescent whiteness of spirit and movement, the dying swan, suffering, wilting, lifting, finally escaping from life, a dancer dancing, a lightness and whiteness rising and falling and passing through death, unforgettable, indescribable, I knew I should never see Pavlova again.

I could not go to her dressing-room. I could not bear to forget the dancer and to see her again as a woman. I wonder if she understood? I wonder?

As I sat by my window in Mayfair I wondered if Pavlova would have liked my book about Fanny Burney. Then I began to think about Shelley. Could I possibly write something about Shelley, the poet? While I was dreaming about him, the dreamer, Shelley, told me a way to stop feeling bored. This was a brilliant idea. Why not go to London University and read English Literature? Well, why not?

To Howard I said: 'Would you mind very much?'

'Of course not. Go ahead and do it.'

'Are you sure you don't mind?'

'I can't say that I understand.'

'You see, I've always wanted to do it.'

'Why?'

'I don't know.'

I did it a little later, with Howard's permission, after attending a preparatory school, because the post-war years were such a disappointment. I suffered from fits of depression. Why did Howard rush home every evening to be with me alone? Why did I feel such a prisoner? I can see now that sex was important to us both. So was talk. Howard would rather live with me than a woman who warmed his slippers. After supper (a delicious meal prepared by pretty little Renée, the French housekeeper), we talked and talked about post-war London.

In a way we had been given what we wanted. In London we now had our classless society, without privilege, a new world with social and economic equality. Yes, it was the century of the common man all right.

We pretended to enjoy the caress of socialism. Somehow it was more like a blow in the stomach. We no longer believed in the control of incomes and prices. The country was still rationed. The people were still short of meat and bread and potatoes and fuel. At the same time, Howard, earning a huge salary, was now taxed into poverty.

Howard used to say, 'I'd be a fool to earn more than I do at present.'

'How much do you earn?'

'I don't know. Six thousand pounds a year, plus my expense account, plus my car.'

'It sounds like a fortune to me.'

'So it does to me.'

'Why can't we manage?'

'I don't know. My boss earns £20,000 a year, but the Inland Revenue takes half of it.'

'Is he in debt too?'

'Yes.'

'It seems ridiculous.'

'Once you get into the super-tax class they only give you sixpence for a pound.'

'You mean ten thousand pounds equals ten thousand sixpences?'

'Exactly,' said Howard. 'It makes you feel sick, doesn't it?'

'No wonder people like Noel Coward prefer to live abroad.'

'Sometimes I feel like doing the same thing,' said Howard.

At least, we told each other, there was no unemployment. And yet everyone knew that full employment led to inflation. It removed the incentive to work.

Howard said, 'Men used to work hard for fear of losing their jobs. They don't any longer.'

'Are they lazy? Or just fed up?'

'Both. At the drop of hat, they all go on strike.'

'What's happened to the wartime spirit? The team spirit.'

'God knows. I think it's easier to make war than to make peace.'

During the war we had dreamed of marriage and longed for socialism. Well, we had been given what we wanted.

'Why do we both feel frustrated?' I said.

'It's all this socialism. It just doesn't work.'

'Let's give it a chance.'

'All right. That's what we're doing. That's why we feel frustrated.'

'Are you happy?' I said nervously.

'When I'm at home with you. Alone with you.'

'Is it going to be all right? Do we still love one another?'

'Of course.'

I often wonder how many war marriages lasted. You love so much when the bombs are falling, and then everything stops. You live together, without children, not young, not old, trying to form an ideal companionship, and while you are doing it the greatness in you begins to diminish. You begin to lose one another.

I used to say: 'The art of living is to make it possible for the other person to behave well.'

This made Howard angry. It was an implied criticism.

'You've got to behave well yourself,' he said.

'Yes, I know, but I can't behave well without your help.'

'Aren't I helping you?'

'Sometimes. Not always. You've got to help me, and I've got to help you.'

'Am I behaving badly then?'

'No, no, I didn't mean to criticize. We must try to get the best out of each other. The art of living,' I repeated (feeling lonely), 'is to make it possible for the other person to behave well.'

'I don't agree. The art of living,' said Howard, 'is to behave well yourself.'

I gave up trying to explain what I meant. I had learnt from Charles how man destroys the thing he loves by trying to change it. I never tried to change Howard. I tried to change myself. This was equally stupid. My blond hair became light brown. It pleased him better. My Bond Street tailored suits with carnation in button-hole became black or grey dresses. These were worn with long dark undesirable coats. I was beginning to look dull and respectable.

'I think you look very nice,' he said. 'Much nicer than you used to look.'

He not only wanted a faithful wife, he wanted a faithful wife who *looked* like a faithful wife.

'All right,' I said. 'I'll try to be what you want.'

To please Howard I no longer saw my Fleet Street friends. I gave up the ones in the film world. Even my beloved Aimée Stuart seldom came to our flat, feeling unwanted. 'I've decided to live in Brighton,' she told me on the telephone. 'You can come and stay with me, dear. Whenever you want me I'm always there.'

'I'd love to come for a week-end.'

'Just telephone,' said Aimée, 'don't bother to write.'

Somehow I never did either. Howard would not have wished me to leave him for a week-end in Brighton. I missed Aimée's affection. I missed my mother's laughter. In my disappearing circle the only ones left were Helen and Andy, with whom I was allowed to spend week-ends (usually without Howard), in order to gallop round the fields on Kitty, my lively little mare. I discovered that Howard was a fisherman, not a horseman. On one occasion I put him on Helen's horse and took him for a ride. He hated it, and so did Helen's horse.

These happy week-ends with Helen and Andy need a bit of explaining. Helen was becoming more and more motherly. She was still my light-hearted lover, my devoted friend, although I had tried in a dismal way to end it when my husband at last came home for good.

'I'm a married woman. I ought to be faithful to my husband.'

'Howard took you from me. I'm the one to complain. Not Howard.'

'He's not complaining. But he would if he knew.'

'There's no need to tell him,' said Helen, 'about something he would never be able to understand. It's beyond his comprehension,' she added.

'Don't you think it's wrong to deceive him?'

'Certainly not. To deceive him with another man would be wrong, but not with a woman. There's no harm in it,' said Helen, 'because the love between two women is totally different. It's a form of friendship, a passionate friendship.'

Of course I knew exactly what she meant. There is little or no similarity between the lusty love-making of a man and the gentle or tender or motherly love-making between women. A male lover is unthinkable for a married woman in love with her husband. A female lover can be delightful.

At any rate they were happy week-ends with Helen and Andy at Quainton, galloping round the fields on our horses, walking our dogs, planting marigolds round the little pond at the bottom of the garden, pruning the roses, mowing the lawns, clipping the hedges, having a game of croquet on summer evenings, laughing helplessly, placing cocktails on the sundial during the game, having supper in the kitchen (cooked by Andy) and finally retiring to bed, still laughing, in the motherly arms of Helen.

'Friendship is what matters,' said Helen. 'You can always come back to us if things go wrong.'

There was a touch of sadness behind the laughter. I knew that she had suffered from moments of jealousy but Helen had never made any attempt to stop or spoil my marriage. She liked Howard. She wanted us to find happiness. As time went by she became more motherly than ever.

'Are you well, Nerina? Are you happy, Nerina?'

'Yes, thank you, I'm well and happy.'

'What about this French housekeeper? Did you say she was pretty?'

'Yes, very pretty. And a very good cook.'

'I don't like the sound of this French housekeeper,' said Helen. 'Do be careful. It might lead to trouble.'

'You're talking nonsense,' I said. 'Anyway, I'm planning to enter London University. Everything will be all right.'

So then, out of boredom, I became a student. I passed the matriculation exam and entered Queen Mary's College, twice the age of my classmates.

Helen said: 'Well done, Nerina.'

Howard said in his gentle voice, 'I thought I had married a sophisticated woman. What have I got? An inky-fingered school-girl!' At this we both laughed. 'What do you get out of it, Nerina?'

'Happiness. Interest. Excitement.'

'Excitement?'

'I want to know what came before the eighteenth century.'

'Is that exciting?'

'Very. How can you understand the present unless you understand the past?'

'Yes, you often say that.'

'You don't mind, do you?'

'I don't want to lose you, that's all.'

'Would you like to have a child?'

'Not really. We're not young enough.'

Howard was the father of two sons, then in their teens. The prospect of teaching an inexperienced wife about nappies and bottles did not please him at all.

'It's better like this. What we both want is companionship.'

'Are you sure that's enough?'

'Let's keep ourselves to ourselves. I shall never change, Nerina.'

'I don't want you to change.'

'Two's company, three's none.'

'I see what you mean.'

I knew he would always be possessive. Let no one disturb the peaceful evenings and the long conversations and the oneness of our lives encircled like a garden by an old and beautiful wall.

I can remember him saying, 'I have never been so happy in my life. You give me what I need.'

'Do I really? Even though I can't cook?'

It was more than flattering. Sometimes I felt like a precious book which no one else must open or touch or read. He disliked other women. He needed only his wife. I must change myself. I must stand on my lonely pedestal. Meanwhile the vitality went out of me. There was no spark. In my home I felt empty. I felt like a run-down battery. But the need for laughter was at last fulfilled when Renée, the little French housekeeper, took her place in our lives. The story of Renée comes later.

One day I announced that I intended to visit my mother. She was gay and amusing. Why was I not allowed to see her?

'I really do miss her very much.'

'All right,' said Howard, 'spend a day with her in the country.'

'Shall I ask her to come and see our flat?'

'No, if you don't mind, I'd much rather not.'

'I'd like a day in the country.'

'It will do you good,' said Howard. 'But try not to get too much involved.'

'What are you worried about?'

'Her husband. I don't like the sound of him at all.'

She had settled with Noel in a pretty house in Crowborough. I found her sitting up in bed. She was wearing a blue bed-jacket, a blue hair-ribbon, a blue silk scarf round her neck.

'I've got a sore throat, dear. Never mind, it's nothing serious.'

I had lunch with Noel, whose manners were perfect. He was gentle and good-looking. Afterwards, in her bedroom, Renie and I held one of those weird and wonderful conversations. It made me feel like an old lady in lavender and lace, my mother like a young girl. It went something like this.

'Of course I know what you're thinking, dear. I can see that you're full of disapproval.'

'I suppose we couldn't expect you to live alone.'

'Of course not, dear. You wouldn't like it yourself any better than I did. Now would you?'

'Perhaps not.'

'In your heart of hearts you're very like me.'

'I think I would have chosen someone of my own age. Noel might be your son. He's twenty-two years younger than you are.'

'He's old enough to know his own mind. I think you're afraid.'

'What am I afraid of?'

'I think you're afraid that I shall disgrace you. You and your well-known husband.'

'Well, you probably will.'

'What makes you think so?'

'This marriage of yours can't possibly last. It's worse than all the others. There's bound to be another divorce, and another scandal.'

'I don't agree. In any case, dear, I've only had two divorces. The other three died, poor things.'

'In a few years time,' I said unkindly, 'you'll be seventy.'

'Well, dear, nobody can blame me for that. One of these days you may be seventy yourself.'

'But don't you see how awkward it will be?'

'It's no more awkward to be seventy than sixty. Once you're over fifty nothing is awkward any longer.'

'What I mean is, your husband will probably desert you.'

'I don't believe he would ever do anything so cruel. He's a *gentleman*,' said my mother indignantly, 'and it's no good arguing about what will happen when I reach the age of seventy. One must live in the present and do what one believes to be right.'

This made us both smile.

'I'm afraid I must have sounded rather pompous.'

'You did, dear. You sounded like your husband. Let's not talk about it any more. You must have some tea with Noel. Afterwards he can show you the garden. The roses,' she added, 'are wonderful this year. You must take some back with you to London.'

In the rose garden I had a quarrel with Noel.

'My mother says you're drinking too much.'

'It depends what you mean by *too much*.'

'You spend too much time in the pubs.'

'Oh, I don't know about that.'

'You come home drunk.'

'Not drunk. A bit tiddly, perhaps.'

'Well, why do you do it?'

'I like you,' said Noel, 'but why must you be so rude and unpleasant?'

I remember feeling angry with him. He reminded me of my elegant father. He was much more boyish than Cammy, with a weak mouth and a weak chin.

'My mother ought not to have married you.'

'Why not?'

'Because you drink too much.'

'Oh, come off it,' said Noel.

After a day in the country London looked very shabby. Even the houses in Park Lane needed a coat of paint. The men and women had no spring in their step. They were down-at-heel.

That evening, talking to Howard, with the sweet scent of the roses dominating my home like the youthful presence of my mother, I tried to explain about Noel. In my mother's cheerful voice I said, 'Perhaps it will be all right. If only she can stop him drinking.'

'I don't like him.'

'You've only met him once.'

'I know his type. I don't like him.'

'My mother does.'

'Why?'

'Well,' I said, 'he's attractive. He's got a way with him. He's out of the top drawer.'

'She ought not to have married him.'

'I quite agree. She always marries the wrong people.'

We had no way of knowing that my mother's mad marriage would last while our own romantic relationship would come to an end. We needed a child. We needed laughter.

I look back in sadness. What I remember most vividly is the strong possessive love, and the reading of poetry, and the emotional voice, and the moments of intuition and understanding which made me adore my dear respectable Howard. I knew I might not be good enough (or happy enough) to give him what he wanted. Dear Howard. Solemn Howard.

Then I began to write about Shelley, the beginning of a new and much more interesting life. Howard took me in his car for a holiday in Italy. We paid a visit to the warm white house in Lerici where the poet and his family were happily living when the little sailing boat was lost in a storm and Shelley was drowned. Howard waited for me while I walked in those sunlit rooms. I stood before those windows overlooking the brilliant blue sea. I found myself longing for news of Shelley as his second wife, Mary, must have done.

Howard was not sorry to go home. He hated the hot sun. It was the fishing season. He was hoping to catch a trout in an English river.

When that wonderful summer was over the rhythm of our existence began to change. Our lives continued not quite as before. My notebook was full of notes about Shelley. Howard gave me love and encouragement. We were two tired people, living in a tired London.

Howard said, 'How do you like being a student at London University?'

'I love it.'

'Where do you get your energy from?'

'I don't know. It's fun.'

'What about Shelley?'

'Shelley can wait.'

But it really was a very strange life, between college and authorship and marriage. It felt busy and complicated and not at all boring. The presence of Renée, my little French housekeeper, who spoke not a word of English, was important to us both, bringing laughter and then tragedy into our lives. I am coming to the story of Renée.

When I left home, on my way to college, I passed beneath the plane trees and walked round the building to a gateway leading to the Connaught Hotel. At a certain point in my walk through the leafy green of the garden I always turned my head and I knew I would see, at the top of the house, framed in my bedroom window, a childish figure frantically waving good-bye. I felt the tenderness of a parent when this happened. I could hear a childish voice calling, '*Au'voir. Au'voir. Au'voir.*'

Of course I forgot all about Renée and her charming childish ways when I arrived by Underground in the Mile End Road to present myself at Queen Mary College. The students accepted me as one of themselves.

'Hello! Good morning! How are you?'

They charged down the draughty corridors and in the 'bun hole', where most people had lunch, the noise was deafening. Everything had to be discussed, from Shakespeare to marriage, in a piercing scream. Everyone knew that I was the oldest student in Queen Mary College. No one, except the professor of English Literature, had any idea what lay behind it. I told him I was starved for books.

'I'm a writer,' I said.

'Then you must be an educated woman.'

'Oh no, far from it.'

I managed to stay in that nice place for three years. (As I failed in my intermediate French exam I did not attempt a degree.) I brought home armfuls of first year books ranging from the works of Chaucer and Lyly, Deloney and Kyd, Marlowe and Shakespeare, Donne and Dorothy Osborne, Swift and Pope, Wordsworth and Shelley, Fanny Burney and Jane Austen to more modern writers like Ibsen and Bernard Shaw. The Mayfair flat was filled with my books.

At night, when Howard came home, wanting refreshment, glad to escape from the disappointing world outside, the world of socialism and strikes, wanting his drink and his companion, I began to believe I had something more substantial to give him. Life in our dull home now held a sparkle. As Renée was an excellent cook and provided us both with delicious French meals I had only to be washed and combed and scented, and to pour out the drinks, and to listen sympathetically to his problems at the office.

He sometimes said: 'Are you happy?'

Helen and Andy asked the same question.

'Quite happy, thank you,' I always replied.

'But you never do anything or go anywhere,' Helen said.

'I go to college,' I said, 'I love going to college.'

'What about the French housekeeper?' said Helen in her motherly way. 'Does Howard like her?'

'We both like her very much.'

'Well, you've always got us,' said Helen, 'also the dogs and horses. Don't forget you've always got us.'

'Thank you,' I said, 'I think of you as my family.'

With Renée, my childish companion, I moved in a small restricted world. She loved to be with me. She and my corgi followed me, and the three of us would walk from the sun-filled flat into the gardens, passing the little elegant church and the flower woman and the expensive china shop in South Audley Street, crossing Park Lane between the scarlet buses, entering Hyde Park, finding a deckchair in the green shade of the plane trees where my father and mother once paraded, arm in arm, on Sunday mornings.

In my imagination I could see this other London which my parents had loved. Men and women now lay on the grass like tired animals, kissing one another, rolling on top of one another, eating egg sandwiches from paper bags.

I could see the Edwardian ladies with cherry-coloured parasols who moved beneath the plane trees and paused, like dancers, to beguile the gentlemen.

I could see a procession of gay carriages, a magnificent yellow-wheeled barouche with c-springs and a powdered coachman. I could see a dazzling Victoria which displayed a lady and her beautiful dress, like an open jewel-box, and finally the royal carriage of King Edward and Queen Alexandra for which all these pretty and pampered human beings were gracefully waiting.

'Don't you get bored,' said Helen, 'when you sit in Hyde Park?'

'No, it's my favourite place. I love it.'

On a hot summer day I sometimes brought a lunch basket, prepared by Renée with tender hands, and a bottle of wine, eating and drinking and reading. With Renée and my beloved Clem I watched the men and women interlaced and intertwined on the grass. Renée was shocked.

'*Ça ne me plaît pas!*'

What would my dear Fanny Burney have said to all this? Shelley, I thought, would have done the same thing. But what would poor little Harriet have said? Harriet, who drowned herself in the Serpentine at the very place where I walked in the afternoons with my dog (throwing sticks in the water for Clem to retrieve) and with Renée, my childish housekeeper, chattering in French.

I heard her saying: '*Tu es toujours toute seule. Ce n'est pas la vie pour toi!*'

'*Pourquoi non? Je ne suis pas jeune, moi.*'

'*Je ne comprends pas,*' said Renée.

I could not explain my loneliness to her. These were the post-war years of disillusion and lost, or half-lost, ideals. I can see now that the war generation had begun to feel confused. Slowly, very slowly, the battered London buildings were in the process of being demolished, or removed, or converted into offices and flats.

The beauty of London was not wanted. Neither was the dignity. Indeed the wartime London we had loved and honoured was rapidly disappearing. We had lost the things we had loved. We would soon become escapists again. Men and women were beginning to feel bored and disappointed because the rhythm of London life had slowed down. Where was the inspiration?

'*Tu ne dis rien. Pourquoi? Où es tu?*' Renée was always saying.

She never learned to speak English and as she was with me for nearly three years I was forced to speak and think in French. This, too, had a certain charm. I enjoyed discovering a friend in another language. And Renée, with pencilled eyebrows and a tilted nose, long curled hair and the gay understanding of a little seductive Parisienne who once was kept by a rich man in a flat in Montmartre, was certainly my friend.

It was the childlike quality I seemed to need.

During the war Renée had lost her mother and father and her two little brothers when her home in Chateaudun was destroyed by a British bomber. She told me that her mother's body had been broken into pieces like that of a doll so that her arms and legs had been found and fitted together for the funeral.

'*Je ne peux pas oublier, madame.*'

Whenever she spoke of her mother, Renée shed tears. I believe she adored her mother and the shock of this terrible ending to her mother's life remained with her like a physical pain.

That was why she left France.

I think it explains why she attached herself to me.

It pleased me to find she was always near me, serving me with delicious meals, mending my clothes, spending her wages on buying me expensive presents, amusing me with gay stories of life in Montmartre before the awful thing had happened to her mother. I found myself treating her with a new tenderness, treating her as Helen treated me.

Renée was in her thirties. Yet she looked and behaved like a young girl. Naturally she had never heard of Fanny Burney or Shelley. We had nothing in common except a desire for laughter. When she was not thinking about her mother she was laughing and playing games, like a child, with me and Clem, and shopping and cooking and chattering to me and confessing all her sins. In the past she had tried to look after her mother. Now she was looking after me.

It seems pretty obvious that I needed and wanted a child of my own. When I had a miscarriage it was Renée who suffered. She found me in my bedroom and served my breakfast, as usual, on a tray, because Howard had long ago gone to his office, and then she discovered I was ill. (The miscarriage was caused by galloping round the fields with Helen, not knowing or believing that I could possibly be pregnant.) At any rate, the haemorrhage had started when Renée found me. I was more surprised than frightened. 'N'ai pas peur! Ce n'est pas grave,' I said.

Renée, who was terrified, appeared to know what to do, and even managed to telephone my doctor. She made the situation understood in explosive French.

'Quelle histoire!' Renée said, 'quelle histoire!'

'Ne t'inquiète pas,' I said.

After a spell in hospital I resigned myself to the certainty that I was not intended to have children, and somehow, when I came home, the presence of Renée became more important than ever before.

I needed her youth and her laughter.

Fanny Burney and Shelley had taken the place of my friends, and now Renée, my devoted little slave, had taken the place of a child. Where was all this going to end?

12 Breakdown

'You look better, Nerina.'
'I feel it.'
'You look happier.'
'So do you.'
'We're getting to be an old married couple.'
'Yes.'
'We're settling down.'
'Yes.'
'Do you think we really know one another?'
'I hope we do.'
'You're a very understanding wife.'
'And you're a wonderful husband.'
'Do you remember how you used to stare?'
'Do you remember how untidy you used to be?'

During the war, at Basildon Court, Howard had undressed at night, not noticing what he did, dropping all his clothes in a pile on the bedroom carpet. I thought it better to say nothing. I left them, and there they sometimes lay for several days until Howard noticed them.

He got the message.

Then he began to pick them up and put them away in his cupboard. It was a silent victory. Without a word being said, Howard became a tidy husband. We both laughed at this memory.

'I'm very tidy now.'
'Yes, you're very tidy now.'
'I think we're lucky people, don't you?'
'Yes, I do.'
'No more cooking problems.'
'And Renée to look after us both.'

Renée had a small apartment with a private bath and also a cat called Mitzie. She lived upstairs, next door to our large old-fashioned kitchen. The food was sent down on the lift and carried by me and Howard to the dining-room. All I had to do was to make him happy. Renée was a help, because her gift of

152

youth and vitality and gaiety was vital to me and offered
through me to Howard.

When I told Helen about this new and surprising relationship
I received a motherly scolding. 'Nerina, this is dangerous; not
wrong, but dangerous. One of these days Howard will find out.'

'But our marriage is so happy now. Much better than it was.'

'You can't take risks like this in your own home,' said Helen,
'not with a man like Howard. He would never understand. Oh
Nerina, do be careful.'

Of course I knew that Helen was right. She herself had found
another partner to take my place in her life, feeling lonely
without me, but the motherly love was still there and the
motherly friendship was untouched. I told Helen all about
Renée. I longed to tell Howard the whole story (as I would have
told Charles) but this, as Helen said, was out of the question. It
would have ended our marriage.

'Oh Nerina, do be careful. Please be careful.'

The most lonely season of the year had always been
Christmas. It reminded Howard of the past. It came, like a black
cloud, soon after Renée's laughing arrival in our dull home. We
solved the Christmas problem by running away.

'Let's go to Paris,' Howard said.

'How wonderful. I should love to spend Christmas in Paris.'

'I can't bear it in London. It makes me feel like an outcast.'

'Do you miss the BBC and the Christmas programme?'

'Yes. Very much indeed.'

'And your family?'

'Yes.'

So Howard took me to Paris, and we stayed like a honeymoon
couple in a small cheap hotel opposite the *Bibliothèque National*.
We escaped from Christmas. We conquered our sense of
loneliness and outsiderness by visiting Montmartre and eating
and drinking and making love. I understood Howard's feelings.
By ending his first marriage he had cut himself adrift from his
family, his fans, even his Christmas Day broadcast, loved and
remembered by men and women all over the world. You might
say that for my sake Howard had become an escapist. Like the
Duke of Windsor, he had thrown down his tools and walked
out.

On Christmas Day he was always attacked by depression.

'I can't help it,' he said.

'It's all right. I understand.'

'Let's go out and spend all our money.'

We filled ourselves with champagne, selected delicious meals
in small but important restaurants and devoured our food, and

then one another, in a hungry and exciting way, in a mutual need for love, and understanding, and compassion.

'You're my wife. I need you more than ever. This is going to be a good Christmas.'

It was. I shall never forget it. In the little hotel, in a bedroom with a hideous wallpaper (I believe it was purple) we became very close, possessed and possessive.

'This is how marriage ought to be.'

'Yes.'

'There must never be another man in your life.'

'No. Of course not.'

'Let's keep ourselves to ourselves.'

At the end of a week we felt tired and glad to return home. What made it so nice was the comfortable knowledge that our flat in London was now being scrubbed and polished by the expert hands of Renée, for whom I had left many little presents and a bottle of wine, or champagne, whichever she preferred.

For Renée I had spent a few shillings on a miniature Christmas tree, about two feet high, and had decorated the branches with silver streamers and golden bells and small shining balls coloured in crimson and emerald. It looked very pretty, placed by itself on a small table. Renée had been forbidden to open her presents until Christmas morning. I think the little silvery tree gave her as much pleasure as it gave me. And when we returned from Paris, charged with adventure like two conspirators, now feeling guilty, glad the party was over, the Christmas tree was still there in its place of honour. The branches were still glittering with balls and bells.

'*C'est magnifique,*' Renée said happily. '*Oui, Madame, ça me plaît.*'

I remember feeling pleased and comforted, as a mother might feel, for life was no longer solitary. In my London home was a new affection and a childish presence and the sound of laughter. I received my exciting inner happiness from Renée, and Howard received it from me. How could this be wrong?

To tell the truth my home had never seemed such a desirable place and now it grew much more friendly to the outside world. We even gave an occasional dinner party. Once we invited Francis Meynell (son of Alice Meynell, the poet) and Bey Kilroy (afterwards Dame Alex Kilroy). They were older than ourselves, a charming and brilliant couple who had married, as we did, for love. I remember that Renée spent a whole day in preparing a chicken. When it was placed before him, Francis tasted it delicately, like a man reading a poem.

'Is it all right?'

'In France,' he said, 'I once travelled thirty miles to eat a particular chicken. It was cooked like this,' he added, 'but not so good.'
Howard was delighted. So was I. So was Renée. In our
dining-room we had never received such a compliment. It
seemed to me that Howard was rapidly becoming a happier man.
For the first time, since I married him, we were both well-fed.
Every meal was a joy to eat. Even his mother approved of Renée.
We had rabbit, I remember, cooked in red wine. We had veal
which melted in the mouth, with mushroom sauce. Each dish
had a special and beautiful French flavour.

I found that Howard came home eagerly at cocktail time,
thankful to end a tedious day at the office, longing to smoke his
pipe and eat his delicious dinner, rest, read poetry, and talk to his
wife about work, and politics, and religion, and socialism, and
books, and people. Renée, upstairs, was equally happy with
Mitzie, the cat.

Sometimes Howard talked about the Duke of Windsor's marriage, and sometimes about my mother's marriage.

'It's unnatural,' said Howard. 'How can an elderly woman
marry a man who is twenty-two years younger than she is?'

'It sounds all wrong, but how does anybody know what's right
and good for other people? In life there's no Golden Rule,' I said.

We sat comfortably in the darkening room, the windows open
to the plane trees and the sky and the church spire. At the end of a
hot day in August we were resting and drinking and talking.

'You're always saying there is no Golden Rule. What do you
mean?'

'I mean there's no Golden Rule for conduct.'

'You've been reading Ibsen and Bernard Shaw.'

'Yes, and I think they're right. Heaven is the home of the
masters of reality, and earth is the home of the slaves of reality.'

'What rubbish!' said Howard.

'Bernard Shaw says, like Ibsen: "Do what you want to do, and
then prove you are right."'

'Don't you believe in a sense of duty?'

'Of course I do. But I believe that duty to self is more important
than duty to the world. And that's why I admire the Duke of
Windsor for his courage.'

'Well, I don't,' said my husband, lighting his pipe, 'and neither
do most of my friends.'

'Well, I do,' said Renie's daughter, and quoted Hamlet:

'This, above all, to thine own self be true,
  And it must follow, as the night the day,
Thou canst not then be false to any man.'

So then we argued for a while about the sad Duke of Windsor, who was living with his bombshell of a wife in Paris. He had made several visits to England to remind the Government as delicately as possible that he was an ex-king without a job. He was met with courtesy and silence.

'Serves him right,' said Howard, smoking his pipe. 'If you break the conventions you've got to *prove* that you're right by making your life a success. Even Ibsen and Shaw would agree with me about that. After all his training as a king!' said Howard in disgust. 'Look at him now!'

'He was Governor of the Bahamas for five years.'

'Why can't he stay in the Bahamas? Can't he stick to anything?'

'Well, he sticks to his wife.'

'Anyhow,' said Howard, 'I enjoy these arguments with you. I enjoy coming home.'

As his second wife I was now accepted by his London friends. The double divorce had been forgotten. In the new socialist London it was not important. And the man they all loved, the broadcaster, the D-Day hero, the poet, the rugger blue, the captain of the Harlequins, the author of a book about Scott's expedition to the South Pole, had entered the new profession.

'What does your husband do?' people used to say.

I replied vaguely, 'He's in the steel industry. He's Director of Public Relations for Richard Thomas and Baldwin.'

'Oh really? What does he *do*?'

At that time nobody had ever heard about Public Relations. Since then it has been described by Malcolm Muggeridge as 'organized lying' and by Harold Wilson as 'a most degrading profession'. For us, in those days, Public Relations was a new ideology, a mystical idea. Not socialism, not religion, not poetry, and yet all of these things could be found, like a new language, in the right understanding of social problems and the use of Public Relations. Night after night we talked about it. Howard's definition of Public Relations was simple. 'Good behaviour, and taking credit for it! It's my job,' he said, 'to insist on good behaviour! Just tell your friends that!'

I believed in Howard as a leader of men. There was greatness in him. He might have risen as a statesman. Sometimes I thought he might even have the quality of a socialist Prime Minister. This I remember telling his parents, who began to think I might one day become a good wife.

But it has to be said that until Renée took charge of the household I continued to feel like a worn-out old battery. Helen and Andy both noticed it.

'There's no life in you,' said Andy.

'You're like a deflated balloon,' said Helen. 'What's the matter with you?'

'I can't help it,' I said. 'I need blowing up.'

I remember the first and only time we were invited by Howard's employer to a dance at the Savoy Hotel. It was a happy little party. I had always loved dancing and that evening, with a man I had never seen before and never met again, I danced three or four times in succession, not bothering to sit down with the others, dancing for the gladness of rhythm, loving it, having fun with it.

Howard was furious. The moment I returned to the table I was taken home in disgrace. 'You made an exhibition of yourself. I won't have it.'

After that, overcome by the dictatorship of love, I made up my mind never to dance with anyone but Howard. I never enjoyed my dancing again, going alone with him once or twice to the Mirabelle, where we danced during the war, but more often talking about it and deciding to stay at home for another quiet evening.

Perhaps it was the turning point. Boredom had set in with a vengeance. I began to feel the long littleness of life which leads to the ending of laughter.

When Renée suddenly appeared, like a ray of Parisian sunshine, I was descending into middle-age. My life was changed by the little French girl. As I have said, she stayed with us for nearly three years, happy years, and it might have lasted twenty years, or longer. She cheered me up. She made Howard smile. She looked after us both, laughing, chattering in French, amusing us like a mischievous child. She was full of vitality. She made us feel young. Even Mitzie, her cat, was a source of amusement, spitting at all of us, especially my dog, in French!

No one could possibly have guessed how it all would end. The human heart is a strange thing. The human mind is stranger still.

One day she had said to me, standing in my small study, with a duster in her hand, '*Madame, j'envie de faire l'amour.*' The next minute she was in my arms.

I can see now that my growing affection for Renée was much like Helen's affection for me. There was something deeply maternal about it. Affection soon became love, and love became the desire to understand and protect. Helen was my protector, and I was the little French girl's protector.

Even now I can hardly believe it or grasp the meaning of it, and yet it happened. I ought to have seen the signs and symptoms. But a mental illness was something quite new to Howard and me. Neither of us had any experience with a temperamental foreigner. There were fits of temper. There were fears and alarms and tantrums. There were mental fixations. Among other things she began to think that Howard wanted to poison her.

I know now because I have seen so much of it since then. The word used when people suffer from it is 'paranoia'.

Then I only knew that something horrible had entered my home. I suddenly found that many months of happiness and laughter and joyous friendship had changed without warning into hatred and suspicion.

One morning she dropped the breakfast tray with a crash. Then she locked herself in her bedroom. When she came out of the bedroom she was terrified, defending herself from me like a small demented animal. I remember she fled downstairs and out of the building and in her handbag she carried a knife.

I remember listening for her all night, and when at last she returned, still trembling with fear, I persuaded her to enter the waiting ambulance and sat by her side holding her hand.

She seemed like my child again. I think we were both crying.

'Madame, j'ai peur!'

I can still hear her childish voice.

'J'ai peur, madame, j'ai peur! Je ne veux pas mourir!'

Afterwards, in the hospital at Epsom, I used to visit her once a fortnight. She stayed there, most of the time in a locked ward, for nine long months. It was painful to see her. The doctor said it was caused by delayed shock, and the root of it was Renée's distress at the death of her mother during the war.

Whatever it was, I suffered greatly at the sight of my poor little friend, distorted and desperate, possessed by evil, like one of those lost souls we remember in the Bible, no longer in the least like Renée, and yet, in her madness, calling out for help, calling me as a child calls for a mother.

'Viens ici! Où es tu? J'ai peur!'

During that terrible time of tears and terror she lost her memory completely. As far as I could tell, her only comfort was the belief that I was her mother. She no longer called me *'Madame'*. I became *'Maman'*. She loved me and quarrelled with me and begged me for help and asked me to tell her about uncles and aunts and cousins and friends whose names I had never heard. She could not bear me to leave her. She was frightened of the other patients, and so was I, for they yelled and shouted and banged one another. The sense of evil was all around us.

Poor little thing! Poor little child!

The sharing of madness and despair with my little French girl diminished me in spirit until I had nothing left.

Howard used to say: 'Well, how was she today?'

At this I would burst into tears.

It really was a very bad time for all three of us. And at the end of nine nightmare months during which I continued to be Renée's mother and tried to tell her the history of her life as far as I knew it, helping her to write it all down, she still could remember almost nothing.

The doctors said she must be sent back to France. She had now received hospital treatment free of charge and a grant of £100 and there was clearly no excuse to stay any longer as a guest of the Government.

There was nothing else I could possibly do.

I remember taking Renée to Victoria Station and leading her by the hand to the seat reserved in her name and kissing her good-bye as a mother would have kissed her. I can see her now. She was dressed in a tailored suit which I had given her. The long hair was curled and carefully combed and she looked even younger than before.

'*Au'voir, Maman,*' Renée said, and then corrected herself. '*Au'voir,* Madame.'

I remember standing on the platform waiting for the train to depart. The window was not intended to open. I could no longer hear her voice. I think she was saying, '*Au'voir, Madame. Je ne t'oublierai jamais.*'

It may have been that, or something else. Whatever she said, it brought the tears to her eyes, and through the thickness of the window I could see a solemn face, deeply wondering, like the face of a hurt child, punished for something unknown, and I could see the tears filling her eyes and slowly running down her cheeks, unnoticed.

Her hurt expression did not change. She did not even know she was crying.

As the train began to move, a part of my life came to an end, and as long as I live I think I shall never forget the tragic figure of my little French girl, not speaking, silently shedding tears, wounded by something, not understanding what she had done to merit all this suffering, rejected, returning to France.

I walked beside the slow-moving train until the platform ended. When the train was out of sight I walked back along the platform and found an empty seat and allowed myself to cry as if my heart would break. I was alone with my grief. I felt more alone than I had ever felt in my life. How could I bear so much suffering alone?

And the loneliness persisted. Sometimes I walked the streets, and longed for a companion. Sometimes I talked to strangers.

At one point, in a moment of despair, I suggested adopting a child. Howard thought it would not be right because our marriage might be coming unstuck. This was something we both dreaded.

We struggled along. It lasted for one more year. At times I found myself thinking about the Duke of Windsor, that brave escapist, that other transgressor, and wondering in a morbid way about the success or sadness of a marriage even more meaningful than mine. Howard felt honour bound to make a success of things. So did I. Was this how the Windsors felt?

One of my problems was the habit of weeping.

I am the sort of person who seldom cries, except when watching a sentimental film. I was rapidly becoming a compulsive weeper. I formed the habit of locking myself in the bathroom, having a weep, then powdering my face and returning to the sitting-room as though nothing had happened. Howard pretended not to notice. Neither of us ever mentioned it.

'Why don't you study something?' Howard said.

My course of study in English Literature had come to an end.

'What shall I study?'

'I don't know. Anything you like.'

'I seem to have lost interest.'

'I think you're suffering from a broken heart,' said Howard, in a tone of surprising insight. 'Can't you get a job? Or write a book?'

In a strange way, because he loved me, Howard seemed to understand the deep pool of loneliness in which I was struggling. I tried not to drown. I tried to fill the days by writing a book about Dante Gabriel Rossetti. I grew fond of the pre-Raphaelites, especially 'Miss Sid'. I wrote a piece about Ruskin which was praised by the poet, Richard Church, who reviewed it.

My work was a form of escape. At least it stopped me from crying. One day, in this empty mood, I went to see my mother in Sussex. Her laughing face looked younger than ever. She had managed to pay the bills. She had performed a miracle. She was living with Noel at Woldhurstlea, the huge Victorian mansion where she had been born and bred.

I remembered it well. I had loved it dearly as a child, before my mother took me to California. In a taxi I passed between the iron gates erected by my grandfather, and up the long drive, which now was rough and stony, and spoiled by huge potholes. Although the garden was wild, and only one of the terraced lawns had been smoothly mown, the long white house looked very much the same as before. It looked bigger, perhaps, with its gables and battlements, and the little white tower and even the flagmast.

The front door was opened by my mother, in a blue cotton dress.

'Welcome home! Isn't it wonderful to be back at Woldhurstlea? Come and see the drawing-room,' she said proudly.

The enormous double room was no longer filled with cabinets and statues and inlaid tables and ivories, but I remembered the Italian Carrara mantelpiece (Carrara marble), at the south end. And then I saw my grandmother's pink Sèvres clock. There was also a pair of cloisonné vases, peacock blue, with gold inlay on the copper, a few Chelsea figures and some Battersea enamel boxes as well as a small Dresden shepherdess.

'I've tried to make it as pretty as it used to be, but of course I haven't much money,' said my mother. 'How do you like it?'

The tea-table was placed by her chair (as it had been placed by my grandmother's chair). It was covered by a lace and embroidered cloth, and the silver tea-tray (one of Renie's wedding presents when she married for the first time at the age of eighteen) was beautifully polished. So was the silver teapot, the cream jug, the sugar basin, and the small silver kettle placed over a methylated lamp, which I remembered admiring as a child.

My mother had even managed to provide a Crown Derby tea-service. A second table, covered by a similar cloth, was laden with dishes of thin bread and butter, rock cakes, sponge fingers, meringues, and a large round iced cake, home-made, with cherries and almonds.

'How do you like it?' repeated my mother impatiently. 'Does it seem like home?'

I managed to smile.

'It seems like a dream. I can hardly believe it.'

'Neither can I.'

'Have you got a butler, and a footman, and two or three housemaids, and a cook? Have you got a couple of hunters and a groom and a few gardeners to mow the lawns and see to the greenhouses?'

'I've got a cook,' said my mother, in a tone of triumph, 'and a charwoman and a gardener aged eighty. The rest is done by Noel and me.'

'How is Noel?'

'Very well, thank you.'

'Is he still drinking?'

'Not as much as he did. You'll see him in a minute.'

I remember noticing the white-and-mauve Belgian carpet, and the gay chintz-covered armchairs, the flower-painted Hepple-white cabinets, the Bechstein grand piano and the Sheraton table arranged by my mother with a cut-glass bowl filled to overflowing with scented dark red roses from the wall in the kitchen garden.

After tea we sat with Noel (whose manners were as perfect as ever) in the comfortable basket chairs on the long rose-covered veranda facing south. We looked with pleasure at the red, heavy geraniums and over the redness and the rich green fields at the changing beauty of St Leonard's Forest, the trees standing in coloured sunlit groups, waiting like dancers to begin the dance.

'Shall we take Nerina for a walk?' said Noel.

The stables were empty now. In the middle of the enormous garage which had been built by one of my rich uncles I noticed a very old Austin car, spotlessly clean, even aristocratic, like an elderly and sensitive bachelor who had seen better days.

'That's our car,' said Renie proudly. 'It looks very nice, don't you think so?'

'Do you drive it?'

'No, dear, Noel drives it. When he's not drinking he drives very well.'

'Thank you,' said Noel.

When we were alone she said, 'What do you think of my husband, dear?'

'I think he's charming. It all seems too good to be true.'

'Why say that? Things turn out well if you try to do what is right. Even if you make a lot of mistakes.'

'By mistakes, I suppose you mean husbands?'

'Well, yes, most of my mistakes were husbands, dear. But if I had taken the advice of other people I should never have married a young man like Noel. When you have the romantic temperament you must do what you think is right. Sometimes it comes off, and sometimes it doesn't.'

'Would you say this is your happiest marriage?'

'Of course it is. He's more like a son than a husband. I've never been so happy in my life.'

'Do you think it will last?'

'Of course it will last. I've never been bored for a moment, and neither has he.'

'I wish I could say the same.'

'Are you bored, dear?'

'Bored to death.'

By this confession my mother seemed worried and surprised.

'You must find something to do. Boredom always leads to trouble.'

'What do you mean?'

'Well, dear, when your father was bored he used to be unfaithful. You know what men are.'

'Were you unfaithful too?'

'Certainly not. When I become bored I simply get married to someone else. Have you been unfaithful, dear?'

'Certainly not,' I said. 'I've never even looked at another man.'

I went home to Howard with the knowledge that my mother had cheered me up. After that, there was less weeping in the bathroom. I tried to forget the little French girl who had managed to bring both of us happiness through love and food and laughter. I tried to forget my poor devoted little Renée.

Howard suggested we should leave our flat in Mayfair, which now was so full of memories, and live, for a change, in Whitehall Court, a magnificent apartment overlooking the River Thames. It seemed at first like a good idea.

13 'Love among the ruins'

It might still have been saved. It was a marriage with an illness like a house with dry-rot.

Our new home in Whitehall Court was majestically depressing. I found I was back in my father's world. It was a stronghold of respectability, an expensive way to live, a huge old-fashioned group of Victorian buildings, overlooking the river, with towers and turrets, which could be seen from St James's Park. It was run like a convalescent home by a staff of waiters and chambermaids and valets and cleaners and carpenters and painters and plumbers. They controlled their elderly tenants with affection and discipline, as nurses control their patients.

Bernard Shaw had moved from the Adelphi to Whitehall Court. He remained there for many years. Perhaps he liked living among the people whose standards he mocked.

In our flat there was a large and beautiful sitting-room with two enormous windows overlooking the river. Each window possessed a little cushioned seat where I used to sit, staring into space, thinking about Renée. There were two bedrooms and a bathroom. There was no kitchen. Either we ordered our meals to be served at the table in our big room, waited on by an elegant gentleman who looked and behaved like a butler, listening sadly to every word spoken, or else we dined and lunched in the restaurant downstairs.

Once I saw my ex-husband, James Wentworth Day, sitting in a corner on the opposite side. Luckily he did not see me, being very short-sighted.

Each day I had lunch by myself in that gloomy restaurant. I felt the glinting eyes of middle-aged women and retired colonels. They might all have been my father's friends. Their eyes were saying:

'Who is this lonely woman? What makes her look so miserable?'

I had escaped from my father's world, and returned to it, and escaped again. Now I was back in it. My last husband had

164

enjoyed it all his life and my present husband had turned to it from socialism, as a man turns from his mistress to his wife.

Sometimes I hated it. I felt like a stranger in this unreal London of riches and comfort and status. And yet Whitehall Court was as comfortable as a feather-bed.

I remember my quick delight at the movement of the river beneath our windows. We could almost see the Houses of Parliament. We could see the river above the heads of the trees, and beneath the trees the couples making love on park benches. During the war, in a moment of passion, standing together in a dark street, we had done the same thing ourselves. An unforgettable moment.

Howard said, 'I like watching them, don't you?'

'I wonder if Bernard Shaw used to watch them as we do?'

'Probably,' said Howard, 'when his wife was out.'

We smiled at one another. Did he know that I was thinking of Renée?'

My mother sent Noel to help us with the curtains and new carpets and all the unpacking. Noel explained that my mother was in bed with one of her ailments.

'She'll soon get well,' he said. 'She told me to give you her love.'

Noel was very helpful. When he departed the flat became lonely because the work had been done. We suddenly realized there was nothing left for either of us to do. If anything was wanted Howard pressed the bell. We were served at once by the waiter or the chambermaid or the valet or one of the others.

'What a dull place this is,' I said. 'There's nothing to do.'

'We shall get used to it.'

'Do you think we shall be happy here?'

'When we get used to it.'

'There's not much privacy.'

'What do you mean?'

'Everyone has a key to our front door.'

It was a fine mahogany front door. They entered whenever they pleased. I remember that moment of astonishment when I walked half-naked out of my bathroom and was greeted by an unsmiling valet. He would like, he said sternly, to press my husband's trousers. I was the intruder, not he.

'Could you come back when I'm dressed, please?'

He frowned at me. 'Very well, madam, I'll come back in ten minutes.'

'Would you make it twenty minutes, please?'

'Very well, madam, twenty minutes.' He looked with annoyance at his watch.

In all my life I had never known the days and minutes to be so long and empty. My book about Rossetti was finished and accepted. I listened to the French programmes on the radio, thinking about Renée. In the daytime Clem was my only companion. I think he hated Whitehall Court as much as I did.

Howard said in a tone of disappointment, 'I thought you would like it here. It's very expensive.'

'I know it is.'

'What do you do all day?'

'Nothing.'

'Tell me what you think about?'

'I think about Renée most of the time.'

Howard sighed. 'What's the matter with Whitehall Court?'

'It's all right for elderly people like Bernard Shaw.'

'It's a very nice place to live.'

'When you get used to the loneliness,' I said.

The longing to escape had returned. The longing for Renée pursued me like an enemy. Boredom led to depression. Finally I felt a desire to die.

I walked with Clem to St James's Park, still thinking of Renée. We looked at the pelicans, and avoided the couples, in the grip of love, who lay with their paper bags on the grass.

To please Clem I sometimes threw a stick, which he retrieved, and then placed at my feet, begging me to do it again. Sometimes my dog and I travelled on a bus, Clem sitting under my seat. We had nowhere to go. The other passengers were always in a hurry to get somewhere else. Clem and I had all the time in the world, and nothing to do with it. We were enclosed in boredom, like goldfish in a bowl.

'Where shall we go, Clem?'

He wagged his tail. He understood.

'What shall we do, Clem? shall we go for a walk in the Park?'

He barked.

I thought incessantly about poor little Renée. After her long illness my little French girl, in London, never had anything to do. Yet she frequently looked at her watch, and then at the clock, pretending she had just remembered an urgent appointment with someone important. She had been trying to copy all the others, the busy Londoners, hoping to find a sense of purpose, a sense of identity. Now Clem and I were doing the very same thing. Renée had lost her reason. We had lost something too.

'What shall we do, Clem? Shall we get on a bus?'

He wagged his tail.

Post-war London looked shabby and sick at heart. The bomb

sites were now used for parking cars. The new buildings were as ugly as matchboxes. somehow, under socialism, the spark and sizzle of London life had entirely disappeared.

'Oh, Clem, what shall we do?'

Occasionally I visited Helen and Andy for a country week-end. I still kept my horse, Kitty, in their field. My devoted friends were just the same, unchanging people, kinder than ever, but Andy, poor Andy, was crippled with arthritis and had given up her work as a surgeon.

Helen said, 'You look terrible. What's up, Nerina?'

'It's difficult to explain.'

'Is it boredom? Have you been quarrelling with Howard?'

'No, no, I love him dearly. He's the best husband in the world.'

'Are you missing the French girl?'

Tears came into my eyes. 'I keep thinking about her. I can't forget.'

'Are you still in love with her, Nerina?'

'I suppose I am. I seem to need both.'

'What do you mean by that?'

'Well, you see, I seem to need a woman as well as a man. Where is it all going to end? Why do I need a woman's love so badly?'

Helen put her arm round me, gave me a kiss and a hug, took me for a walk round the garden, and tried to explain things to me as though talking to a young sister. Helen was thirteen years older, and many years wiser, and far more experienced than her weeping companion.

'You need a woman's love because you need to be mothered,' said Helen.

'Why am I in love with poor little Renée?'

'Because Renée needs to be mothered. It's the other way round, don't you see? Both of you need to be mothered.'

'Is it wrong to love another woman?'

'Of course it's not wrong. But it's dangerous when you have a jealous husband. Some men understand these things. Most of them don't have any idea what it's all about. That's why you've got to be careful, as I've told you before.'

'I would never be unfaithful to my husband with another man. Loving a woman is different. You don't feel unfaithful to a man when you love a woman, and you don't feel unfaithful to a woman when you love a man.'

'Exactly,' said Helen. 'You don't feel unfaithful to me, and you don't feel unfaithful to Howard. I understand you but Howard doesn't.'

I knew that Helen had found another partner, someone to replace me in her need for an intimate friendship, but Andy did not mind and neither did I. The close understanding between us remained untouched.

'You always have us,' said Helen. 'You can come here whenever you like.'

'Of course you can,' said Andy. 'People make too much fuss about sex,' she added with a smile. 'Friendship is what matters.'

'Thank you,' I said. 'Sorry to be such a misery.'

'Can't I make you laugh?' said Helen.

'I wish you'd try.'

'I've never seen you like this.'

'I feel suicidal.'

The weeping fits in London continued. In the morning, which was the bad time, the depression was like a physical pain in the stomach. I lay there rigid, stiff and tense, staring at the ceiling, tortured and frightened, unable to face another day in such a dull and dreary world. Why should I dress? What for?

I believe there is a medieval word for this mental state of apathy and despair. It is 'accidie'. I believe it was once one of the seven deadly sins.

When men and women feel like this they are tempted to commit suicide. In 1955, when I lived in Whitehall Court, an Anglican clergyman called Chad Varah started a rescue service and named it The Samaritans. Unfortunately no one told me about it then, but years later I joined it as a volunteer.

Today, in my peace of mind, it is difficult to explain, even to myself, the meaning and depth of my depression at that time, my angry and lonely despair.

'Are you all right?' Howard used to say. 'Shall I find you a job?'

'What kind of a job?'

'I don't know. What would you like to do?'

'Nothing in particular.'

'Haven't you any ideas?'

'None at all. I'm bored.'

'I can't understand it. How can any intelligent woman feel bored?'

Howard was working so hard at his own exciting job as Director of Public Relations for the steel industry in Wales. He was broadcasting once a month for the Commonwealth. At the same time he was preparing for the biggest event of his life since D-Day. By this I mean the Coronation. Londoners were keenly patriotic and Howard, like everyone else, was longing for the big event. Every evening he talked about it. And what, I said to myself, did he get out of it?

In his fine apartment, admired and envied by visitors, he came home to eat and drink with a miserable half-dead woman whose eyes filled with tears. I pitied Howard. He deserved something better from his partner.

But I moved in a world of unreality like a sleep-walker. Somehow the light had gone out, leaving me in an empty world where the trees and flowers stood still, without colour. The birds had no song. When I looked at it there was no magic in anything, anywhere. In such a world there was no point in existence. I wanted to escape. I would rather be dead.

Since then I have seen it happen to many other people.

It is not now called accidie. When you get it badly it is called a nervous breakdown. It may take years out of your life. You behave like a different person. You hardly know in your bad moments what you are doing or why you are doing it. You lose your identity.

At that time I had no idea what was wrong with me. The sense of drifting was horrible. Perhaps the sleep-walker had somehow managed to change personality. Even this, I thought, would be no more difficult to understand than a sudden fit of insanity when men and women do strange, inexplicable, outrageous, and faulty things.

Lonely people are close to insanity.

I think Howard saw the danger. He helped me to get a job with a publisher, and this was certainly a means of escape from the chambermaids and valets in our flat. I forced myself to write a report on education for Richard Church. It led to numerous interviews with teachers and parents and children. I discovered that one in three 15-year-olds could not read properly. I then wrote a series of articles for *John O'London's Weekly*, which were published later in book form. The title was *Favourite Books For Boys and Girls*.

'Well done,' said Howard. 'Well played.'

But the sleep-walker was incredibly unhappy.

'I made myself do it,' I said.

'Why?'

'To overcome boredom and depression.'

'Have you succeeded?'

'No, not quite.'

'What has happened? *Where are you?*' said Howard. (He said it as Renée had said, '*Où es tu?*')

'I don't know. I don't know. I seem to be lost.'

One day we had lunch with Richard Church in his country home, a converted oast-house in Kent. The poet had a silvery voice and a silvery face. His wife, who loved him, interrupted

him when he spoke. After lunch, because of this, he took me
into his study and talked about my work as a writer. I remember
him saying in his silvery voice: 'You must follow your star!'

'What is my star?'

'I think it's your sense of humour,' the poet said.

I was deeply impressed. I knew he meant it because, in a
review, he had described my book about Rossetti and especially
the passage about Ruskin as 'wildly funny'.

But I now felt I had lost my sense of humour. There was no
sparkle. There was no magic. There was no beating of drums.

'Thank you for noticing my sense of humour,' I said.

'I like your work. Don't lose confidence, Nerina.'

On the way home, in the car, Howard talked about our
marriage.

'Richard is happy because his wife loves him,' I said.

'That's how it ought to be. I hate these untidy marriages.'

'Is our marriage untidy?'

'Whatever happens we must never be unfaithful.'

'No, of course not.'

'We must never debase the coinage,' said Howard.

'That's a good phrase. I know what you mean.'

I realized that Howard was doing his best to help me. On
another occasion he invited Pamela Hansford Johnson and C. P.
Snow to dine with us in our flat. It was done for my sake. In the
past, if such a thing had ever happened, I would have sparkled
with pleasure. Howard's entertaining wife had changed. The
sleep-walker had nothing to say to our nice friends.

Pamela Hansford Johnson talked brilliantly about the
problems of a novelist finding material. C. P. Snow looked at me
with fatherly interest because I was suffering from sciatica. I said
nothing when I was standing up tall and straight beside Howard
but when I sat down I emitted a shriek of agony. I think they
forgave me because of that shriek. It made everybody smile.

'Are you in pain?' said Howard lovingly.

I nodded, without speaking.

'Never mind. Have another drink.'

I am thankful to say that Howard's father, who was fond of
me, had died a little while before these happenings. He gave me
the title *Georgian Lady* for my book about Fanny Burney, which
he read and enjoyed. He died after an attack of jaundice.

Howard's mother lived in a state of weepy despair and then
died, mercifully, without seeing the end of our marriage. (She
had never spent a single night away from her husband.)

Before I left my beloved Howard, we had to face the
excitement of the Coronation, an event I remember as through a

glass darkly, as a sleep-walker might remember an interesting dream.

Richard Dimbleby was the man chosen by the BBC to compère the television programme. Howard was the radio man.

In those days not many people had television sets. It was still a novelty. It prevented conversation. We had a set and Howard loved it, and yet the sleep-walker refused to allow it in the sitting-room. Even my mother was against it. She was converted to it (like so many others) by the Coronation programme.

'Come on, Nerina. Try to take an interest in my work,' said Howard.

'All right,' I said, 'tell me about the new Queen.'

In 1953, in London, there was still a public adoration for the Royal Family. Londoners adored the new Queen. We felt a special sentimental tenderness and worship for the calm young woman about to be crowned, given the title and hailed before her subjects as 'Her Most Excellent Majesty, Elizabeth II'.

We knew so little about her then. Even today she has never held a press conference. Howard taught me a lot about Buckingham Palace. He said the Queen lived on the first floor in the rooms overlooking Constitution Hill, the nursery above, the offices below.

'The men-servants are dressed in a kind of blue battledress, Nerina.'

'How many servants are there?'

He said the whole household, not counting servants, was no more than sixty people.

'They say she is the third richest woman alive, Nerina.'

Howard used to believe, and so did I, that the Queen was a symbol of something. The Queen was a sign of stability. The Queen represented a way of life and a dignity and a true integrity in which we continued to believe and tried in a small way to imitate. If we lost our Queen each of us would die a little. This is what I still believe today.

And yet, at that time, I could not take part in Howard's pleasure for the sleep-walker took charge and most of the time I felt I was floating and drifting, no longer myself.

'I wish you would take a little more interest, Nerina.'

When the big day arrived at last our flat was filled with BBC people. To me they were all strangers. They seemed to be very busy with lights and cameras and suitcases which had to be left or delivered or changed. I listened to Howard's velvety voice on the radio. Then I turned to the television. I looked with wonder at the solemn face of the little new Queen beneath her huge and heavy crown.

This part brought tears to my eyes.

'Well, did you enjoy it?' said Howard.

'Some of it. Especially the Queen and her crown.'

'What about me?' said Howard anxiously. 'How did I sound?'

'Wonderful. You always do. I think you're the best in the world.'

When it was all over most of us felt exhausted. Londoners continued to talk about it for weeks, as you talk about a birth or a death in the family. Finally there was nothing more to say. The dullness and littleness of an empty life became too difficult to bear and I wondered how to end it.

Had I the courage to commit suicide?

I remember on a Sunday morning going by myself to the service at St Martin-in-the-Fields. I was thinking as usual about poor little Renée. My mind came back to the church service and I heard those words which were intended for me.

'Take not Thy Holy Spirit from us.'

It seemed to me then that the Holy Spirit had been taken from me. Renée had lost her mind. I had lost my serenity, or my soul, or whatever it is that puts the spark of magic into life and fills you with radiance.

Since I had no wish to live, Howard would be better off without me.

I went home. I locked myself in the bathroom so that I could cry undisturbed for fifteen minutes, and then powdered my face, hoping against hope that Howard would not notice.

'Hello,' he said. 'Where have you been?'

'Nowhere,' I said. 'Well, I went to church.'

The weather was very cold and Christmas was approaching. There was no point in preparing even a small Christmas tree. Who would want it?

At Christmas-time the lonely people become lonelier than ever. They learn to dread Christmas. The pointlessness of their wasted lives becomes sharp and cold. I have seen all this many times in men and women I have tried to befriend.

Then, it was happening to me.

I remember visiting the children's ward in the Charing Cross Hospital bcause Howard was one of the Governors. The children were opening their presents on Christmas morning. It should have made me happy. Instead I began to cry, and at Whitehall Court I could not control my grief. When I came out of the bathroom it started, to my shame, all over again, in front of Howard, in front of his son.

A psychiatrist might have known what to do, what to say.

I forgot to mention that when I was very young I went to one for advice. I was told (after six visits) that I was a well-balanced person and had better go home and stop fussing about myself and my faults. Yes, but a well-balanced person can become suicidal. It could happen to anyone. Until Christmas Day I had not realized how much I needed a child. And then, like a sick person, wanting to end my life, I found myself ending my marriage.

On New Year's Eve I had a violent row with my beloved husband and told him the truth about my love for Renée.

'You have been unfaithful to me! I can never forgive you!' said Howard.

'But I have *not* been unfaithful. Don't you understand? I love you with all my heart. I've never had anything to do with another man since the day we met, and you know it.'

'You've been unfaithful with Renée.'

'No, no, that's different! Loving a woman is quite different from loving a man. You don't feel unfaithful to a man when you love a woman because it's another kind of love. It's a motherly love.'

'I don't understand it,' said Howard, 'and I never shall.'

There was no need to tell him about it, and yet I did. An inner voice was whispering: 'To thine own self be true.' As the little French girl would have said: *'C'était plus fort que moi!'*

Perhaps, in my heart, hoping against hope, I thought my husband would try to understand. How could he understand? How could he possibly understand?

Afterwards, in a frenzy of passion, unable to resist one another, we went to bed and made love for the last time. It was unforgettable. It was thrilling.

When it was over I heard my husband say, in a heart-broken voice, 'Love among the ruins! Love among the ruins!'

14   *Retreat*

I could not possibly tell my mother the whole story about poor little Renée and yet, in her own way, she was most understanding. We discussed the situation in her bedroom because she was ill. We talked about it as one escapist to another.

'Why did you leave him, dear?'

'He said I was unfaithful.'

'Did you tell him about it?'

'Yes.'

'That was a mistake, dear.'

'He insisted on total fidelity for both of us.'

'Then why did you tell him, dear?'

'It was stupid of me but I felt I had to confess. I was hoping he would understand how it all happened but I knew it would end my marriage, and it did.'

'Do you mean you were tired of your marriage?'

'I was bored. I was fed up with everything.'

'Do you mean you wanted to escape?'

'Yes, I suppose I did.'

'Well, dear, I know *exactly* how you felt. I would have done it a long time ago. To tell the truth, I don't know how you stuck it so long. Why didn't you do it before?'

She was perfectly serious. Her immediate sympathy made me smile for the first time.

'Well, you see, I've left three men.'

'I've only left two,' said my mother, 'because the others died, poor things. But I *would* have left them if they hadn't.'

I can see her now, sitting up in bed beneath a pale-pink counterpane. As usual the blue hair-ribbon was tied in a bow round her curled hair. In spite of illness the large blue eyes were sparkling with life and love and defiance.

'Never say die. Two heads are better than one. Between us we'll think of something. Don't worry, darling.'

At first she thought that my dog and I had come to stay for a week. When I arrived, on that bitter cold New Year's Day (it

174

was 1 January 1954), I pretended to believe it myself.

I told myself that Howard would forgive me. One of these days he would learn to understand that certain women need the love of another woman even when they love their husbands. I would make him understand. I would force myself to live at Whitehall Court when my nerves were better, and the fits of weeping had been overcome. Everything would be all right. I loved my husband, and he loved me.

When Howard telephoned, I said: 'I need a rest. Let me stay with my mother for another week.'

But I never was able to return. I could no more have gone back to Whitehall Court than a prisoner could return after breaking out of prison. The mere thought of it reduced me to tears.

My mother said, 'Never mind, darling. Have a cup of coffee. There is always something round the corner.'

I knew she had been through it herself. In California, in my childhood, she had tried to commit suicide by taking an overdose. But mine was another form of despair. I was trying to escape from myself, and my longing for poor little Renée, as well as from London and marriage and a jealous but adoring husband, who would never comprehend my loneliness or my need for a woman's love.

Meanwhile I listened for the telephone.

When it was Howard my heart began to thud. He was kind and gentle. He wanted me at home, even if he had told me to go. Would I come back, please, when I felt better? We would move from Whitehall Court to Sheffield Terrace. Would I like that? I thanked him for his kindness. The end had come, but we went on pretending.

'I don't feel well enough to come back. I still feel very upset.'

'Do you miss me?'

'Yes, of course. I still love you.'

'When will you come back?'

'I don't know. Are you sure you want me?'

'It depends on you,' said Howard. (In other words, I must never again have a close friendship.)

'No, it depends on you,' I said. 'Please try to understand what has happened. I never had any wish to be unfaithful.'

I know now it is possible for incompatible people to love one another very deeply. My mother could have told me that. Instead she lay in bed and smiled and offered me cups of coffee and waited to see what I would do next.

'You need a change. It's lovely to have you with us. You must think things over, dear. Noel, give her some more coffee.'

Noel did as she told him. He was now like an affectionate son, always in her bedroom, attentive and charming. I had come from luxury to poverty. My mother had been forced to leave Woldhurstlea, on which she had spent so much money. The family home had been bought from the family trust by the Crawley Corporation. The fields and woods and avenues and houses on my grandfather's estate were soon to be swallowed up and destroyed and forgotten by the planners and developers.

Crawley, poor Crawley, was turning into a parasite town.

So my mother was living in a bungalow in a village called Rusper. It reminded me of a houseboat on the River Thames.

'It's very small,' said my mother, 'but Noel likes it, and so do I.'

A long corridor ran from end to end of the wooden building and the five little rooms opened from it like cabins. My mother's desire was to sit on the white wooden veranda overlooking the lupins and roses in the flourishing garden. In summer this is what we did. Of course I was still with her. We sat like passengers on deck even when it rained. We looked down over the white wooden railing into a wet green lawn, a dripping oak tree, a damp green hedge, and the soft, swishing, rivery movement could almost be felt beneath and around our table as we sipped our tea.

'Isn't it nice?' said my mother. 'I like the smell of the rain, don't you?'

It was the wettest and most miserable summer that anyone in Sussex could remember. The sound of dripping water continued like the ticking of a clock. I still had no wish to go back to London. The telephone calls from Howard had ceased. Without any bitterness we had decided to live apart, always to be friends, each of us to find another partner, or a new way of life, if and when we stopped loving one another.

'Take care of yourself,' said Howard.

My mother said, 'Don't worry, dear. You'll get over it. There's always something round the corner.'

We then had the wildest and stormiest winter that anyone in Sussex had ever beheld. No one could understand it. Noel and I (beginning to behave like brother and sister) were astonished to find enormous trees suddenly and violently uprooted. They lay like bodies across the country lanes.

'Never mind,' said my mother, 'winter will soon be over.'

She spent most of her time in bed, or lying on the sofa, contentedly watching the television. I often wondered why she had bought such a matchbox of a house. It really was a jerry-built place, with tiny rooms, and every conceivable disadvantage. It even had dry-rot under the floorboards. This we did not know and would have angrily denied, because, for some reason, we all loved it.

'It's such a nice little house,' my mother said.

In cold weather it was very snug and warm, no one knew why, and in summer it was surrounded by tall delphiniums and voluptuous lupins and large flamboyant roses, like chorus girls, all of them bigger and better than anyone thought possible. There was something about that bungalow. It never let us down.

After the magnificence of Whitehall Court it seemed unbelievably small, and to make matters worse each room was stuffed with unsuitable furniture. My mother had filled it with large beds and wardrobes. The poor little drawing-room was bursting with antiques.

'Never mind, dear, Noel likes it, and so do I.'

Outside we still had storms of thunder and rain. Inside we always had illness and poverty. And yet in my mother's bungalow we lived with kindness and courage and laughter.

My mother was now seventy-six years of age. She did not suffer as I did from a sense of guilt. But she was beginning to suffer from blood pressure and heart attacks, and during the second winter one of the bedrooms was occupied by a resident nurse whose salary was £8 a week.

'Isn't it a nuisance, dear? I don't feel old in the least. I believe I could still ride a horse. And yet here I am,' said my mother indignantly, 'battling to keep out of the grave!'

I forget how much the housekeeper was paid. Doctor's bills were enormous. Even worse, the Inland Revenue had now learned about my mother's dealings in property and that, for ten years, she had omitted to pay tax.

This was a blow to us all.

Exasperated letters from inspectors and collectors arrived at critical moments, when Noel was shaving, or when my mother was having a heart attack. Long and soothing replies had to be composed by Nerina.

'What on earth are we going to do?' said my mother, between her attacks. 'They can't get blood out of a stone. Have you told them that, dear?'

When I wrote to Howard I always received a sympathetic letter in reply. The relationship was one of affection. But he refused ever to meet me again.

'He's quite right, dear. It's better to make a clean break,' said my mother.

'What do you mean by a clean break?'

'Well, you've got to get over one husband before you can find another.'

'I don't want another.'

'You probably will. You're like me in some ways.'

'I don't think so.'

'Never mind. I'm glad you and Howard are good friends. He's much more sensible than some of *my* husbands, dear.'

Sometimes I left my mother, to spend a country weekend with Helen and Andy, who still kept Kitty, my horse, in their field. Helen told me that my unhappy husband had called on her several times in London to talk about his broken marriage.

'He still loves you,' said Helen.

'I still love him.'

'Why did you make that silly confession?'

'It was madness,' I said, 'but I wanted him to know what was happening. I wanted to make him understand. So then we had a row, and it all came out.'

'It seems such a pity,' said Helen, still my devoted friend. 'I feel so sorry for both of you. I was afraid this would happen.'

In her motherly way she put her arms round me and gave me a kiss. Then we saddled our horses and went for a ride, which made me feel better.

'You've always got Andy and me,' said Helen.

I returned to my mother and Noel with a smile on my face. Even if boredom had departed (and it had, for how could anyone feel bored in my mother's bungalow?), the financial problem was serious. The guilty mood continued, the sorrow for my husband, the longing for little Renée. It was like the beat, beat, beat of the pelting rain.

And yet my mother's bedroom was a place of laughter.

'Shall we go bankrupt?' said my mother, when the Inland Revenue threatened us with High Court proceedings.

'I refuse to believe it,' said my mother, sitting up in bed in her blue silk jacket. 'We must sell the furniture and pay them by monthly instalments. Had you thought of that, dear?'

'Well, no,' I said, 'but the inspector in Horsham has invited me to see him.'

'Offer to give him the furniture, dear. Don't give him my bed. I need it,' my mother said cheerfully, 'to have heart attacks in.'

A form was sent to her by the Inland Revenue and my mother was instructed to sign her name and give her occupation.

'How silly these officials are!' said my mother. 'Keeping out of the grave is my *only* occupation.'

The centre of life and gaiety was always the bedroom where my mother lay. When she was well enough we helped her down the long narrow passage to the drawing-room at the other end.

In the evenings she lay stretched on the sofa, lost in her love for the good-looking television announcer.

'I'm perfectly happy. So long as the Inland Revenue doesn't take my television I can bear anything. Don't let them take it, will you, dear?'

I promised to cope with the income tax collector. I painted the bathroom, which was easy, and the front of the bungalow, which was difficult. Something had to be done about payments to creditors.

'What shall we do?' said Noel.

'I've got a wonderful idea,' said my mother. 'What about selling some of the furniture?'

'Who shall we sell the furniture to?' said Noel.

'To the dealers in London. Nerina can do it,' said my mother.

I never thought much of this idea. The car broke down (costing us a lot of money in repairs) and when at last her treasures were delivered to a scornful salesman in London, I was told they were unacceptable.

'It's a load of rubbish,' he said.

I returned to Rusper with all her things except a gold and black lacquered sewing-table with mother-of-pearl fittings. For this a small offer had been made.

Now it was my mother's turn to be scornful.

'I'm sorry, dear, but I can't let my beautiful table go for a song. They must send it back. I love that table and so does Noel. Don't you, Noel?'

'Yes, I do,' said Noel.

We all felt we had been disloyal to the sewing-table.

It cost us more than we expected to get the poor thing back to Rusper. When it arrived we placed it thankfully in the long passage where, as before, it was much in everybody's way.

'What about money?' said Noel. 'What are we going to do now?'

'Nerina will think of something. What about writing another letter to the income tax people?' said my mother.

When she had been young my mother had made so many mistakes. We had all blamed her, including myself, for treating my father badly and neglecting me and refusing to come home when I wanted her and selfishly husband-hunting in middle-age. At one time she and I had a love-hate relationship. Now she was old and ailing, and I thought she was wonderful.

In her bungalow, crowded with furniture, uncomfortable, circled by creditors, haunted by doctors and nurses and poverty and illness, threatened by death, she made me laugh again. It pleased her. I think it gave her more pleasure than anything else.

My mother said, 'It's no good fretting about the past. When you've spilt the milk, you've spilt the milk. The thing to do now is to find another husband.'

'But you know I don't want another husband. I've told you that before.'

'Well,' said my mother, 'the next best thing is to buy a house.'

'I don't want to buy a house.'

'Nonsense, dear, everyone wants to buy a house.'

'Everyone except me.'

'Don't be silly, dear. You know what I mean.'

Of course I knew what she meant. The shortages of houses during the post-war period was something my mother had foreseen. In ten years she had bought and sold thirty houses!

She had moved into them with all her furniture, repairing them bit by bit, persuading local carpenters and plumbers and buildings to do what she wanted. Noel had helped. Had I not watched her moving with him from house to house?

'I always sell at a profit, dear. The trouble is I spend the profit on the next house. I never quite know where the money goes.'

She loved houses as she loved horses and dogs. She could never see an old unwanted one without wishing to own it and love it and live in it.

So now we had the problem of the Inland Revenue. After ten years of buying and selling, the amount demanded by the income tax collector in Horsham was £2,000.

'What on earth are we going to do?' said Noel.

'I don't know,' said my mother, 'but something will turn up.'

She had a small income from the family trust. It was hardly enough to pay the interest on the mortgage, and to feed herself and Noel, let alone to pay for a resident nurse and a housekeeper and all the bills for doctors and medicines. She had no more capital. Her profits had long ago been spent. There seemed to be no solution.

'Never mind. It's no good worrying. Take my advice, dear, and buy a house.'

'But I haven't any money.'

'Borrow it,' said my mother.

'I've never borrowed money in my life.'

'Then it's time you started, dear. You can easily get a mortgage. All you've got to do is find a nice house, if possible with windows looking south, and a view of the forest.'

'Do you really mean it?'

'Of course I do.'

'All right,' I said.

'And try to be more cheerful, dear. There's always something round the corner. Are you still thinking about Howard?'

'Sometimes,' I said.

I forced myself to read the proofs of my new novel about Rossetti. It was difficult to concentrate. I went with Clem for long walks over rough fields and through the woods. He slept beneath my bed. I remember talking to Clem, who whined and growled and barked in reply. I remember reading the Bible right through from cover to cover. I might have been reading Chinese. Then I sent for my horse, Kitty, and found her a new home and went for rides in the Sussex lanes.

All this time I was trying to understand what had happened to my marriage. Why had I left Howard? Why had I made that confession? Since poor little Renée was living in Paris the dangers of the friendship no longer existed. Why tell Howard what had happened in the past?

I could now be living with Howard in a beautiful old-fashioned flat in Sheffield Terrace. Before I left him Howard had signed the agreement. After I left him, poor Howard had moved the furniture to Sheffield Terrace and had camped there alone, not bothering to arrange it, only waiting to get rid of it.

What muddles are made by people who love one another. I had lost Charles by imposing restrictions. Howard had done this to me. But I was the transgressor, not Howard. I had escaped from marriage. I had not escaped from myself. Why had I lost my husband by making that foolish confession? How could I expect him to comprehend?

My mother understood what had happened better than I did.

'It's no good loving the wrong people, even when they're kind and good.'

'What happens if you do?'

'You leave them, of course.'

'Do you?'

'Of course you do.'

At the end of the first summer, when it seemed that every tree in Sussex was rhythmically dripping, we went for an afternoon drive in the old car. It was one of her good days, and my mother was dressed in a tweed suit.

'We'll go house-hunting in the rain. We'll take a picnic basket. Noel, what happened to that basket?'

She possessed two small white poodles and they sat, to the annoyance of Clem, on my knee. Noel drove the car along the lanes, and at Faygate, the neighbouring village, at the end of the line of chestnut trees, a very large house was discovered. It had no gate. The winding avenue of lime trees had not been used for a long time.

'Do be careful of the poor old car,' my mother said, as we bounced up and down.

'What an enormous house!' I said. 'Do you really want me to buy this one?'

Faygate House had twelve acres of land as well as a cottage, a garage to hold four cars, a number of sheds, an overgrown tennis-court, an orchard, a kitchen garden, a rose garden, hundreds of trees, and two gigantic greenhouses which my mother adored. It had four sets of fine bow windows. On the south side it had a rose-covered porch where my mother at once decided to have her tea.

'It faces south. It has a wonderful view of St Leonard's Forest! What could be better?'

'It has no view at all,' I told her. 'It's completely surrounded by trees and you can't see anything from any of the windows.'

'Don't be so silly, dear. All you've got to do,' said my mother impatiently, 'is to cut the trees *down*!'

We were told by a cottager that the house had been empty for two years. It had no electricity. Inside it was filthy. In the drawing-room I remember finding a scarlet cloak with a rich brocade lining, a top hat, and a dead bird which had fallen down the chimney. One of the ceilings had fallen when a pipe had burst.

'I think it's absolutely charming,' my mother said. 'If you have any sense, dear, you'll find a way to buy it and put the place in order. It will keep you occupied for quite a long time.'

'It certainly will.'

'The first thing to do is to persuade somebody to give you a mortgage.'

'Who?'

'I don't know, but God helps those who help themselves, dear.'

'But where is the money coming from?'

'You can sell the cottage and the garage.'

'How can I sell the cottage and the garage before I've even bought them?'

'You can sell that big field,' said my mother, without listening, 'and then, of course, you can sell the trees. All you want, dear, is a little initiative. Oh yes, it's a perfect house, and you can easily buy it if you make up your mind.'

'I haven't made it up.'

'Then do so at once, dear.'

'But this house,' I said, in desperation, 'is more like a hotel. Do you really want to live in such a big place?'

'You will have to find about £2,000 for electricity and decorations, dear.'

'Where am I to find £2,000?'

'I don't know, dear, but something is bound to turn up. It always does,' said my mother, in a tone of certainty.

I soon discovered she was right. To my astonishment it became possible to borrow the money, and to buy the house, and finally to sell the cottage and the garage. Later, much later, it even became possible to pay the mortgage, just as my mother had said.

'It's easy, dear, when you know how to do it.'

Of course my mother made most of the plans. The butler's pantry was to become her bathroom, and the dining-room her bedroom. There were some huge trees blocking the view from her window. These must be marked by Nerina with a white cross. They were to be cut down at once.

'I don't like doing it because they're such beautiful trees. Still, it's got to be done,' she said.

In the end forty-five fir trees were sold and removed by the man from the lumber-yard. As usual my mother was right. Faygate House, like a bride unveiled, was found to have a perfect view of the forest.

'It's a delightful house. It's worth twice what you paid for it. You see, dear, there's always something round the corner,' said my mother.

But I shall never forget the cold. While the work was going on my mother was too ill to be left, and so Noel sat by her bed. Each morning Clem and I drove to Faygate House. It was so cold that I dressed in trousers and rubber boots and several pairs of socks and three sweaters, in addition to a thick tweed coat and a woollen scarf. I worked all morning as a painter, Clem by my side, and returned to the bungalow for lunch. Then I rushed back to continue my painting until tea-time, when it grew dark. (We still had no electricity.)

The second winter away from London was passed in this way. There was no time to visit Helen and Andy. I can hardly believe it now. I painted all the doors and windows and the wainscoting in that enormous house, and also the outside paintwork on the cottage. The workmen painted the walls and ceilings. I did the rest.

When I bought the house I had only £200 in the bank. Before the property became mine I arranged to sell a six-acre field, and in this way, prompted by my mother, I was able to pay the necessary deposit.

'You see how easy it is?' said my mother happily.

The bank manager refused to help us. He said the property was a white elephant. So I raised the money, still prompted by my mother, with two private mortgages. One of the mortgages, the one for £3,000, I promised to redeem at the end of one year. And this I did, after many sleepless nights, although I could hardly believe it myself, by selling the cottage at just the right moment for just the right amount.

'I wish I could help you,' said my mother. 'If only I could get out of bed. Oh well, never mind.'

She had so many ailments. She suffered from hardening of the arteries as well as heart attacks and high blood pressure and a hint of potential cancer which none of us then understood. She had pains and alarming attacks. Her temperature went up and down from day to day.

I used to wonder what would happen if she died. What would I do with Faygate House? With Noel? With myself?

'I know what you're thinking,' she said. 'But I'm not going to die. Don't worry.'

In my mother the spark of life was so faint, and yet she was the inspiration, the flame behind the flame in us all. Somehow we kept her alive. In April we decided to move in the furniture.

From the modest little bungalow, nearly bursting with pictures and antiques, my mother's treasures were gently extracted. They were delivered by lorry in six loads. Places were found in the blue drawing-room for the precious gold and black sewing-table, not to mention the flower-painted Hepplewhite cabinets and the life-sized portraits of Cleopatra with a seventeenth-century gilded-oak frame (the picture was not really by Guido Reni but my mother believed it was) and the cloisonné vases and the Dresden shepherdess and the pink Sèvres clock which I had known since childhood. My mother kept saying, 'I shall be all right for the move. I refuse to die. Don't worry about me, dear.'

Finally the nurse left.

In the evenings I still rushed back to her bedroom and she still used to say, 'How does the drawing-room look with blue walls? What about the electricity? What about the plumbing? Are you sure the lavatories are in order, dear? Have you finished your money? Can't you borrow more?'

At the end of the second winter she lay with closed eyes, white and exhausted. To lift her out of bed now seemed almost impossible. Would she not prefer to stay in the bungalow until she was better? Would she not consent to be moved in an ambulance? No, said my mother emphatically, she would be driven to Faygate by her husband.

'There's nothing to worry about, dear.'

So we did as we were told. One morning in April, after the

gold and black sewing-table had been safely placed in the blue drawing-room, we moved the furniture from her bedroom in the bungalow to her bedroom in the big Edwardian house. Then we moved my mother. She was carried triumphantly from the car and replaced, with two hot-water bottles, in the warm bed from which, like a baby, she had just been taken.

'Do you feel all right?' said Noel.

'Would you like a glass of brandy,' I said, 'in case you have one of your attacks?'

'I'm not going to have an attack,' said my mother impatiently. 'What about the drawing-room, dear? How does it look with the Hepplewhite cabinets? When can I see it?'

'Tomorrow,' I said.

'Why not today?' said my mother.

15 'Come into the sunlight!'

It was a superb April.

On the first morning, in my wonderful bedroom, I opened the huge bow windows and there, like a page in a fairy tale, was the garden, the field, and the sunlit forest.

I can see it clearly. At the edge of the lawn, close beside a thick little shadowy wood of budding rhododendrons, grew a tall Wellingtonia, a green skyscraper which dwarfed all the others, elegant and slim, perhaps a hundred years old. And around this magnificent tree, in a yellow semicircle, like a greeting of joy, as though waiting for my eyes and my window to open, I noticed for the first time a family of daffodils.

It seemed too good to be true.

The first morning I had breakfast on the balcony which opened from the room next door to my bedroom, soon to be my study. It was warm. The birds were singing. The daffodils gleamed in the green. Could this be the beginning of a new life?

Happiness was in the air. It gave us all a new feeling of reality. The spring sunshine was so delicious that my mother grew better. Noel was delighted. For several weeks she lay in bed in the panelled room which had once been used as a family dining-room. From her pillow she could see the daffodils. She loved the pinkish stem of the Wellingtonia and the changing colours in the forest she had known all her life. The big bay windows were always open to the scent of spring.

I knew her illness was incurable. I watched her battling with it and laughing at it.

'I'm getting better every day. I'm determined to get better. What are you going to plant in the greenhouse? And *when* are you going to prune the roses?'

I wrote to Howard in a mood of deep affection. His kind replies came from London by return. They were loving letters. I wondered how soon he would find someone else?

My Edwardian mother did not believe in analysis. She believed in will power. You laugh. You carry on. You ignore the pains and the glooms and the miseries. You learn to enjoy life as you learn to hunt your horse and take your falls.

At times she could see or feel the guilt and sadness behind my fits of depression and my mother, sitting up in bed, her hair tied with a blue ribbon, in charge of things, the head of her family, gave me a lecture.

'Why do you worry about the past?'

'I've made so many mistakes.'

'Not nearly as many as I have, dear. I've been making them all my life.'

'I'm not complaining,' I said. 'What happens to people is nearly always their own fault. I blame myself.'

'You've got to break away from one husband to find another,' said my mother with her usual enthusiasm. 'And there's *always* something round the corner.'

'Is there?'

'Of course there is. Now Ibsen had the right idea. Do what you think is best – leave your husband, shock the neighbours, desert your children, break up your home if necessary – but *always do what you think is best.*'

'Even if you have to go it alone?'

'Yes.'

'Is that what you did?'

'Yes, dear, but the trouble is you can't tell if you're right or wrong until after you've done it.'

'Done what?'

'Broken the conventions.'

'Is that why you've broken them so often?'

'Yes, dear, I believe it is. Ibsen never told us what happened to Nora after she left her husband. My own belief,' said my mother, 'is that she probably made as many mistakes as I did.'

Once a week letters arrived from Paris. Each letter, written in French, was a tale of delusion and fantasy, angry thoughts about men and women who were trying to deceive or poison poor little Renée. Clearly she had lost her memory and lost her reason. For this little French girl I had ended my marriage.

I still had no desire to return to the noise of London. In Sussex, in my true home, I would find my true self. My mother would help me. For two years I paid regular visits to the income tax inspector in Horsham. After a time I persuaded my mother to become a National Health patient.

'I don't like it, dear, but I suppose you are right.'

In this way we saved the large sum of £3 a week. My mother received the same treatment from the same doctor and the same pills.

Noel said: 'Nerina likes coping with problems.'

'Not money problems. I hate being in debt.'

'You like being in charge. You were born clever.'

'What about you?'

'Me? I was born stupid,' said Noel.

I had other decisions to make, with our huge garden, six acres of it, including orchards and shrubberies, not to mention the sale of the cottage in order to redeem the mortgage. At night I took sleeping-pills. Even then I dreamed about my mother's illness and about the mortgage.

'Don't look so worried,' said my mother. 'It will all come right.'

There was not much time for literary work and yet I started to write another book. It was called *Come Into The Sunlight*. It told the story of my mother's astonishing life and her six husbands. It was partly a tribute and partly an attempt to understand and share my mother's philosophy of high spirits and hope. I did not know that after her death Noel would become my close companion. I treated him as a brother.

'She loves you more than anyone else,' Noel said.

'She loves us both.'

'You're the one she relies on to get things done.'

'You're the one she needs. You're a wonderful husband now that you've given up drinking.'

'Thank you,' said Noel.

My mother still loved her television. It gave her something to talk about. It renewed her joyous interest in life at the end of each day. The three of us watched it in her bedroom. Noel sat close to the bed, sometimes holding her hand. Clem sat beside me. The poodles were allowed on the bed.

'This is so nice. What a lucky woman I am,' she said.

London was far away. In her bedroom I felt protected from danger. It was better to watch life on television than to take part in it. Harold Macmillan, for example, was like one of the family.

As my mother said, 'He's such a gentleman, isn't he?'

I forgot to mention that when Churchill resigned she wrote a letter of sympathy to Lady Churchill and reminded her that when they were girls they had met and made friends and my mother had taught 'Clemmie' to play billiards. Lady Churchill replied with a formal letter of thanks. It gave pleasure to Noel and me because it made my mother so happy.

But during the second summer at Faygate House the weather was not so beautiful. At tea-time we sat beneath the other Wellingtonia. From a certain place we could see the rose arch, the cedar tree and the thick little shadowy wood of rhododendrons where I had placed an Italian statue like a shrine among the green. We could also see the forest and some of the herbaceous border and a second stone statue belonging to my mother.

'It gets more like Woldhurstlea every day,' she said proudly.

She now had an air of dignity. No one would dream this beautiful elderly lady had once been the dashing young woman who left my father, the escapist who passed like a film star through six unsuitable husbands. She was an English gentlewoman having tea with her family in the garden. She had found her true self at last.

Would I follow my mother's example? Would I find happiness too?

We all felt that something delightful was coming to an end. The new Crawley was nothing but a factory town. The new cottages, built for factory workers, with large windows and brightly coloured front doors, were filling the lanes and the fields and all the places of beauty.

'I think they're hideous,' Noel said.

'Oh, well, never mind,' said my mother. 'They make nice little homes.'

We knew that the dower-house would soon be pulled down. Our beloved Woldhurstlea would follow. Would anything be left of the world my mother had loved? It was her idea to buy the Woldhurstlea gates. It was an exciting day when the wrought-iron gates and also the old lanterns, put there by my grandfather to light the carriages at night, were sold to me for £5. Soon they stood at the entrance of Faygate House, just as my mother had planned.

'Thank you, dear. They give me such pleasure.'

'Me too,' said Noel.

It rained almost daily that second summer. When it was not raining we pushed my mother in a wheelchair round the garden. She visited her favourite flowers in the greenhouse. She looked very pretty. She always wore a big straw hat with a bending brim, a blue silk scarf and blue earrings. Noel became more devoted each day. As a child, I discovered, his mother had sent him to a prep school but never to a public school. She had kept him by her side until the day of her death.

'I enjoy nursing,' he said. 'I did it for my mother.'

For the first time in his life he had given up drink. 'I don't seem to need it any more. There's too much to do at home,' he said.

'Isn't he wonderful?' said my mother.

Noel had never been attracted to women of his own age. Now his time was spent in my mother's bedroom, sitting by her bed, reading to her, holding her hand, watching television with her.

She said to me once: 'I always think of him as *little* Noel. He is so weak, and you are so strong. Still, dear, he's a man.'

'What do you mean by that?'

'Nothing, dear.'

I think she wanted me to take care of him. I think she knew that when she died neither of us would wish to go on living, and so she continued to fight with her illness, and sometimes she seemed to be winning the battle.

'I feel much better today. Let's go round the garden before it starts raining again. Come along, dear. *Come into the sunlight!*'

That became the title of my new book. Howard thought of it. In one of his letters he told me to think of a title which would express my mother's philosophy, and between us we arrived at *Come Into The Sunlight.*

At last my light-hearted mother had settled down. I had not always admired her. She had deserted my father, taking me, her favourite, to California, where she had lost the remains of the family fortune in a gold mine, distressing all her family, especially me, with a succession of faulty stepfathers. What she had given her dear Nerina was a most unhappy childhood in California, little or no education, and a great deal of love. Now, at the end of her life, she was behaving like a saint. The light in her was a great deal stronger than the light in me, or Noel, or anyone we knew.

Another who learned to love her was a little French girl. It was Renée, who came to us for a holiday. In that second summer I paid her expenses from Paris.

'*C'est une femme magnifique. Elle me plaît, cette femme, je te jure. Comme elle est belle, ta mère!*'

Neither of them had any idea what the other was politely saying, but somehow they understood one another.

'She's like a child. She's lost,' said my mother. I suffered when I saw the change in Renée. Followed by Clem and the poodles, we pushed the wheelchair beyond the garden and along the woodland path. Whatever she found in the woods she brought to my mother as a gift. It might be a pretty stone or a flower. She trusted my mother, but not Noel. Sometimes her fears returned, and then she trembled from head to foot. She firmly believed that someone, an enemy, perhaps Noel or my husband, was trying to poison her. Sometimes the enemy was trying to poison me as well. I told her there was nothing to worry about. I told her I had left my husband. She had no idea that she was the cause of my broken marriage and of course I refrained from telling her. Poor little frightened Renée. For a time she became one of our strange family. Clem used to follow her round the garden. She talked to him in French. He barked in reply. At the end of a happy holiday (happy for Renée, not happy for me), she returned to Paris, not quite herself, always a lost child, and there, in a small room, spotlessly clean, she lived and suffered and smiled for the rest of her life. No one was able to help her.

At that time, when she left me, I wrote a long letter to Howard. I was feeling lonely. I remember sitting by myself beneath the Wellingtonia and building up the picture in my mind until I could see and hear and feel his presence. He was near me. He was in the garden. I began to believe that he was in the mood to forgive me, that we had not been parted after all. So then I posted my letter in the scarlet pillar-box at the end of the chestnut trees in the lane, and sent with it a little prayer. Perhaps it was not too late. Perhaps he still needed me.

In my heart I knew what would happen. I received a long letter in reply. I read it many times. He told me in gentle words that he loved someone else.

How could I change? How could he change? I knew that the art of living is to make it possible to behave well without anyone changing. I knew something else. We were incompatible, and Renée, a French girl, had come between us. But it might have been an English girl. Howard was not like Charles. He could never understand the need of a woman for the love of another woman.

And yet I loved my husband, and I knew very well that no other man would ever take his place. Howard was still my lover, my hero, my favourite companion. When I told my mother about my strong sense of guilt she sprang to my defence.

'Why do you always blame yourself? You're not the only unfaithful wife. You were too much alone at Whitehall Court. He was too possessive. I'm surprised you stood it so long.'

'It was my fault. I'm not the marrying kind.'

'Well,' said my mother, still defending her child, 'you must have got that from your father. You didn't get that from *me*!'

I continued to write him friendly letters, and tried not to grieve, and my mother tried, for two more years, not to die. We dreaded the winters. In December Noel and I said to one another: 'There won't be another Christmas. This will be the last.' Once again I decorated a small Christmas tree and surrounded it with presents for my mother. She opened them with joy in the blue drawing-room.

'I feel so happy. I feel quite young again.'

'Do you? Is that true?'

'Don't worry, I'm not going to die. I'm getting better, dear. How can I die when all these exciting things are happening?

What about the Suez Canal? What about Anthony Eden?'
  She felt sorry for Anthony Eden and delighted when Harold
Macmillan took his place in the Tory government.
  'Thank goodness that *nice* man is our Prime Minister. I feel
safe with him, don't you? Tell me, dear, what's happening about
the Inland Revenue?'
  'There's still no news,' I said.
  I shall never forget the morning when a buff-coloured
envelope was delivered by the postman. I had been expecting it
for days. I knew it came from the Inland Revenue. When I ran
downstairs, still in my dressing-gown, I found it on the hall
table. I sat on the stairs, holding the wretched thing between
thumb and finger, unable to open it. It was like holding a
stinging nettle. This is how you feel when you have battled for
two years, visiting the income tax inspector once a fortnight,
believing that your mother owes £2,000.
  I had argued and bargained and haggled. As she had bought
and sold thirty houses in ten years it was a problem to work out
expenses. Most of the accounts had been lost. She would
suddenly remember a staircase, or a chimney, or a garage, or a
new roof, on which she had spent a great deal of money.
  'I can't remember how much, dear. It might have been £500 or
it might have been £800. What does it matter?'
  'It matters a lot. What shall I tell the inspector?'
  'Tell him I can't remember. Smile at him,' said my mother,
'and see what happens.'
  'Nothing will happen.'
  'Oh yes, it will, if you know how to smile.'
  'I don't know how to smile. The income tax man wouldn't like
it.'
  'Oh yes, he would.'
  'How do you know?'
  'I've been doing it all my life, dear. I know by experience.'
  I took my mother's advice. I had now been smiling at the
inspector once a fortnight for two years. We had worked out
approximate figures on each house. In the end we had no idea
what the final result would be, and the inspector said I must
wait for it, because all these details and approximations must be
sifted and analysed by members of his staff. When we parted we
shook hands. I smiled. He did not. He said he was sorry about
my mother's illness. He said it might not be £2,000. It might be
no more than £1,000.
  So now the moment had come. The buff-coloured envelope,
large and fat and alarming, must be opened. When I got the
thing undone a thick sheaf of documents unfolded themselves.

They revealed a mass of figures. I leafed through them with mounting horror.

The top document appeared more simple. I gained the impression it was a summary of some kind. At the end of some mystifying figures I found this uncomplicated one of £17 10s. 6d. When the thought came it hit me so hard that I leapt to my feet and dashed upstairs to my bedroom. Within half an hour I arrived at Barclay's Bank in Crawley and demanded to see the manager.

He saw me at once. I handed him the sheaf of documents.

'Am I crazy? What does it mean? Does my mother owe them, or do they owe her?'

The bank manager was surprised. He seemed to understand the financial situation at a glance, and immediately said, as though such things happen every day., 'The Inland Revenue owes your mother seventeen pounds, ten shillings, and sixpence. Is anything the matter?'

'I shall be all right in a minute,' I said.

And when I returned home, and rushed into my mother's bedroom to tell her what had happened, she looked up with her usual smile and happily said, 'I *knew* it would be all right. Isn't life wonderful? Thank goodness there's no need to talk about it any more. Tell me, dear, how are you getting on with your book? When can I read another chapter?'

The Inland Revenue was already forgotten. The demand for £2,000 might never have been made.

'Weren't you worried about it?' I said.

'Not a bit, dear. I knew it would be all right. Let's talk about your book. I'm longing to see how you end it.'

Come Into The Sunlight, the story of my Edwardian mother, was published in 1957. It was chosen by the BBC critics as the Book of the Week. I think my favourite memory of my mother is the day when she sat up in bed, the radio close beside her, and listened with shining eyes while Margaret Lane and the other critics described and discussed the events of her life.

'One man called it a *tour de force*! Did you hear that, dear?'

She looked very frail now. She was seventy-nine. Her hair was carefully curled, tied round the head with a sky-blue ribbon, and her nails were manicured. For the particular pleasure of sitting with Noel and me and the BBC critics, on this exciting day, she was powdered and scented and radiant as a girl.

16   The Chelsea Set

My mother's life was coming to an end. I was frightened. I could feel death standing behind me. It seemed that everything I loved would be taken from me. Even my horse had been killed.

In the winter of 1957 I went into the field to catch Kitty. She must have been eighteen years old. Led by a wild young pony, full of life, she was galloping round, slithering and sliding in the mud.

I spent nearly two hours in the attempt, a bridle on my arm, a saddle waiting on the gate. To catch her was impossible. In the end, following that pony, she fell on her side with a thud. The pony galloped to the other end of the field, then stopped and turned to watch, interested, surprised. Five minutes later Kitty died, with her head on my knee.

My mother said, 'Never mind, dear. She had a good life. We've all got to die, haven't we?'

Then came another death. I was loaned a horse by a friend and this other mare escaped from the grounds of Faygate House and was killed on the railway line by a passing train. I cried as though my heart would break when I found out what had happened. Death was over my head. I remember that moment, in my study, stretched on the divan bed, sobbing, with my face buried in the cushions. I felt Noel's hand patting my shoulder.

'Never mind,' he said, in my mother's voice. 'It wasn't your fault.'

'I'm frightened.'

'What of?'

'Death.'

'So am I,' said Noel.

I felt we were threatened by danger. Worst of all, unthinkable, was the loss of my mother. She grew so frail. There was nothing left of her except the blue eyes and the spirit of laughter.

It was a sad bad winter. That was why, when the telephone rang, I felt so delighted by Helen's voice, loud and kind and cheerful, like the ring of a bell. 'Look here, old girl, I want a secretary. Why don't you come back to London and take the job?'

It seemed like a call from another world.

I had been separated from London during four years of exile and now I felt hostile to it, scared of the place where everything horrible had happened. I wanted to escape from London. So I just said I would think it over and sleep on it, and asked Helen to give me twenty-four hours.

'Are you all right, Nerina?'

'Yes, thank you, quite all right.'

'Do come if you can,' Helen said. 'I need you so badly.'

My mother thought it a good idea. 'You need a change, dear. You ought to go back to London.'

'I don't want to go back.'

'You're a Londoner. You belong in London.'

'Not now. I feel like a foreigner. I'd rather stay here.'

'Why not enjoy yourself? I'm not going to die for quite a long time. You need a bit of fun, dear.'

Noel said: 'I don't mind. So long as you come home every week-end.'

'He's right,' said my mother. 'It will cheer us up. You will have such a lot to tell us about.'

'Are you sure you want me to do this?'

They persuaded me to take their advice. I had now acquired two elderly lodgers. Even this was not an excuse to stay at home. The housework was proudly done by women from the village and the cooking was nicely done by a resident housekeeper.

'Noel can look after the lodgers, dear. You *must* go back to London.'

'What about Clem?'

'Clem can sit in my bedroom. Think how happy he'll be on Saturdays when you come home.'

'All right,' I said.

Helen was delighted to see me, and the first week was not as alarming as I expected. As my mother said, I belonged in London. Now I was part of the stream of humanity, rushing for buses and trains. Instead of sitting with my grief in Whitehall Court, I was one of the thousands of human beings, employed and useful, loving the city streets, needed in a certain place at a certain time, endlessly rushing from Underground to office.

Of course Helen had not changed. She was dressed as always in her white linen coat, light and bright with starch. She greeted her distinguished patients like members of her father's parish, kissing some of them, telling stories to others, pulling out their teeth between jokes. No wonder they loved her. Some of the older ones I remembered meeting at Helen's pre-war parties.

Now their children and grandchildren rang the front door bell
(the door was still painted green) and I, the secretary, led them
with a broad smile to the waiting-room.

'Are you Nerina?'

'Yes, I'm Nerina.'

'I remember you well. You haven't changed much.'

'Oh yes, I have. I'm much more sensible now.'

I sat in a small office answering the telephone. From time to
time I heard a shout of laughter in the hall, then a burst of barking
from the dogs in the bedroom above.

'Shut up!' Helen shouted.

The dogs barked louder than ever. No one minded. The dogs
enjoyed dentistry and so did the distinguished patients. As one
man said to me (I forget his name but I believe he was an Earl),
'She's a marvellous dentist, and I like it when the dogs start
barking. 'Don't ask me why.'

Even Andy, crippled with arthritis, had found ways to make
life amusing and enjoyable. She could still drive a car. She could
still entertain her friends at opera and ballet.

'All the porters and barmaids know me,' said Andy. 'When I go
to Covent Garden they treat me like royalty.'

I did not realize how much London had changed because
Helen and Andy were the same as ever.

'You're the world's worst secretary. Never mind,' said Helen,
'the patients like you, and so do I.' That was when I forgot the
sterilizer and it nearly exploded.

'If you were ugly as well as stupid,' said Helen. 'I should give
you the sack.' At the end of a day with Helen, tired and laughing,
we sat down together for a drink and a talk. 'Look here, Nerina,
it's nearly five years since you left your husband. Why don't you
find another man?'

'I don't want another man.'

'Then why don't you find another woman?' (Of course Helen
had found one.)

'I don't want another woman.'

'Aren't you lonely?'

'Very lonely. But I still love Howard. I shall never marry again.'

'There was no need to leave him,' said Helen, in her motherly
voice, 'and why you told him about Renée I shall never understand. After all, the relationship was finished.'

'Renée was in Paris,' I said. 'Renée had lost her reason.'

'So why did you have to confess?'

'I was hoping against hope that he would forgive me. I was
feeling suicidal. I suppose I wanted his help. I wanted to tell him
the truth and share things with him.'

'You can't do that with a man like Howard. As a matter of fact, you hurt him very much, and now you've lost him.'

'I've lost them both. I've lost Howard, and I've lost Renée. What shall I do now?'

'Oh, come on,' said Helen, giving me a quick kiss, 'you must have another drink, and find another woman. That's what you must do.'

Somehow she always made me feel stronger and happier. After that little talk, and others like it, I discarded my wine-coloured uniform and walked contentedly from New Cavendish Street to the Underground. I loved the crowds. I enjoyed the London smell. I remember feeling the beauty and glory of Sloane Square on a bright wintry night, the lamps glittering between the branches of the plane trees, the fountain glittering between the lamps, the pigeons hovering, the scent of the streets after rain, the sound of traffic and voices and running footsteps.

I crossed Sloane Square and walked with a new sense of confidence along Lower Sloane Street to the flat I was sharing with another pre-war friend. This was Moie Charles, playwright, producer, theatre manager.

I found her resting on her bed. Although she was ill at the time I laughed with Moie as I laughed with Helen.

'Have a drink. Tell me more about Faygate House. Tell me about your mother.' When I had finished she said, 'I think it's a wonderful story. If you'd stayed with Howard, what would have happened to your mother and Noel?'

'I don't know.'

'It's just as well you left Howard.'

'Let's not talk about that.'

'Your marriage would have lasted if Howard had let you go out with your friends. Boredom set in. That's all it was.'

'Let's not talk about that.'

Moie was to have an operation and was waiting for admission into hospital. During the period of illness and convalescence I was to look after her flat. Meanwhile, until moved out by the doctor, she was sharing it with me. I was sleeping on the sitting-room divan.

I soon discovered that Moie was a marvellous cook. She had written a cookery book. She reminded me of a glamorous boy, always in trousers (at that time considered Bohemian), always immaculate. She had an elegant boyish head, beautiful hands, long nails like scarlet almonds and a style of dressing, a studied untidiness, a youthful style not yet discovered by the fashion shops in the King's Road.

'I love the way you dress,' I said.

'It's nice to have you in the flat. I like you because you never interfere.'

She had a need for privacy. Sometimes her bedroom door was closed in the evening, which meant that I must not disturb her. She was writing something, or talking to a friend, or resting, or not feeling well. One night she told me she had fainted. In case it should happen again she wrote the name of her doctor and his telephone number with a piece of chalk on the kitchen slate and this was hung on the wall beside a string of onions and a bottle of Chianti.

'Just phone him if you want him. I'll try not to pass out again. Anyway, I'll soon be in hospital.'

'Are you in pain?'

'Don't worry. It's nothing serious.'

The thing happened on a Wednesday. I believe it was my third week in London. I came home feeling tired and cheerful, in Helen's mood, laughing at my troubles. My friends still loved me. Howard was still in my life, writing me affectionate letters. Aimée Stuart (living in Brighton) had invited me to spend a week-end. My mother and Noel and Clem were waiting for me at Faygate. Why feel depressed?

There were many stairs in that tall Victorian house. I arrived at the top flat in a breathless state, unable to speak. I saw at once that the bedroom door was closed. Moie was engaged. So I went in silence to my room, the sitting-room, and noticed a smell which made me think I had forgotten to turn the tap firmly on the old-fashioned gas fire.

After a few minutes I went to the kitchen. The smell of gas was coming from the stove, a strong and horrible stench. Moie was stretched on the floor, face down, the gas lighter a few inches from her hand. I noticed a tray prepared for lunch and a frying-pan ready for an egg. Had Moie fainted again?

I turned off the gas. Then I opened the window, and knelt in the kitchen beside my friend, tried to lift her, and eventually dragged her across the linoleum and placed her in a sitting position against the wall.

She was very heavy. She was dead.

A little later, in a voice I did not recognize, quite calmly, I telephoned the doctor. A girl answered the telephone. I gave my name and address. I asked the girl to send someone as soon as possible. The waiting period was bad. I wanted to run away. Instead I sat beside Moie on the kitchen floor.

Moie's doctor turned out to be a young man, and he looked at me curiously. 'You seem very calm,' he said. 'Are you used to this

kind of thing? Has it happened to you before?'
'Of course not.'
'How can you be so calm and collected?'
'I don't know. It doesn't seem real.'
'To me it seems very sad,' the doctor said.
In the new permissive London such things were not unusual.
This I did not understand.
'I just can't believe it,' I said.
Someone helped me to pack my clothes in a suitcase. I was
taken by car to New Cavendish Street where Helen and Andy
looked after me during the night. The next day I still behaved
like a normal person. I listened to my steady voice, and watched
my haggard face in Helen's mirror, and observed Helen's
secretary with interest as she dressed and fed herself and did
what was wanted by people concerned with death.
'Are you all right?' said Helen.
'Yes, thank you.'
But the gift of calm was taken from me. In the weeks which
followed I dreamed about the body of my friend as it lay on
the kitchen floor in her London flat. It haunted me. I can see it
still. Was this heavy and helpless thing my glamorous
companion?
My mother understood. She tried to protect me from death by
staying alive a little longer.
'You must learn to enjoy yourself, dear. Don't worry about
me. Have a good time in London.'
Clem, my beloved corgi, lay beside her bed when I was away.
There were joyful reunions on Friday evenings. At Faygate
Station I always found Noel waiting, with three excited dogs, in
the old car. I said to my mother, 'I don't like London any more.'
'You will when you get used to it.'
'I'd much rather stay at home with you and Noel and the
dogs.'
'No, no, London is where you belong. I want you to live in
London.'
'Why?'
'It's interesting, dear. I want you to tell me all about it.'
'About what?'
'All the scandals, dear. I want to know about the Chelsea set.
How do people live? Do young people really take drugs and try
to commit suicide? I want to know what's going on!'
'All right,' I said, 'if that's what you want.'
'Stop looking so miserable! Come into the sunlight!' she
added with a smile. To please my mother, I worked for Helen,
found myself a bedroom in a London flat with a girl called Ann

Wells, and told my mother that Ann was a member of the Chelsea set. She belonged to a new generation of escapists. She might have been my daughter.

'Does Ann wear good clothes, dear? Is she pretty? Have you met her friends?'

'Indeed I have.'

'What are they like?'

'For one thing,' I said, 'they slash their wrists.'

'Good heavens, dear. Tell me more. I can hardly wait.'

I was surrounded by pretty girls and yet none of them attracted me. Ann's greatest friend was an Italian Princess, a beautiful girl whose parents were divorced and whose mother was English. I believe her name was Maria. She was a girl who had slashed her wrists more than once with a knife or razor. Ann, who admired her friend, could never discover what caused these fits of despair, or whether it was all done in an effort to attract attention.

'How can she be so *stupid*?' said my mother. 'Doesn't she see how exciting it is just to be *alive*?'

'I'm afraid she doesn't.'

'Why not?'

'She's unstable. She's insecure.'

I remember telling my mother that Maria had plenty of money, a title, a beautiful face. She appeared in London in the pre-Beatle period. I dined out on some of my stories about the Chelsea set, and somehow I made it all sound funny and light-hearted. Some of the boys were homosexuals, but not the girls.

'It's thrilling, dear. I'm so glad you live in London,' said my mother.

On one occasion I arrived on a Sunday night to find Ann's flat in darkness. It was 10 p.m. I switched on the lights, and called Ann's name. Suddenly I noticed dark patches on Ann's carpet. They were outside a bedroom which was used now and then by Maria. I entered the room, and found the bed was unmade and the sheets stained with blood. It was clear that the stains on the carpet were bloodstains. I had blood all around me.

My mother said: 'What did you do? Call the police?'

'Certainly not. Ann would have been so annoyed.'

'Hurry up,' said my mother. 'Tell us what you did.'

'I waited for something to happen. I waited for two hours.'

'What time did Ann come home?'

'About midnight.'

'Go on, tell us what happened. Noel is longing to know, and so am I,' said my mother.

Following Ann was a young man called Edward, whose name, at that time, was constantly appearing in newspaper headlines. Edward had eloped with the daughters of at least two millionaires. He took them to Gretna Green. Sometimes he went to prison. Furious parents did their best to stop it but Edward and the daughters enjoyed it.

'This is Edward,' said Ann, with affection.

In a tone of apology Ann explained to me that Maria had slashed her wrists all over the flat in a fit of loneliness. 'Of course, if *you* had been present, Nerina, she would never have done it. Her manners are perfect.'

'Yes,' said Edward, 'she has beautiful manners.'

Apparently the polite Maria had slashed her wrists, telephoned for an ambulance, and was now resting and reading quite happily in hospital.

'I'm sorry you came home to all that blood, Nerina. I'll clean it up in the morning. Good-night, sleep well,' said Ann, giving me a kiss.

At that time she and her friends took the stage in London. They were proudly different from the beatniks and beautiful people and hippies who followed them, and still parade, sometimes, in the King's Road, Chelsea. In Ann's day the escapists had style. Ann herself was pretty and snobbish, with long Titian red hair and a taste for titles. She wore a broken pair of horn-rimmed glasses which no one else could possibly have worn. She spent hours working on her face with creams and lotions and eyelash make-up. She looked and behaved like a well-bred gipsy. She said to me several times, 'What you need is a boyfriend, Nerina.'

This, then, was the Chelsea set.

It was the parent of the teenage world of free love and drugs and pop music in which Londoners are taking part today. It had a different accent and a pedigree and the leaders of it had the touch and charm of outcasts and aristocrats. What appealed to me was Ann's sense of humour. She lived in a world where boys and girls used mental homes like luxury hotels.

'Don't you understand, Nerina? To get your son into a good mental home is just as important,' she told me, 'as to get him into Eton. My friends enter their sons for both,' she added, 'the moment they are born!' At this we burst out laughing.

I repeated the joke to my mother, who enjoyed it as much as we did. One day my dear little snobbish Ann drove in her bubble car to Faygate in order to see my home. She had lunch with me and Noel. Afterwards she walked round the garden, and her Titian-coloured hair was admired by my mother from her bedroom window.

'What a pretty girl! Why doesn't she get married and settled down?'

'You didn't settle down, and neither did I.'

'Is Ann like us?'

'She seems to be an escapist,' I said.

Helen was equally curious about Ann. When we had drinks together, after a long day's work, Helen raised her eyebrows and then raised her glass.

'Here's to your new friend in the Chelsea set. Are you in love with her, by any chance?'

I was shocked at this suggestion.

'Of course not. She's much too young.'

'Do you want an older woman then?'

'Yes, but not as old as you.'

'There's no need to be rude to your boss. I shall give you the sack.' Helen smiled at me. 'As a matter of fact you need an older woman to take care of you.' She then suggested a white-haired woman with an understanding husband, both of them known to her for many years as patients and close friends.

'The husband,' said Helen, 'is very understanding indeed. Not like Howard.'

'No, thank you,' I said. 'Not interested.'

I did not tell Helen that at last I had found a beautiful woman who might possibly be the answer to all my problems. That would come later.

In the summer of 1958 I was waiting for my mother to die. The time had come, the dreaded moment. When a middle-aged woman is alone and frightened, and apprehensive, how does she find a new way of life? How does a middle-aged escapist escape? One day, while sitting by Helen's telephone, I made a personal call to the *Dancing Times*.

'I want to join a dance club. Can you tell me the name of a good one, please?'

Just before my mother died I took up ballroom dancing. My mother was delighted.

'Enjoy yourself. Have a good time. Come into the *sunlight*, dear.'

The night before it happened I was watching the international dancing competitions at the Albert Hall in which the world champions dance each year, and among the famous people who were present I could faintly see the beautiful woman I so much admired. I felt indescribably happy at that moment. I remember thinking how my mother would have loved such a scene of gaiety and grace.

Beside me in the stalls was an elderly white-haired lady, not unlike my mother, wearing diamond earrings and splendid rings on her manicured fingers.

'I love dancing,' she said. 'I am seventy-three but I still have dancing lessons twice a week.'

The next day I was back with Noel in my mother's bedroom. She died on 5 November. It was the day we three had been dreading and fearing for such a long time.

17   Phyllis

I sat beside Noel in the back of the big black car. I felt close to him and loved him, as a human being, because the two of us were deep in our grief. We were nearly there.

For me the approach to Ifield is now spoilt by the modern houses, each with a garage and a blue, pink, yellow or scarlet front door. The building development had spread like a fever from the factories and bungalows in Crawley New Town. Nothing is left of my mother's world except the church, the vicarage, the pub and a row of cottages.

They are protected, thank goodness, by some trees and a country lane, and they are hidden from the road.

'Come on,' said Noel, as the car stopped. 'Are you all right?'

I was not all right. Neither was he.

My mother had been married to her first husband in this little church. I had been christened here, and so had she. Beneath the white Victorian tombstone my grandfather and all the others were buried. She had often told me about it. On icy Sunday mornings in winter my grandmother came to church in her carriage, driven by John Reade, her coachman, family servant for forty years. My grandfather preferred to walk. He and she and their five children sat in the second pew on the left. My mother, as a little girl, used to stroke the crossed legs of the stone crusader while listening to the sermon. So did I.

'Come on,' Noel said.

We walked from the big black car to the lychgate, into the church, and down the fourteenth-century aisle to the pew on the left, where I sat, once again, beside the stone crusader with crossed legs.

There were not many people at my mother's funeral. Helen came from London by car. The others drifted round me like shadows and as we moved through the pageant of death I could feel the sufferings of Noel by my side, frightened, lonely, needing help.

Afterwards, in the blue drawing-room, surrounded by my mother's possessions, looking through bay windows and beyond the garden to the line of gold and brown forest which my mother had loved all her life, I felt unreal. My guests departed. Helen said,

'Good-bye, old girl. Have I lost you as a secretary then?'

'I'm afraid you have. I can't leave the house, I can't leave Noel.'

'Why not?'

'He might start drinking again. He's very upset.'

'I shall miss you. I shall never again find a secretary as bad as you!'

One of the last to go was the family solicitor, Mr Godfrey. What he said about death duties and income tax was more than depressing. I felt suicidal. Then he pointed out the difficulties of selling a Victorian mansion because everyone wanted a small house with central heating.

'But I've no intention of selling this house.'

'How are you going to live?'

'I shall take paying guests. I shall turn it into a private hotel.'

It might have been my mother speaking. It sounded quite cheerful. Mr Godfrey left, shaking his head, and I wondered if I could possibly do it. Until the death duties and probate were settled, I should have no income from my mother's estate. Mr Godfrey said this might go on for twelve months or longer. Mr Godfrey thought I was unrealistic, not to say mad. And then I saw Noel across the drawing-room. I felt his unhappiness.

'I know I can do it,' I told Mr Godfrey. 'Everything will be all right.'

That was the beginning of a new relationship with Noel. To look after him was clearly my job. He needed me more than anyone else. But how do you cope with an alcoholic?

When I asked Helen for advice, speaking on the telephone, she laughed and said, 'An alcoholic is like a bad tooth. You only know your *own* alcoholic.'

After my mother's death I had a telephone call from someone very important. It was the beautiful woman in London, the one I had seen at the Albert Hall, the one I fancied, with whom I began to think I was falling in love. Everyone in the dancing world knew her name. It was Phyllis Haylor. I was thrilled when I heard her voice. I had met her in London several times.

One day, to Noel's delight, she arrived on the train from Victoria, more elegant than anyone we had ever seen at Faygate. She lunched with us, looking rather shy, and gave immense pleasure to the elderly gentleman, my first lodger, who still had an eye for a pretty woman. He was sitting at the table, his back to the hot stove, and suddenly announced, in a grave tone of voice, with his eyes fixed on the dignified Phyllis,

'Madam, I think I have reached boiling point!'
Phyllis laughed until she cried. Somehow it broke the ice. I ceased to feel nervous.

After that she became a regular visitor and her laughter gave me the courage and understanding to cope with Noel, with whom I felt like a new acquaintance. The stranger in Noel was an alcoholic who looked at me with annoyance. It was as though I had never met him before.

'Don't worry. I've given it up,' he used to say.

'There's no need to feel guilty about it.'

'I don't want people to know.'

'Why not?'

'I don't want to feel different from everyone else.'

We tried the experiment of talking about it and we told all our friends about Noel's problem. I thought it would help him. Without my mother Noel was a changed man.

'You were wonderful,' I said, 'when my mother was ill. I shall always be grateful to you.'

In a tone of resentment he said: 'Don't worry, I've given it up.'

Needless to say this was not true. During my mother's illness Noel had given up alcohol but now I was anxious about him. In that difficult time we were training ourselves to be host and hostess in a private hotel. As a start, I had to paint the lavatories and bathroom. Then I had to attend the local sales to buy curtains and linen.

Noel developed a bad cough. We were told by the specialist that he was suffering from cancer of the lung. He endured an unnecessary operation.

'I'm fed up,' he said.

After that empty bottles were discovered in unexpected places, hidden under mattresses or behind cushions or concealed in clothing.

'What about all these bottles, Noel?'

'I don't know. It's not me.'

'Who is it, then?'

'Not me.'

'Can you suggest anyone else?'

Noel grinned. 'It must be a ghost.'

In the end I told Doctor Matthews, Ronnie, whose father and grandfather had both attended my mother's family as physicians. Noel was given a daily pill (Antibuse), an insult which every alcoholic seems to resent, like a child when given castor oil.

'Have you taken your pill, Noel?'

'Yes.'

'I don't believe it. Come on, take another one.'

'Why should I?'

'Doctor's orders.'

I was beginning to realize that to look after someone is part of my nature. It was not easy. But to live with the wrong person is better than to live with no one, and I now had the help of Phyllis Haylor. My deepening love for my new friend gave me strength. She was unmarried, and dedicated to her work as a teacher of dancing. She was a few years older than myself but we looked about the same age. She spent a great deal of money on her glamorous appearance, on her evening dresses, on her exquisite shoes, on her powders and perfumes, on her immaculate head of blond hair.

'I would rather have ladders in my stockings than a bad hair-do,' she said.

My father would have loved her, so would my husband. She had all the English charm of a pink and white Edwardian lady. Like Helen she had a strong sense of humour but she was a private person, which Helen was not. Like my mother she had the gift of high spirits and gaiety and courage.

So that was how the new life started, a lifelong friendship with Phyllis and a perilous partnership with Noel which continued (to the surprise of other people) for nine years. Two more opposite characters would be hard to find. And yet I needed Noel as he needed me, as we both needed the smiling support of Phyllis Haylor.

He still said, 'Don't worry, I've given it up.' I still gave him his daily pills. Until the paying guests arrived we had a financial problem. Then I advertised in *The Lady* and immediately obtained what I wanted. One was a retired banker in his fifties, the other was the elderly gentleman, once an artist, whose wife lived in America, who quickly fell in love with Phyllis. He required Noel to bath him.

'Must I really do this, Nerina?'

'If you don't, I shall have to do it for you.'

'Oh well,' said Noel, 'I suppose I must.'

It was a queer life. We both wondered what to do when the elderly gentleman came downstairs naked. But we grew fond of him. In the summer he collected wild flowers and grasses with which he filled his bedroom.

'Do you think he's happy?' I said.

'Well,' said Noel, 'he's a bit senile, isn't he?'

'He can't help that. Do you think he's happy?'

'Yes, I do.'

In the room which had once belonged to my mother the

retired banker sat before a pile of books and papers dedicated to
horses and racing. He was working out a system which would
earn him a fortune.

After tea my strange family gathered on the lawn. We played
croquet. For a stretch of time we moved like actors across the
green silky lawn between the sundial and the silvery stone statue
of the stooping boy, between the dark bushes of rhododendron
and the golden border of flaming dahlias and chrysanthemums
and Michaelmas daisies. The tapping of croquet balls for an hour,
two hours, even three hours, on a sunlit evening, became part of
the unreal beauty of the little world of teacups and escape which
existed, like a perfume, in the garden. After supper, in the blue
drawing-room, we watched television. Noel and I both liked a
group of young boys with long untidy hair. They were called the
Beatles.

'I should like to live in London,' Noel used to say.

'Why?'

'I have never lived in London.'

'I'd rather live in the country.'

'No, you wouldn't. You belong in London, Nerina.'

It was Noel, a countryman, who urged me to sell Faygate
House when the death duties at last were settled.

He kept saying, 'Why don't we move to London?'

'You wouldn't be happy in London.'

'Yes, I would. So would you. Then we could see more of
Phyllis.'

Strangely enough, Noel understood my need for Phyllis. He
encouraged me in every way. I had formed the habit of visiting
London once a week to keep up my dancing lessons and also,
which was more important, to see my beloved new friend.

'I wish I could have lessons too,' Noel said. 'What makes you so
fond of Phyllis?'

'We make each other laugh,' I said.

By this time the Beatles, on television, were becoming bold and
sophisticated. There was also a nice young man called Cliff
Richard. Mary Quant was another new character. She was just
starting her first boutique in the King's Road at the time when
Noel and I were playing croquet.

As we watched these wonderful people we began to see how
rapidly the world was changing. London was the centre of it, the
crazy new culture of drugs and mysticism and sex.

'I wonder what these people are like in real life?' Noel used to
say. 'Do you think they are happy?'

At that time, on television, we used to see Phyllis at the national
dancing competitions, among her friends at places like the Albert

Hall and Blackpool.

Noel admired her as much as I did. She was quite surprisingly elegant, as well as dignified, visiting the hairdresser two or three times a week, immaculate, stylish, every blonde hair in place. She took us both under her wing. 'Why don't you learn to dance?' she said to Noel. 'Why not dance with Nerina?' The world of ballroom dancing, her world, beginning now to be my world as well, had its own tradition of movement and grace. Phyllis Haylor was recognized as one of the stars, an adjudicator, a hostess, a public figure.

I could never see any resemblance between myself and this glamorous, hard-working woman. Other people noticed it though. When I entered her London ballroom, filled with dancers, I was frequently mistaken for her sister. Her real sister found this amusing.

'It's because you go to the same hairdresser,' said Noel rudely. 'It's the bleach that does it!'

And then, in the month of June, her sister tragically died. Phyllis had lost a lifelong partner and companion. I began to see that I was now needed by someone else.

The three of us went for a holiday together, taking my car, and drove in the heat of August through France, into the château country, along the valley of the Loire to the coast, and finally to Sables d'Orlonne, a little cheap hotel where I and Howard had once spent a happy holiday.

'I love this place. It's all so clean and simple,' Phyllis said.

'It hasn't changed a bit,' I said.

Indeed, a watercolour painting, a sketch of the little square and the buildings which Howard had quickly done to please our host, still hung in a place of importance near the front door.

'*Bonjour, madame,*' they said. '*Comment ça va? Où est monsieur? J'espère qu'il va bien?*'

They expected him to be somewhere in the town, perhaps shopping. When I told them we had parted they expressed their sympathy. They behaved as though someone dear to all of us had died.

'It makes me feel sad,' I said.

'Me too,' said Phyllis. 'I wish I had known your husband.'

'Oh well, never mind,' said Noel, in my mother's voice, 'we're having a wonderful holiday.'

The three of us got along very well. Noel seemed to understand the sadness and shyness and loneliness of my new friend, who was grieving for her sister. Every day we rested on the long clean white beach, or played ball together, or went swimming, or went to a cheap restaurant for a fabulous meal, and then returned like a family to the little cheap hotel which Phyllis loved. Every night, very tired, I lay in her arms.

Thus ended a beautiful summer, the hottest in many years, and Noel kept saying, 'What about living in London?'

'You don't know what it's like.'

'Yes, but I want to try it.'

'Why?'

'I want to see a bit of life.'

'But I don't want to sell Faygate House.'

'It's far too big for you and me. It's all very well to have paying guests who walk downstairs naked. Enough is enough,' said Noel.

'How can I possibly afford a house in London?'

In my mother's voice he said: 'You'll manage. There's always something round the corner.'

Even when I heard of a house in Cadogan Place, and received at the same time an offer for my big Victorian home which the solicitor still said would be impossible to sell, I felt unwilling to do it.

'Go on,' Noel said impatiently, 'let's live in London. Let's have a good time.'

'I'm sure you won't like it.'

'Of course I shall like it, and Phyllis will like it, too. Don't you see? We've got to do it.'

One by one our paying guests departed. We were left, he and I, with our two dogs, his poodle and my corgi (my mother's poodle had died) and the two white pigeons. They had belonged to my mother. And now, with a new owner, they gave me a look of reproach when I said good-bye. A few days later one of them died. The other soon followed. Something with beauty had been ended.

But Noel was delighted by the change, and so was Phyllis.

'Well, that's that,' he said, as we drove for the last time beneath the lime trees in the avenue, through my grandfather's heavy iron gates and along the lane of chestnut trees into the road leading back to London.

'You may not like the London life. You may start drinking again.'

'Don't worry. I've given it up,' he said sharply.

When we arrived in the King's Road, Chelsea, passed round Sloane Square into Sloane Street, and turned right into Cadogan Place, I felt sick with nerves. We were to live for three months in a small basement. Later we would move to the top flat overlooking the trees.

'It feels poky and horrible,' I said.

'We shall soon get used to it,' said Noel.

'You'll soon start drinking again.'

'Oh, shut up!' said Noel.

He did, of course. He was tempted by the pubs all round us. But in June we moved upstairs to the lovely flat in which I continued to live for twenty more years.

'It's beautiful up here,' said Noel.

I remember his nervous excitement at the thought of freedom, and my own excitement at the thought of Phyllis, living nearby, needing my friendship. We had our antique furniture in the sitting-room, the silver bits and pieces arranged on the old gateleg table, with my mother's photograph, in a silver frame, in the place of honour.

'This is a real home,' said Noel.

In spite of his pleasure we both felt troubled. Each of us was starting a new life in a new world with a not very suitable partner. Oh well, never mind; perhaps Phyllis would help us to help each other.

18   The Swinging 60s

In 1960 I hated the new swinging London. Who were these monsters parading in the streets? Who were these dreadful boys and girls with long untouchable hair and grimy untouchable clothes? Could they be the new escapists?

'I believe you're shocked,' Noel said.

'They behave like animals. I don't like them at all.'

'When you were young you managed to shock everybody. What's the difference?'

'It's a question of style. Charles and I were deeply in love. We gave each other a wonderful experience.'

'Rubbish,' said Noel. 'Young people always give each other a wonderful experience.'

'But somehow it's different now. You sleep with everybody. There's no danger of having a baby. If you're stupid enough not to take a pill you just have another abortion.'

'I thought you believed in all that.'

'I believe in sex. I also believe in love.'

'So does everyone else. Everywhere I go in London I see people kissing and touching bodies.'

'That's what I mean. They're not like adults. They're more like puppies or rabbits.'

'What's wrong with puppies and rabbits?'

'They're not civilized. They don't know the meaning of adult love.'

'You mean they're permissive,' said Noel, 'like you used to be when you were young.'

'That's true.'

'Then why are you shocked?'

'They look so scruffy. I don't like to think of dirty boys going to bed with dirty girls.'

'You're being unkind.'

'I like instant coffee but I don't like instant sex.'

'Now you're being unfair.'

'Do you like the permissive society?'

'Not much.'

'The worst of it is that we were the ones who started it.'

'Not me,' said Noel. 'I didn't start it. I couldn't start anything.'

'Well, me and my friends and people like us. In London, in the thirties, we were the ones who introduced the permissive society.'

'Did you take drugs?'

'No, of course not.'

'Why do they take drugs now?'

'Because they're escapists. I think the young escapists are trying to escape from the old escapists,' I said.

I decided that the boys and girls of the drop-out generation had been given all the sex they wanted. So now, out of boredom, they took drugs and objected to war. They were blaming the rest of us, the war generation, Winston Churchill, those who had loved him and followed him.

To me they seemed a stupid lot. How different were these hippies and hooligans from the boys and girls in the 'Chelsea set'. Ann Wells and the Italian Princess and the other stylish young things had already disappeared. Dirty untidy London was full of the new ones. We had given birth to a generation of squatters and layabouts. They infested London like a plague of locusts.

That was how it seemed to me in 1960. Today I love London more than ever. It is difficult to describe the horror I was then feeling at the changed and changing skyline, the hideous skyscrapers, the beatniks in the King's Road, the noise and bustle, the alarming sense that no one had time to help anyone else.

Noel was usually taken for my husband, or lover, or brother. It was a sexless relationship. It was close and kind and domesticated. Both of us were suffering from depression, two unnecessary people in a city of computers and commuters.

'I should hate to live alone. Especially in London,' I said.

And yet I knew that my true home would always be in the centre of this noisy, dirty, turbulent, disturbing city. I wanted something nice to happen, wishing to become part of it, the new horrible classless society.

'I like the coffee bars,' Noel used to say.

They were opening everywhere. In the coffee bars and small eating places gathered the nouveau riche. Some were pop stars. Some were in the rag trade. Some were actors and artists. Others were photographers and hairdressers and television characters. (Today we call them 'Yuppies'.)

The homosexuals were far more noticeable than they are now. Their tinted hair and bright-coloured shirts distinguished them from other people like a race of canaries. Today, in the King's Road, mingling modestly with hippies and punks, most of them look more like squares. I suppose you could say that in 1960 a new moral attitude was born. Perhaps the first signal was the Wolfenden Report. From this publication we could all see a changing point of view. Most of us began to believe that homosexual relationships between consenting adults were not criminal. They might even be happy unions, a form of marriage between two men.

As Noel used to say: 'Everyone is talking about it. Even old ladies sitting on a bus.'

'How do you know?'

'Because they tell me what they think.'

'What do they think?'

'They think pansies are charming.'

Books, films, plays and general conversation were based on this fascinating subject. In the thirties we had hoped against hope that one day homosexuality would become acceptable, understood by the man in the street, no longer considered a crime or a form of perversion. In the sixties this actually happened. The Wolfenden Report made it happen.

But alas, there was and still is a feeling of dislike for the lesbian tribe. Respectable married ladies, pillars of the church, devout bridge players, members of the Conservative party, take pleasure in befriending nice young men with pretty shirts and clean hands who are known to be 'gay' and will gladly tell you all about it. Lesbians are different. For some reason boys are allowed to be 'gay' but girls are not. This is something I fail to understand.

'Oh well, never mind,' as my mother would say. '*Ça n'a pas d'importance,*' as Renée would say.

In the sixties, at any rate, these questions were frequently discussed by Noel and myself and all our friends. In Britain, we were told, there were over a million active homosexuals. In London the meeting-places were known as 'cottages'. An evening could be happily spent 'cruising the cottages' in search of a beautiful boy.

'You didn't tell me London was like this,' said Noel.

'I didn't know.'

We passed the time by exploring and finding things out. We listened to the talk of Africans and Indians (who came frequently to the flat). We went to church. We listened with pleasure to Leslie Weatherhead, who was then preaching at the

City Temple. On Sunday mornings we sometimes joined the homosexuals.

'It makes a change,' said Noel. 'It makes me feel young again.'

Their meeting-place at the time was a pub in a mews only five minutes walk from Cadogan Place. They were all so excited and gay and brilliantly coloured. They were like something in a painting by Lautrec. Both of us were frightened by what we saw. We began to feel like nervous tourists.

One day Noel came home with a teenage haircut. He said it was the latest thing to wear a forelock, a hill of hair which rose up skilfully and fell in a careful curl over the forehead. He wore it like this for several months. It gave him a look of permanent surprise. Was it the forelock, or was it the way he felt?

I was still trying to understand him. He was a good-looking man. In many ways he was feminine, extremely attractive to elderly women, possibly an undiscovered 'gay'. To be amusing, to make people laugh, he said waspish things behind my back. But there was an intimacy between us and he was my charge, 'little Noel' as my mother used to call him. How could I stop him from drinking?

Since then I have met so many alcoholics. I know that most of them are escaping from something; marriage, or sex, or fear, or just from themselves. In Noel's family there were several compulsive drinkers. His brother, my mother told me, went down on his knees, begging her not to marry Noel. 'Yes, dear, down on his *knees*,' she said.

Anyway, as a cure for boredom I persuaded him to have dancing lessons. He began to feel better, and so did I, both of us in the gift of rhythm and grace of movement, taught by Phyllis Haylor, learning to dance as though for the first time. And then, as was bound to happen at intervals, Noel lost his confidence.

'I'm no good at dancing. I'm no good at anything, Nerina.'

He went back on the bottle.

'Oh Noel, what shall I do with you?'

At that time I knew what was happening. When you suffer from the glooms you lie awake half the night with a lump in your stomach like a load of lead. When the alarm-clock rings you are unable to leave your bed. There is no reason to lift up and dress your lazy body because there is no purpose in the tedium of living. Why should you get out of bed? What is there to get up for?

When I discovered empty bottles beneath his mattress I knew how Noel was feeling. All he could say was: 'Don't think I get any pleasure from drinking, because I don't.'

'Why do you do it?'

'I get this craving.'

I was then learning more about Antabuse tablets. (There are others with a different name which have the same effect.) It is no good dosing your patient from time to time. You must give him one tablet a day, sometimes two. Always dissolve it in water and watch him swallow it. Unless you do so, your patient will tell you a lie, or pretend to swallow the tablets and afterwards spit them out.

As Noel said, an alcoholic is a person with a craving. You learn this, as I did, after years of trying to understand.

'Let me have one drink, Nerina, only one drink. What harm can it do?'

'All the harm in the world,' I said.

To get them to admit they are alcoholics is difficult. To persuade them to take one tablet each day is more difficult still. They say, as Noel used to say, 'Why can't I be a social drinker, like you?'

The answer is that no alcoholic can ever be a social drinker. Either they give it up or they die of it in the end.

Sometimes Noel tried to give it up. When I forced him to fight against it, he hated me. Alcoholics are like that. He and I, such unsuitable partners, were struggling to help one another to find jobs, to understand, if we could, the new point of view in our changing London.

'What do you make of it, Nerina? Is it right or wrong to live as young people live? What do you think of the permissive society?'

'When I was nineteen I believed in it. That was why I wrote my first novel.'

'Do you believe in it now?'

'What is right for some people is wrong for others. I still believe that.'

'But that's what the young believe today, isn't it?'

'Yes, but they've got it all twisted.'

'In what way?'

I remember the words of my husband. 'Well,' I said, 'they've debased the coinage.'

'What do you mean by that?'

'It's all sex and no love. The girls are too easy to get. The only way to have a rich experience is to take drugs.'

'Did you think the permissive society would turn out like this?'

'No, I didn't.'

'Are you shocked?'

'Yes.'

'Well,' said Noel, 'I enjoy hearing them talk about themselves.'

'So do I.'

That was why we brought people home to tell us their opinions. We found them in a coffee bar, or a club, or walking in Hyde Park. We asked them questions and studied them and tried to join ourselves with the life of London. For example, there was a girl of sixteen. I will call her Penelope, which was not her name. She told us about the teenagers in Hampstead, and this is what she said:

Every Saturday night there's a party. We don't wait to be invited, we gatecrash. Well, why not? The object of a party is to meet people, isn't it? So we take a bottle of wine and hand it to the host.

Sometimes we are thrown out. Jewish people make us pay. They give the money to charity.

In Hampstead we meet in coffee bars and pubs. The one I like best is in a cellar. On Saturday all you have to do is to say to someone: 'Where's the party tonight?' You are given an address. If you're desperate for a party, that's all you have to do.

Some of us take opium for kicks. Some of us use four letter words like they do in the East End. Bad language is part of it. That's one of the things our mothers object to.

We like Africans and Indians. We can't stand anyone with colour prejudice. If I loved an African of course I would marry him. My mother would have a fit. Mothers don't understand.

I am glad I wrote it all down. I then went with Noel to a place called The Witches' Cauldron, which Penelope said was her favourite dance club. We sat on hard benches round the wall. It was dark and warm and friendly. The teenagers, wearing jeans, were sitting and standing and twisting their small bodies in jerky movements to the sound of pop music. Boys and girls stood close to each other and remained in the same place and occasionally twitched one leg or one arm in a spasmodic jerk or kick. It was not like dancing. It was not like anything either of us had ever seen.

'Don't they look silly?' said Noel.

Penelope was copying the mods and rockers, who were then attempting to imitate the Beatles, and all of them, rich and poor, were learning to speak an international language based on pop music and fashion and sex. Good old sex!

Noel and I, middle-aged escapists, were watching the new London with amazement. I found myself longing for the London I had known with Howard as my lover, wartime

London, heroic flaming London, a place of glory and greatness, now forgotten. I thought about gallant London when the war was over, the face of the city scarred by bombs, men and women still suffering, exhausted, haunted by memories.

Nothing was left of all that glory. Even my husband's name had been forgotten. How would we, at our age, identify with the get-rich-quick teenage world, or the gay homosexual world, or even the busy professional world of Helen, the dental surgeon, or Phyllis, the professional dancer?

Helen informed me that she wished to meet my glamorous new friend. So this was arranged. On the night of a party at the ballroom, Helen was introduced to Phyllis Haylor, who was looking beautiful in a glorious evening dress, taking care of all her friends and pupils, dancing with some of the men, presenting the women, offering drinks to all and sundry when the music ended. As usual the ballroom was a-dazzle with lights and laughter. The dancing couples, well dressed and well trained, moved in complicated beauty as they whirled and twirled and circled round the room in magical rhythm.

Helen was enchanted.

'What a delightful ballroom! What superb dancing! Come on, Nerina, introduce me at once!'

Of course they liked one another. Both were professional women, both worked hard, both had a strong sense of humour. Another meeting was quickly arranged while watching a foxtrot. It took place, I remember, in Phyllis Haylor's private flat, above the ballroom, and Helen with a glass in her hand made a strange little speech. It was something about her lasting affection for Nerina. She could see that Nerina was deeply happy and she wanted us both to know that our friendship gave her pleasure. I remember feeling slightly embarrassed. We were drinking champagne. It was rather like listening to a speech at my wedding with Howard.

At the time when this happened I was having trouble with Noel. He refused to take his pills. Phyllis noticed that Noel was drinking. She had rescued many people from the backwash of divorce and separation and grief and loneliness, and now, doing it as though part of her job, she set about Noel and me. Noel was made to learn his quarter turns in her beautiful ballroom. I was persuaded to dance every Tuesday, wet or fine, having joined the Mardi Club for regular dancers.

Phyllis Haylor at last made me understand that ballroom dancing gives you confidence. It gives you the joy of rhythm and movement and style and control, depending for perfection on two people becoming united, even in thought, rising and falling and flowing into the music as though born to do nothing else.

'You're still too tense in the shoulders. You're full of rhythm,' she used to say, 'but you lack poise and co-ordination.'

Noel thought my new friend was wonderful.

She seemed to have a date every week in the north or south of England, or in Germany, or Scandinavia, as well as in and around London. She was wanted everywhere to judge competitions, to lecture and examine students. She had toured Australia and South Africa and later would be touring America.

'I've never met anyone like her,' said Noel.

We both depended on this busy, shy, unusual person for help and understanding. During one of his bad times Noel did something he regretted. I was in Brighton, spending a week-end with Aimée Stuart (retired now, living with a woman friend, watching television with the eye of an expert) and Noel was drinking.

Aimée said, 'If he's an alcoholic, you ought not to leave him, dear.'

'I can't be tied to him like a mother with a young child. He would hate it and so would I.'

'You seem to understand one another. You seem much more happy than you were in the past.'

'That's because I have a new friend.'

'It seems to be a very good friendship, dear. Do you still miss your husband?'

'Very much.'

'Do you still write to him?'

'Of course.'

'I remember you telling me that Howard had lunch every day with his famous friends while you stayed at home and never met a soul. Do you remember that?'

'Yes, of course.'

'Noel is different. You enjoy things together, don't you?'

'When he's not drinking.'

'I'm glad you've got Noel and I'm glad you've got Phyllis.'

Aimée had not changed. Motherly, affectionate, with clean, silky-white hair, she refused to grow old or dull or bored. She dressed like a girl in trousers and bright-coloured sweaters with earrings and chains. She still had many friends who came to see her for advice, as I did.

'Well, dear, you'd better go home and see what Noel is doing. If he's drinking he needs you. Anyway, he's a nice alcoholic, isn't he?'

Noel was in a bad way. Once again the craving was on him. I

found he had borrowed money from Phyllis. She told me afterwards that she had placed the money in his hand (I believe it was £20), and then caught the gleam in his eye, surprised and gratified, not expecting so much, like a child robbing the larder. This was a Noel she had never seen.

I was furious with him.

By the time I returned home he was full of drink and the borrowed money had already disappeared. In order to repay Phyllis I made him sell a valuable antique chair which had once belonged to my mother. I filled him up with pills. I made him apologize.

'Nerina, I can't help it. I'm an alcoholic,' said Noel.

Phyllis had never met one before.

'What is the difference between an alcoholic,' she said, 'and a person who drinks heavily?'

Noel said, 'For one thing, we never tell the truth. When we are drinking we will do anything to get it.'

'Poor old Noel,' said Phyllis. 'I'm sorry you lost your beautiful chair. *Why* did I lend you money?'

After that he and I both tried to get jobs. Noel became a kind of messenger and packer of brown paper parcels in a small shop selling curtains and materials. He hated it because no one had ever taught him to knot a piece of string in the Boy Scout manner. Phyllis tried to teach him. So did I. Noel's knots either slipped or came undone.

While Noel was working as a packer I was working as a part-time secretary for Ann Todd, the film star.

'I am sure we shall both get the sack,' I said.

We did.

'Oh well,' said Noel, 'it's nice that you got the sack too.'

'Thank you very much.'

Noel still said, from time to time, after a drinking bout, when I returned from a holiday with Phyllis, or a week-end in Brighton, or a couple of nights with Helen or Andy, 'Don't worry, Nerina, I've given it up.' We both knew he would never give it up. He could only keep off it for six months if forced to do so by me.

As he said, with a smile, using all his charm, 'You can't believe a word an alcoholic says. Not a word, Nerina.'

'Don't you ever tell the truth?'

'Sometimes.'

'When?'

'Not when I'm drinking,' said Noel. 'Why don't you smile?'

'It isn't funny,' I said. All the same I smiled.

19 Soho

My beloved little dog died at the age of fourteen. He was too old to get up and down the long flight of stairs to my flat. He hated to be carried. One day, in my absence, he was given an injection by Noel and the vet.

'I sat beside him and stroked him,' said Noel, 'until he died.'

'Thank you.' I believe I said it with tears in my eyes.

'I didn't think you could bear to watch him die.'

I looked at Noel with affection. 'It was kind of you to do it.'

Soon after that my novel was published. Pamela Frankau liked it. Phyllis hated it. Into *Malady of Love* I had written all my loneliness and lack of purpose and placed them in the lost soul of the young girl who loved a homosexual. One of the characters committed suicide. They moved like puppets in the London world of ballroom dancing (which annoyed Phyllis), and some of the dialogue was considered funny in a black, ironical way.

Phyllis said: 'I wish you hadn't written it. Are you still unhappy?'

'Sometimes. But I'm never unhappy when I'm with you.'

'Thank goodness for that.'

When the book appeared in print I was invited by Christina Foyle to one of those literary luncheons at the Dorchester Hotel and sat beside Denise Robins at the top table. The guest of honour was Cecil Roberts. The Duke of Bedford made a speech, so did Beverley Nichols.

Christina Foyle gave *Malady of Love* a window in the Foyle's book shop in Charing Cross Road. I was flattered to see a whole window filled with copies of my novel.

'It's up to the minute,' Christina said. 'It belongs to our time.'

But for once she was wrong. It was not a success. After publication I had an attack of the glooms.

Phyllis said: 'A holiday in Italy will do you good. When your mouth turns down at the corners it means you're unhappy.'

So I joined her in Positano. On the first blissful morning we lay on our backs in the warm blue sea, side by side, smiling at each other, staring at the cloudless sky. We gazed up at the sheer beauty of the mountain above our heads, the Italian houses clinging to it like pink and yellow flowers among the cactus plants on the rocks. Lazily we dried our white bodies in the sun. Slowly we climbed up the steep flight of rocky steps to the hotel bedroom where we had spent one wonderful night.

'Are you all right?' said Phyllis anxiously.

And then the pain started, about an hour later, during lunch, and Phyllis said, 'Perhaps it's lumbago. You'd better have a rest on your bed.'

On the second day the pain increased. Assunta, the chambermaid, nursed me like a baby. When Phyllis returned from her morning swim, anxious and tired, climbing by herself up the rocky steps which yesterday had exhausted us both, she found me on my bed, weeping with pain. I remember that scene very well. My dignified friend, still in her swimsuit and beach robe, immediately took me in her arms and began to cry. Like a couple of children we sat there sobbing, unable to speak.

On the day I was taken to hospital Assunta gave me a bottle of pills and a kiss. The doctor gave me a *puntura* (injection) to reduce the pain. Then I was carried in a chair along a tunnel of grapevines to the doctor's car, and there followed a nightmare journey on a twisting narrow road which clings like a serpent to the side of the mountain.

I heard Phyllis saying: 'Can you stand the pain? Do you want another pill?'

'Yes, please. Can I have two?'

'No, you can't. You've had three already. You'll end up as a drug addict.'

'Never mind. Give me a pill.'

'Oh, dear,' said Phyllis, 'what a horrible holiday we're having. How shall I get you home?'

In the hospital, in the X-ray room, I was told I had a displacement of the spine and would need a *corsetto*. The Italian doctor departed, taking Phyllis with him. The Italian nurse refused to give me a *puntura*. My pills were finished. Presently I was placed on a trolley, faint with pain, and when I opened my eyes I saw three white-coated Italians and a tall metal thing which reminded me of a gallows. Quite soon my head was encased in a leather helmet, and the helmet was attached in some way to the metal crossbar which was part of the gallows. Next they made me stand on tiptoe, my arms held high, like a diver.

'What are you doing?' I said indignantly.

I screamed and groaned with pain. My body was stretched out and suspended. The next job was to wind me up in plaster-covered bandages, which would dry and stiffen and finally become a *corsetto*.

In agony I said: '*Puntura! Per favore! Puntura!*'

No one took the slightest notice.

'Does anyone speak English? *Parlez-vous français?*'

They shook their heads. At last, in a moment of excruciating pain, I managed to remember an Italian phrase. '*Non posso respirare!*' I said.

It worked like magic.

'*Es vero?*'

'*Si, es vero.*'

The chief surgeon, persuaded at last that I was telling the truth, gave me a *puntura*. He was not a heartless man, as I discovered later. It was just that in Italy a patient pretends to be in pain when he is not. Italians are born actors. When I moaned and groaned he thought I was enjoying myself as an actress, pretending to be in pain as Italians do when in need of sympathy. Later, to complete the treatment, he made love to me. (I decided not to mention this to Phyllis.)

I remember that I lay in a bath of sweat for two whole days. My *corsetto* was lined with cotton wool, which made me feel much worse, and I begged the nurse to wash me. The nurse told me she was only sixteen years of age and had never washed anyone before. Which part of me was it necessary to wash?

'*Tutto,*' I said. '*Tutto.*'

I made her understand what was wanted but the nurse was filled with misgivings. In broken Italian I asked her who washed the other patients? Oh, said the nurse, the *sorella* washed them when she had time. The nurses only washed the floors. When the *sorella* was saying her prayers she could not be disturbed.

So then I discharged myself from hospital. Over my *corsetto* I managed to dress myself in a blue cotton shirt and a pair of jeans. I telephoned for a taxi. Back in the hotel I said to Phyllis, 'I couldn't stand it a moment longer. I like Italians. I don't like Italian hospitals.'

'Let's go back to London where we belong!' said Phyllis.

At Milan, where we changed planes, the shy and dignified Phyllis Haylor became involved with an airport official, a big and splendid Italian. He took her for a long walk round the buildings. When at last they returned her face was pink with embarrassment.

'Really,' she said, 'I'm too old for this kind of thing!'

'You're never too old in Italy. Anything can happen in Italy.' We both began to laugh. 'Wait till they get you in hospital!' I said, 'wait till the chief surgeon gets you in bed!'

This horrible holiday brought us very close. We laughed a great deal. I can see now that my friend's light-hearted charm was much like the charm of Helen, the charm of Renée, the charm of my mother when I was a schoolgirl in California. Women have mothered me, and I have mothered them (especially poor little Renée), and between us there has been a depth of understanding which is difficult to describe. You can mother your husband, but how can your husband mother you? In the end, after the inspiration of this horrible holiday, I grew to love my gentle Phyllis more than anyone in the world. Our love continued for twenty-two years.

I remember the return to London, still in pain, still laughing, and Noel's face when he heard the story. The three of us became much better friends than before. While I was ill he gave up drinking. He nursed me and cherished me for about six months. Phyllis helped us both with telephone calls, laughter, unfailing friendship.

'Don't be depressed. You'll soon get better,' said Noel, in my mother's voice. He was not in the least jealous of Phyllis and he seemed to encourage the love between us. To my surprise, I was beginning to love him and like him as a person. I never thought of him as a man. I thought of him as a child.

This was a strange period in my life. When I was well enough to think of work, something made me put an advertisement in *The Times*. It was very short, a few words about an educated woman seeking a charity job with a small salary.

'I wonder what will happen to you next?' said Noel.

I found myself in the House of St Barnabas, a hostel for unmarried mothers and women in distress. It lay behind Christina Foyle's bookshop, down the lane, beyond the chapel, beneath a low and sinister archway known to Charles Dickens. I was in Soho, in London's underworld. The door was suspiciously opened by Mary, the housemaid, a little human being with the appearance of a gnome.

'Oh, it's you. The warden is ready to see you. Come this way, please.'

The warden was called Mrs Gibbs and she stood, like a tall grey rock, defending something from her visitor.

'Why do you want to work here? Are you a do-gooder?'

'I don't even know what a do-gooder is,' I said.

So then I became her secretary. On the first day I walked slowly from the bus-stop in Shaftesbury Avenue and entered Soho like a tourist. I passed two striptease clubs, a betting shop, several pubs, countless restaurants and cafés and bistros and coffee bars. Inside a beautiful old house, part of eighteenth-century Soho, belonging to it as Soho belongs to the heart of London, I found the young girls with huge bellies, tragic eyes and foul tongues. They were rejected human beings. They were escapists who could not escape. They were supported in spirit and prevented from committing suicide by Mrs Gibbs, who appeared to love them.

She had lived among them, night and day, for five years. She was the widow of a parson. When I found her she had been submerged, or nearly submerged, in the stream of hatred and jealousy and lust and alcoholism and suicidal despair which swept through the house like a tidal wave. She was governed by the girls, unable to leave them because she loved them.

The little housemaid always called her 'Madam'. The others were rude to her. They quoted her, copied her, lied to her, deceived her, obeyed her wishes reluctantly, stuck out their tongues at her, felt proud of her sometimes, in a secret way, as some girls feel proud of the Queen.

'She's all right. She's a bloody bitch,' they used to say, 'but she's all right.'

I liked Mrs Gibbs. I brought her home to meet Noel. I enjoyed my afternoons in the big pleasant shabby room, with open windows, sunlight spearing through leafy plane trees in Soho Square. It was peaceful, like a room in a vicarage. But the door might burst open, and the voice of an unmarried mother might be heard shouting: 'You bloody bitch!' to another unmarried mother.

One afternoon, when I happened to be alone, a girl entered whose name was Sally. Her first words were, 'I never thought it would happen to me.' She sat on the sofa and began to sob.

'Poor Sally,' I said, 'did they take your baby away?'

She was the only married girl in the house but her latest baby, illegitimate, had now been adopted.

'What happened, Sally?'

'They took my baby, see? After the baby was took my husband come to the hospital. I done it to please him, see? I gave up me baby to please him. So then he come to the hospital and brought his girlfriend. Right? I lost me baby, see, and now that bloody bitch has took me husband. You can't win, can you?'

Sally burst into tears.

'Christ, I never thought it could happen to *me*!'

I was beginning to understand these girls, and their syncopated moralities. It might be a centre of vice and crime but Soho had a heart. I liked it. Sometimes I loved it.

My friends held different ideas about life in London.

'I don't like all these hippies,' said Phyllis, safe in her ballroom.

'I don't know what young people think they are doing,' said Helen, safe in her surgery.

'I'm afraid I'm a square,' said Howard in one of his letters. 'The world is getting more and more sad.'

'I'm too old to live in London,' said Aimée Stuart (approaching ninety), 'but I love these girls in their mini-skirts. Are you feeling happier, dear?'

My love for London had now returned. I said to Noel: 'The pendulum will swing the other way.'

'What will happen?'

'We shall go romantic. We shall realize what we're missing. Romantic dress, beautiful manners, charm, elegance, dancing to romantic music, moonlight, perfume, love, marriage, the joy of living.'

'What nonsense!' said Noel. 'You sound like your mother.'

'The girls will stop popping into bed with every boy they meet. They'll suddenly realize it pays a woman to be hard to get.'

'I don't believe a word of it,' said Noel.

At that time we knew nothing about AIDS, now changing the permissive way of life. I remember being taken to one of the high-class striptease clubs and telling the story again and again to all my friends.

'How did you get in?' said Aimée Stuart enviously.

'Well, I know the woman in charge of the bar.'

I remember looking out of the taxi window at the glittering sunlight on the trees in Green Park. Why go to a striptease club on a beautiful afternoon? But I soon discovered it was not a den of vice. At 2 p.m. there were only half a dozen customers, tired businessmen, some of them standing at the bar, their backs turned to the stage. 'How rude!' said I to myself.

I was given a glass of champagne. I felt sorry for the Italian girl, very young, as she crawled on her belly down the walk-out stage, then turned on her back like a small dog. She endeavoured to excite the bored gentlemen at the bar by rolling and squirming to the music of an old piano. A moment came when she leapt to her feet and whipped off her black lace pants. Only one man clapped. So the poor girl retired, carrying her pants, reminding me of a cricketer who leaves the field with bowed head.

Later we had the gorilla dance, and this I enjoyed very much. The curtain went up on a dark stage and the piano rattled in the darkness. Against a background of palm trees and sinister shadows we could see a young woman with long blond hair. She was struggling to free herself. Apparently she was in the jungle. To make matters worse, some evil person, no doubt a rapist, had tied up her arms and legs with a heavy rope.

Then we noticed (and so did the young woman) a huge black hairy gorilla, emerging from behind the palm trees. The young woman uttered a scream. (Beneath my breath so did I). In imagination I struggled as she did with the wicked gorilla. The piano rattled. The audience loved it.

I forgot to mention that the young woman was wearing nothing but a flimsy grass skirt. The gorilla tore the ropes from her beautiful legs. He placed a great hairy hand on her pink breast, at the same time tearing her grass skirt and growling savagely.

'No, no, no!' cried his victim. The piano rattled louder than ever.

When this charming love scene was over the audience applauded. The leading lady returned, hand in hand with the gorilla. She bowed. She smiled. She was completely naked, calm and satisfied. To judge by her dignity, she might have been Sybil Thorndike, the first lady of the stage.

'But tell me,' said Noel, when I tried to describe this delicious entertainment, 'what kind of girl is she?'

'Oh,' I said, 'she's a married woman.'

'Who is she married to?'

'She's married to the gorilla, of course.'

'Are they happy?'

'Very.'

All my friends, including Phyllis, laughed at the gorilla story. I dined out on it. When I told them about the rope dance some of them said they had seen it in Paris. This other girl was a dancer with a very white body and a silvery veil. She danced an erotic and beautiful dance with a length of rope. The little smoky theatre was thrilled and deliciously excited by the slow soul-sufferings of the dancer, the rope between her legs, tortured by love, caressing her sensuous body, in love with her own beauty. There was nothing obscene. Every movement was beautiful. It was quite the most suggestive performance I have ever beheld.

As I left the theatre, (longing to tell Noel about it), another collection of middle-aged men were crowding at the swing-doors. The girls must have been tireless. They went through this amazing routine three times a day. But they were a happy lot. Each day the Italian girl's mother came to the stage-door with a basket of delicious sandwiches. She boiled the kettle. The girls, when not on the stage, gathered round a television set, munching and drinking tea.

Noel said: 'What about the girl in the rope dance? What's she like?'

'She's prim and prudish. She wears no make-up. The only thing she drinks is bitter lemon.'

'Is she married?'

'She's engaged.'

'Who to?'

'Oh, he's such a dull young man. He collects her every night and she always wears a mackintosh. She might be a suburban housewife.'

'All the same, I'd love to meet her,' said Noel.

He and I had developed a strange understanding. He worked now in temporary jobs as a male nurse, or companion, to elderly ladies and gentlemen. (He liked the elderly ladies best. Young men appealed to him but not old men.) Most of the time I was able to keep him off the bottle.

We had in common this great desire to know more about human beings. From my point of view it was delightful to share things with Noel. From Noel's point of view, it was good to be protected and supported and reprimanded and sometimes punished, and to know that the bills would be paid by Nerina.

There is something to be said for a sexless relationship. It might not have worked, but it did. Noel was still a good-looking, delicate man. He took pains with his grey hair. He matched his blue eyes with a blue tie, blue socks, a blue pullover, or sometimes a blue silk handkerchief. (Blue had been my mother's favourite colour.)

We never kissed one another except when I left him, or returned from a holiday (with Phyllis) in France or Italy or Corsica or Malta. I waited on him. He waited on me. I did the cooking, which I hated. Noel laid the table, and washed up, which he hated as much as I did.

Coming home from a dance or a party I would find my bedroom arranged by Noel, curtains drawn, covers turned back, pillows and nightdress all ready. In the morning I would say, 'Hello Noel, thank you for doing my bed.' That was all. It meant a great deal to us both.

But to live with an alcoholic is not easy.

'Why do you criticize me to my friends? Why do you say such horrible things when I leave the room?'

'Because you deserve it. You bully me,' said Noel.

'My friends don't like it.'

'Anyway, it makes them laugh,' said Noel unkindly.

So we rubbed along, and occasionally quarrelled, and put up with one another, and when I came home from the House of St Barnabas he was always there, waiting for me, ready to say: 'Well, how did you get on? Are you tired? Tell me what happened.'

I was Noel's Nanny. I guarded him and protected him. I enjoyed telling him stories about my life in Soho.

For example, I was by myself in the warden's sitting-room when I heard a loud scream, followed by a bang. The door burst open. Little Mary said in her squeaky voice: 'Come at once, please! They're at it in the lounge!'

I started to run across the room, then stopped myself, remembering that the warden always behaved with dignity, as though nothing worried her, not even screams and bangs. This was important. To run was bad for morale. Then I heard another shriek, and Mary squeaked, 'Come on! Be quick! They're killing each other!'

Two girls were rolling on the floor in the lounge while the other girls stood in a circle, eagerly watching.

I said in a stern voice: 'Stop screaming. What are you doing?'

Anyone could see what they were doing. What a stupid thing to say! Then Mary, in a moment of inspiration, rushed from the room and returned with a jug of cold water. The fighters on the floor had cold water flung in their faces. They were biffing and bamming and pulling hair. It all stopped when Mary did this sensible thing. But one of them, Blondie, was hysterical. She continued to scream and swear and hurl abuse. To cause more trouble she even telephoned the police.

The next day, which surprised me more than anything else, Blondie came forward to make an apology.

'It must have been very embarrassing for someone like you. After all,' Blondie said, 'anyone can see that you're *a lady*! You're not *a bitch*!' At this I smiled broadly and so did Noel when I was able to tell him.

Noel said, 'She's dead right. You *are* a lady, whether you like it or not.'

'Well, it's not a crime, is it?'

'Don't be silly, Nerina. Why do you work for these daft girls?' In my mother's voice he added, 'Why don't you get married?'

'Because I still love Howard. Anyway, I've had two official husbands, and one common law husband. Enough is enough.'

'Do you like helping these dreadful girls?'

'Yes.'

If nobody helped them, what would they do?'

'Some of them would commit suicide.'

'I suppose they would. Tell me,' said Noel suddenly, 'what makes it worthwhile?'

'What do you mean?'

'Have you got a man in your life? A lover?'

'Mind your own business. I wouldn't tell you if I had.'

'Oh well,' said Noel, 'I only wondered.'

Of course he knew about my love for Phyllis but we never spoke of these personal things. I believe Noel was probably a latent homosexual. Perhaps that was why we understood each other so well.

20 *The Good Samaritan*

In the sixties we were living through our best and most interesting time, Noel and I. These were the good years. He liked to be, as he called it, 'in the swim'. He liked listening and learning and joining himself with the life of London, as I did.

In addition to Noel I had the love of Phyllis, who lived with us at Cadogan Place for about twelve months, perhaps longer, and made both of us happy. It was almost like a *ménage à trois*. In my heart I longed for Howard and wished I could exchange my husband for Noel, but these were thoughts I kept to myself.

At any rate, I had a man in my life and also a woman in my life. It was wonderful. And then, to make my existence still more interesting, and quite by accident, I joined the Samaritans.

In the summer of 1964 I went with Rachael Grieve, a writer friend, to look at the little churches in the City. These little churches contain something as flowers do. They give you courage unexpectedly. They stand there, half-hidden by enormous modern blocks of stone and glass, the little power-houses, waiting there to give you what they have.

You find the little churches when you start looking for something. Usually you are looking for happiness, or lost youth, or a lover, or a friend, or a sense of purpose, or just for the meaning of something, or something to live for.

They have beautiful names. Some of them are hard to find. We ended by sitting on the steps of a little one called St Mary Woolnoth.

I remember looking at the sky and feeling the presence of the little churches all round me so closely, like flowers. Because it was Sunday most of them were locked. We knew they would all be open on Monday. At lunch-time they would be full of music, and prayer, and people from the offices. St Mary Woolnoth seemed a friendly one, always open, a bit too rococo for some of us, like an architectural barmaid, but very charming all the same.

Rachel said she knew of a little church called St Stephen Walbrook. It sprouted in a narrow City lane behind the Mansion

House. It had a beautiful small dome, the parent of the great dome of St Paul's Cathedral. We went to it from St Mary Woolnoth via Lombard Street and the Royal Exchange. It seemed a long distance. I felt excited. It was like making a new friend. Working in the crypt of this little church, built by Sir Christopher Wren, we found the Samaritans.

Afterwards we drove in my car down the narrow lane called Walbrook into Cannon Street, passing the magnificence of St Paul's Cathedral in the sunlight, washed white, like a piece of china, and into Queen Victoria Street and down the hill and under the bridge and along by the lovely dirty old Thames, alive and bright and glittering between the trees, not forgetting the old gas lamps with their rounded glass globes, shaped with beauty, and their small crowns, worn proudly, as if each gas lamp belonged to Queen Victoria.

It really was a lyrical experience.

When we left the river and came to Westminster Bridge we turned sharp right beneath Big Ben and found ourselves in St James's Park. Across the velvety water we could see the white pelicans. They stood, as they always do, in magnificent attitudes, resting on their island rock, large, languishing, looking at themselves, looking down at their beautiful reflections in the water.

I said: 'I would rather live in London than anywhere else in the world,' and added, half to myself, as if thinking aloud, 'I should like to work for the Samaritans.'

After that I found what I wanted. Somebody gave me a pamphlet about the Samaritans, which I read, discussing it with Noel, and then, a few weeks later, I was given a temporary job as a not very suitable Volunteer. (My job lasted for twenty-five years.)

I shall never forget my first success as a voluntary social worker. She arrived, a middle-aged woman, too nervous to communicate, trembling, lost, like a child, like a whipped puppy. I took her to one of the interview rooms. I was almost as nervous as she was.

'Try to tell me what happened,' I said. 'I do want to help you. I do care. Please tell me what happened.'

She refused to see a doctor, and yet, as we both believed, she was on the verge of a mental breakdown. She had come to the church for help because she wanted love. She wanted friendship.

In this way I found myself being used for the first time as a power for human help. I was this woman's life-line. Later I found myself being used as something between a friend and a mother and a psychiatrist. Every day we talked on the telephone. Sometimes there was no conversation. The woman would cry her heart out and expect me to listen lovingly to the sobs and moans because neither of us was able to communicate in words.

In desperation I used to say, 'I will ring you back in half an hour. I can't talk to you when you are crying.'

'Don't go, Nerina.'

'It's all right. I promise to ring you back.'

Finally she began to feel better and we were able to say good-bye. It was like the parting between a patient and her nurse. From time to time I received a note or a small present but I saw her no more. Others took her place. The one I loved most was an alcoholic. I seem to be good with alcoholics. They come to me as if attracted by a kindred spirit. The woman I am speaking of now ended by committing suicide. For more than three years she and I were friends. She was adored by her husband and her two children. The temptation always returned at Christmastime and the drinking bouts lasted for three months, or longer.

I can still hear her pleading voice on the telephone. 'Nerina, I feel very suicidal. Can't you help me?'

I tried, I tried. It was one of many conversations, always the same, this time on a dark and dreary morning.

'Yes, I know how you feel. You have felt like this before. But you can overcome this drink thing. You can, you can, you can.'

'Nerina, I can't.'

In the afternoon she took yet another overdose. Without meaning to do it she committed suicide. I went to the funeral with her husband, still hearing her voice: 'Nerina, I feel very suicidal. Can't you help me?'

This poor woman had been to my home many times and of course she became friendly with Noel, who perhaps understood her even better than I did. Noel was a great help in moments like this. I still hoped he would join my working group.

'No,' he said, 'it would drive me to drink.'

'But you might enjoy it. Look what you did for my mother when she was ill.'

'No, no, I couldn't do it for anyone else. Why do *you* do it, Nerina? What do you get out of it?'

'It gives me a purpose in life. I feel I am being used. It gives me what religion gives to churchy people.'

'Do you believe in God?'

'Of course I do.'

'Do you believe in an afterlife?'

'I do.'

'Do you really believe that you and I will meet in spirit when we're dead?'

'I do.'

'I do too, but sometimes I don't,' said Noel, 'if you know what I mean.'

'Sometimes I believe in reincarnation and sometimes I don't. But I believe in the other things firmly.'

'So do I,' said Noel, 'most of the time.'

One night, when he was already in bed, I was summoned to the telephone. Would I go by car to Leicester Square immediately please? I would find a man in one of the telephone boxes, a man who needed help. He was swallowing pills while he talked on the phone to one of my friends. Would I be quick, please?

Poor Noel was hauled out of bed and made to come with me to Leicester Square. We noticed a couple of hippies lying in a doorway. And there, sure enough, in the second red booth, opposite a cinema, still using the telephone and peacefully swallowing his pills, was a short, thick, heavyweight of a man, too big for me to manage by myself. He was dopey. He seemed quite glad to see me, followed by Noel. I remember noticing the pills which were scattered on the floor. The pill-box was still in his hand. He had one in his mouth. Noel took him by one arm, I took the other, and between us, half-carrying his heavy body, we dragged him to the car.

'You sit in the back and talk to him,' said I to poor Noel.

Somehow Noel managed to restrain him when he tried to escape.

'Don't take me to hospital!' the man kept shouting. 'No, no! Don't take me to hospital!'

Noel did the talking. I did the driving. We spent half the night in miserable conversation, driving round and round London, and I now forget where we went. But we managed to buy some sandwiches, and the man was persuaded by Noel to eat them. When he at last became more reasonable we handed him over to the nurses and doctors, who pumped him out. He spent the early hours of the morning in Guy's Hospital, where we left him.

'Well, that's that,' said Noel. 'Can we go home?'

'Thank you so much for what you did. We saved him, didn't we?'

But the man did the same thing on the following night. Someone else rescued him. I believe he did it every night for a week. He was like a child screaming in the dark.

'Aren't people extraordinary?' said Noel, when I told him. 'I suppose he's a bit like me, isn't he?'

'No one is quite like you,' I said.

At that time I did not realize how much I loved him.
Compared with my husband he was nothing but a child. He sat
in his armchair by the fire, and read the newspapers from cover
to cover, and watched television, and deplored the socialist
government. For everything unpleasant which happened to the
British people he blamed Mr Wilson.

'I think he's a dreadful little man. No wonder we've got
hippies in Leicester Square!'

'You find hippies all over the world,' I said.

'I wouldn't mind if they weren't so dirty and scruffy.'

'I think they're getting cleaner.'

'What makes you think so?'

'Because fashion is changing. Even hippies wear better
clothes. The genuine ones are people with ideals.'

'I doubt it. They're a bunch of anarchists.'

'I don't believe it. They're just escapists. I think the world is
getting better and better,' said I, in my mother's voice.

'Anyway, Nerina, I love living in London.'

I still remember how thrilled he was when introduced to
Pamela Frankau, who was perhaps our best-known novelist. I
had met her during the war, and then at Helen's parties, and
now, because I admired her so much as a writer (so did Noel),
we were invited by a mutual friend to meet her again. I
remember being given a surprisingly beautiful stemmed glass
filled with gin and martini. Noel was given tomato juice.

'How are you?' said Pam. 'What are you writing? I liked that
book called *Malady of Love*.'

'No one else did,' I said. 'It wasn't a success.'

She knew she had cancer. I remember she made a joke about
the surgeons cutting her to pieces. I remember the charm, the
wit, the courage, the brilliance, the raised eyebrow to stress the
point of a crack about Beverley Nichols, the warm heart, the
dazzle and sparkle of Pamela Frankau, so hard to describe, so
difficult to forget. She could charm a bird off a tree. I can see her
dark, illuminated face laughing at me. Holding in her hand
another exquisite glass half-filled with gin, she talked about the
novel as a work of art, a thing, she said, of the past.

The Willow Cabin is usually considered her best novel,
although she herself preferred *The Bridge*. I wish I had one tenth
of her talent. When we left her (it was the last time I ever saw
her), Noel said to me, 'What a wonderful person! She puts you at
ease, doesn't she? Now that's the sort of person I should like to
be.'

'You don't think much of yourself, do you?' I said. 'Is that why
you drink?'

'Partly,' said Noel.

He and I were beginning to feel at the root of things. We belonged now in the new swinging London. We were a piece of it. We were beginning to understand ourselves and each other.

At Christmas-time I wrote to Howard. My letters to my husband were increasingly happy, full of my life with Noel, my exciting work among alcoholics and other sufferers. I wished with all my heart that my husband could share my life and my work. If only Howard could make friends with Phyllis Haylor! I knew they would like one another. And Howard, so different from my weak Noel, so reliable, such a rock in a storm, replied to all this with letters of affection and kindness. His health, he said, was not so good. He preferred to live in the country because London had become too noisy and turbulent. Fishing, he said, was still his favourite occupation. I expected him to ask me to give him a divorce but this he never did. I wonder why?

'He's not like me,' said Noel. 'I may not be a Londoner but I do like a bit of life.'

'So do I.'

'Do you mind living with an alcoholic?'

'Well, it's better than living with a drug addict.'

'Thank you very much.' With a smile Noel said, 'I haven't given it up, but I'm not so bad as I was.'

I had several holidays with Phyllis which were spoilt by the home-coming, the return to my dear alcoholic Noel. It was fine if we took him with us to France or Italy, which we did three times. When he was left, for a short time, with relatives or friends, he assured me it would be all right. 'Promise to take your pills!' I used to say.

'Don't worry,' said Noel, 'have a good time with Phyllis. I shall be as good as gold when you're away.'

One summer I went with Phyllis to Provence and we stayed, I remember, in a gentle village called Grimaud, in a small hotel almost hidden by flowers, overlooking the sea, perched like a bird on the side of a mountain. Of course we both sent postcards to Noel in London. We thought he was happy and occupied, planning a holiday abroad with the parents of a young friend, a Swiss boy, who was with him during my absence.

I said to Phyllis, 'I've got a feeling something is wrong. Things are too good to be true!'

'I do so hope he's all right,' Phyllis said.

These holidays were blissfully happy. When I think of her now I always remember that smiling face beneath a large straw hat with a bending brim (like my mother's hat), and there is always a blue sky, a blue sea in the sunlight, a range of blue mountains somewhere in the distance, a blue swimming-pool, a blue summer dress, a blue scarf, as blue as her eyes. Phyllis loved this colour; so did I, so did Noel, and so, of course, did my mother. We all had blue eyes.

At any rate, from the flowers and sunlight in Provence I returned to the bottles of whisky in Cadogan Place. The Swiss boy was trying to look after him. I telephoned to say I was home. When I arrived Noel was expecting me.

It was eleven o'clock in the morning, and I found him on his bed, fully dressed, showing that pale pathetic face, furtive and defiant, a child confronted by his Nanny after doing a shameful deed, a child caught out, and confused.

There was no mistaking it. I had seen that expression before. Wondering what to do, or say, I walked round the bed and sat in a small chair by the window. As I sat down, my eyes lowered, and there, on the floor, beneath the bed, standing in rows, I saw them and counted them, twenty-nine empty bottles.

I said, with a sigh: 'Oh dear! What a lot of bottles!'

Noel was annoyed. He did not realize the bottles were visible, and started angrily to deny their presence.

'Bottles? What bottles? What are you talking about?'

I brought them out, one by one, and laid them, like dead bodies, beside him on the bed. This was, to Noel, a highly objectionable action. He had no wish to see the bottles, or to be reminded of them, let alone to have them on his bed. I understood his anger, and shared it. And yet the situation was so ludicrous that I wanted to laugh. What was I to do? I told myself it was Nanny's job to scold, and not, certainly not, to laugh. So then we had one of our quarrels. I shouted and stormed and worked myself into a towering rage. This was expected of me, and it happened, after a drinking bout, once or twice in a year. It had to be done in order to establish morale.

'If you behave like this,' I stormed, 'you must leave my flat!'

We both knew that I did not really mean it, and the next job was to search the chest of drawers. As the top drawer was pulled open by my furious hand, he protested bitterly. 'You won't find anything under my socks!'

Of course I found some more bottles under his socks, then immediately opened another drawer, filled with shirts and underwear.

'There's nothing in there,' Noel said, 'you're wasting your time.'

I expected it. Each drawer in Noel's large oak chest contained bottles of whisky, some empty, some half-full, deep down under the socks and sweaters and ties and pants, and as I brought them out, and piled them up, the owner continued violently to protest.

'What's the good of looking in there? You won't find anything in there. You're wasting your time.'

He looked at me with hatred in his eyes. The last bottle was buried beneath his mattress. 'Well, are you satisfied?' he said.

I understood that Noel was terribly indignant. What right had I to search his bedroom? On the other hand, I could see the look of relief on that white and wasted face, the expression which told me how thankful he was to see Nanny doing her job. He knew I would make him stop drinking. As he often said, when a drinking bout had been ended, whisky gave him no pleasure at the time when the craving was on him. To begin with, whisky gave him courage and gaiety. Afterwards, compelled to continue, driven by the craving, he felt frightened and bored.

So I found his pills, the ones he had promised to take while I was on holiday with Phyllis, and dissolved a couple in water. He swallowed them at once.

'Good for you,' I said.

This was a victory. We both knew that Noel was unable to drink whisky with two pills inside him. Sickness and nausea and spells of dizziness would immediately follow if he did. Yet he swallowed his medicine without a murmur.

The struggle between us went on like this for a week, and I had never seen Noel look quite so fragile. He was skeleton thin. His delicate skin now became dead white. He was obviously not fit to travel. But in order to keep his promise to spend a holiday with the Swiss boy's parents, he actually bought a bottle of male make-up, with which he browned and beautified his wasted face and forehead. I thought he looked like an elderly actor in search of work.

'I wonder what that Swiss boy thinks? I saw him staring at my face,' Noel said, with a smile.

But he went to Switzerland in spite of everything. It was his last holiday. Poor little Noel, poor old Noel, poor battered Noel. While he was away I spent as much time as possible with Phyllis. In fact she returned to me every night, after a hard day's work, to comfort me and make me laugh.

21 *The Happiest Years*

Those last years with Noel were the best. Even if we quarrelled we understood one another, we became close friends, and sometimes I was tempted to tell him the story of my life, my secret problems. He questioned me about Phyllis.

'Supposing I died, what would you do? Would you live with Phyllis?'

'Don't be silly. You're not going to die.'

'Why don't you find another husband? Don't you need a man in your life?'

'Perhaps I need a woman more than a man.'

Noel smiled. 'I know what you mean. You need Phyllis.'

'A *ménage à trois* might be the answer. What do you think?'

'You will end by living with Phyllis. That's what I think.'

My friend was then living in her own flat, not far from a new ballroom, but sometimes I stayed with her, as I stayed with Helen sometimes, and Aimée Stuart. When the Swiss boy returned to Switzerland I found another nice young man, a paying guest, to keep Noel company when I was away. This was a good idea. In his gentle feminine way Noel seemed happy and contented. In the next few years I had several paying guests, partly to pay the bills, partly to please Noel.

We had a great deal to talk about.

Winston Churchill died in January 1965. Even General de Gaulle, while keeping us out of the Common Market (unable to forgive Britain for liberating, or helping to liberate, France), came to London for the funeral. Noel and I watched it on television. We both had tears in our eyes. We loved Churchill for what he had given us. This old and wonderful man had believed in the courage of his people and had cherished it like a growing plant until each man felt it within him, as my husband did, in the hour of danger.

'He made us feel like heroes. Good-bye, Churchill,' I said.

'It won't be the same without him,' said Noel. 'I expect he hated that awful little man as much as I do.'

Needless to say, the 'awful little man' was Mr Wilson.

239

'We must move with the times,' I said severely.

I remember defending the socialist government when I visited Helen and Andy in their new country house at Boxmoor. They had sold the horses and the house at Quainton. Poor Andy was now quite crippled with arthritis and yet full of spirit, contentedly quarrelling with Helen, who was, of course, an ardent lover of Churchill. She was seventy, and yet she was gay and active, a young woman still, a dental surgeon with a flourishing practice in the West End of London, a huge circle of distinguished friends.

'I can't stand socialists,' Helen said. 'It's no good defending them because I don't believe a word you say. As for hippies, I think they're the end.'

'I don't like the hippies myself.'

'They're bonkers,' said Helen. 'Have another drink.'

Because Helen knew my husband very well, and had counselled him when I left him, I was able to talk to her about my broken marriage.

'Was it my fault for telling him the truth?'

'Yes, it was. You should never have told him about Renée.'

'I did so hope he would understand. Do you think my marriage would have lasted?'

'Yes, I do. Howard loved you so much. Never hurt your husband by telling him the truth.'

'Some husbands would turn a blind eye.'

'Yes, but not Howard.'

'Some husbands would understand the need of a woman for the love of another woman.'

'Yes, but not Howard. You were much to blame for telling him the truth. Husbands don't like the truth. Have another drink,' said Helen, 'and stop grieving, there's a good girl.'

'It's no good crying over spilt milk,' I said.

'Of course it isn't. Have another drink.'

'I'm not grieving. I'm very happy with Phyllis.'

'Thank God for that. Now do have another drink,' said Helen.

'The trouble is I'm not very good at deceiving people.'

'Have another drink and shut up,' said Helen.

When I visited Aimée Stuart in Brighton we had long conversations about London life, about my friendship with Phyllis, about drugs and homosexuals.

'I think young people are going in the right direction,' I said, 'but they're on the wrong path.'

'What do you mean by that, dear?'

'I think they've taken to sex and drugs as a means of escape. I blame the hippies.'

'Why do you blame them?'
I repeated the words of Howard. 'Because they've debased the coinage.'

Aimée smiled. 'I like that phrase,' she said. 'Now tell me about yourself and Phyllis. Are you happy, dear?'

'Happier than I've ever been in my life.'

'What about Noel?'

'He's happy too.'

Aimée found the world a fascinating place, as did my mother, until the day of her death. I hope to do the same. But Howard, writing gloomily, in reply to one of my letters about life in London, summed up his views in one short sentence.

'The world gets more and more sad.'

Phyllis, perhaps the most stable person in London, still safe in her ballroom, teaching men and women to dance as though life depended on it, believed in self-discipline. With indignation she said, 'What are all these hippies on about? What makes them think life is harder for them than it was for you and me? Why do young girls have to take drugs? Why don't they learn to dance?'

One morning, working for the Samaritans, I met a nice young girl, a drug addict, who told me all about it. Her favourite drug was hashish.

'Well, why not? There's no harm in it, as long as you know when to stop. I like smoking hashish better than drinking. Have you ever tried it? What's your name?'

'My name is Nerina. No, I've never tried it.'

She was a pretty little girl, very clean, with silky dark hair, cut short and straight to look like an urchin. She was wearing a spotless white dress. She appeared more like a child of twelve than a tragic young woman of nineteen.

'Well, why don't you try it then? It's wonderful. It's better than alcohol. It makes you feel so happy and gay. It gives you a feeling of escape. It turns you on.'

While we were talking I gave her a cup of coffee. This was a mistake. She had started the morning with a smoke, which I did not realize, and the coffee had a strange effect. The girl went 'high'. Suddenly she was on her feet, dancing, laughing, fluttering round the interview room like a bird, talking nonsense, telling me in a tone of ecstasy that her chair was a beautiful work of art, a magnificent, charming, devastating, entrancing, delicious little seat, delightful to sit upon, a remarkable chair, a divine piece of domestic gear.

'Look at it, Nerina. Don't you see what I mean?'

She seemed to be having a love affair with the chair. While she danced and fluttered and laughed she told me in a childish voice

that all her sensations were enchanting, and now, because of the
chair's great beauty, she was her true self, liberated, the
happiest girl in the world.

'It's wonderful, Nerina. It's wonderful.'

She then fluttered out of the interview room and into another
room where my colleagues were holding a meeting. This she
quickly broke up. She flung her arms round one of their
astonished necks, and laughed like a child, and had to be sent
home, with an escort, in a taxi. The next day she returned to
apologize.

'I'm sorry I gave you so much trouble, Nerina. It must have
been the *coffee*,' she told me.

This little story gave much pleasure to Noel.

'I like them,' he said, when I told him, 'but why, oh why, do
they have to take drugs?'

All my friends were asking Noel's question.

'It's a form of escape,' I said.

'But why? What are they escaping from?'

'From life. From responsibility. Like you do when you drink.'

At that time I was still trying to work out the difference
between the young escapists and the old escapists. The Duke of
Windsor, who meant so much to my generation, gave up his
crown for Mrs Simpson. He escaped from kingship into
marriage. Not long before his death, when I heard him
discussing the youth of today on television, holding hands with
the Duchess, he gently and humorously remarked, 'I was a
young man once. I was *with it*. Oh yes, I was *with it*.'

But the boys and girls who are drugging themselves with
hashish and heroin and LSD are not like the Duke of Windsor.
They are escaping from something into nothing. They are like
the girl who fell in love with the chair. Before he died, I was
always discussing this problem with Noel. He used to say: 'Why
do young people look so miserable? What's the matter with
them all?'

'I know what you mean. When I was young there was a
feeling of gaiety. I don't mean homosexuality. I mean *joie de
vivre*.'

'When I was young, we danced all night,' said Noel.

'Anyway, they're not hypocrites. No one calls anyone a
"pervert", thank goodness.'

'Of course not. Homosexuals are now respectable,' said Noel,
'like housewives.'

'When I was young, we were always talking about the "brave
new world". Now we've got it, so what are we complaining
about?'

'You're the one who's complaining.'

I said, as though thinking aloud, 'I like the girls and boys who insist on trial marriages. I like the young men who live together like married couples. It's all so natural. This is what we were hoping would happen. Before the War, in Aimée Stuart's sitting-room, I was supposed to be a modern girl with modern ideas.'

'Don't you think modern girls have gone too far?'

'I'm not sure about that. They're struggling for equality. And yet lesbians are still not acceptable.'

'Perhaps they will be in another fifty years.'

'I wonder if you're right? I'd love to be alive in the year 2000.'

But the situation was puzzling. When I was young my elders had been shocked by that book of mine called *Another Man's Poison*, and then by that wartime book, *We Mixed Our Drinks*. Now, talking with Noel, I knew that I was the one who felt shocked.

'Why do teenagers dress like dirty children?' said Noel.

'Because they don't want to grow up,' I said crossly.

'And yet most of them are so talented.'

'Yes, I know, but they want to be treated like babies.'

As soon as I had said it, I knew I was being unfair. What about the work of Task Force? What about the youthful volunteers who were making it their job to serve and help lonely old people? What about Caroline Coon (director of Release), who was working among the drug addicts?

Of course the drug situation was increasingly awful. Whether they did it with hashish or marijuana or purple hearts, or whether they got their kicks more dangerously out of cocaine or heroin, they belonged, nearly all, to the drug-taking circle. They wanted to legalize marijuana. They told you triumphantly that Islam prohibits alcohol and permits marijuana. They explained to you that composers of pop music found drugs inspiring. The Beatles did it. The Rolling Stones did it. A teenage pop star with a gift for writing songs could turn over as much as twenty-five thousand pounds a year. So why not take drugs and get rich quick?

'What will happen to them,' said Noel, 'when they get older? Will they settle down?'

'Why not? I settled down.'

'What were you like when you were young?'

'Awful.'

Noel smiled. 'In some ways you still are,' he said.

These conversations took place in the late sixties.

Even now, after Noel's death, which I shall be forced to

describe before I end this book, I am still trying to understand the good and bad changes which are taking place in permissive London. From Chad Varah, an Anglican priest, I have learnt much about tolerance, as well as from the novelist, Monica Dickens. She came to London to write a book about the Samaritans, which was founded, of course, by Chad Varah.

I remember that happy evening, after Monica's book had been published when I gave a party in my flat. Chad Varah was the guest of honour, Monica Dickens, like the rest of us, was there to listen and learn. Most of us sat on the floor because there were not enough chairs, reminding me of youthful days when we sat on the floor discussing sex with Aimée Stuart and Miles Malleson and many others.

Chad talked (at my request) about reincarnation. He said he believed in it. He told us why. I remember wishing that Noel could have been with us.

I am coming to the way Noel's life ended, and remembering the good years before it happened. Of course, I was always under strain; sometimes Noel might be found lying on the floor at the bottom of the stairs. Once he was picked up in the street, taken to hospital, and brought home in an ambulance. I never knew what might happen next. If I spent a week-end away from home what would I see on my return?

Noel died in 1967. The truth is, that although I loved him and needed him, the happiest years of my life came later, in the seventies, when I lived with Phyllis.

But we found a pleasant way of life, Noel and I. We managed to share my blissful friendship with Phyllis, the elegant Phyllis, who loved him as I did, because he was kind and sympathetic and gentle. As I have said, there was a feminine streak in Noel, and it made him attractive to older women. For example, I was trying to befriend an alcoholic lady of seventy-four, and so Noel came to my aid.

'I'll help you,' he said. 'Leave her to me.'

Noel's old lady was living in a miserable room in the Portobello Road and to raise her spirits she frequently turned, as Noel did (when I was away), to a bottle of whisky. One day, no one knew how, or why, she managed to blow herself up while cooking herself a meal. We only knew that she was standing by the kitchen stove, a glass of whisky not far away, and was taken to hospital by ambulance.

Anyway, she adored Noel. She was a pretty old lady, come down in the world, and at Christmas-time, when she discharged herself from hospital, Noel said: 'Let's give her a party. How shall we get her up all those stairs?'

I forgot to mention that Noel's old lady had broken her hip while in Kenya, and now, among other problems, she was very lame. At Cadogan Place there was no lift. My flat was approached by a steep and narrow staircase with seventy-six steps.

I said: 'What about getting a policeman to carry her up?'

'What a good idea. She'd love it! Especially if the policeman is good-looking!' said Noel.

So we found a good-looking policeman, and Noel's old lady was successfully carried upstairs. I shall never forget what happened. It was a cocktail party, followed by a small dinner party with roast turkey and Christmas pudding. Among our guests were three alcoholics, in addition to Noel. That night all my alcoholics were supposed to be drinking lemonade but Noel made a mistake. He filled his lemonade glass from the cocktail jug, swallowed half of it, and then came to me with a chalky-white face, and said, 'Oh, Nerina, I feel so ill. Do you know what I've done?'

'You've taken your Antabuse tablet, and now you've been tempted to have a cocktail. What do you expect?'

'It was a mistake. Everyone makes mistakes.'

I said impatiently, 'Oh, Noel, what an idiot you are! You had better go to bed before you pass out!'

So he missed the turkey and plum pudding, and for two days he felt so ill that he was forced to remain in his room.

After that we saw quite a lot of Noel's old lady, who continued to worship him. Before we met her she had planned to leave her luggage at Paddington Station and to end her life on the night train to Edinburgh.

'I do hope she won't do it,' Noel used to say.

'Don't worry. She's too fond of you to do it.'

Since then Noel's old lady has disappeared. As I write about the Christmas party given by Noel and me for charming alcoholics I am wondering where she went and what happened. I shall never know.

All of that seems a long time ago, and Noel has gone.

In my imagination I can hear Noel saying: 'Then why do you feel so hopeful, Nerina?'

'Well, I do feel hopeful. Manners and morals will improve. Romantic love will return. Hippies will be forgotten. I wonder what London will be like in the year 2000?'

Perhaps I see the world in glowing colours because my personal life, after Noel's death, became so extremely happy. Before he died Noel said to me, 'I wish I could be a bit more stable. I wish I could help other people.'

'You do help other people.'

'How do I help them?'

'I don't know, but you do.'

The last summer was a bad one for all of us. As usual I went with Phyllis for a holiday, this time to Majorca. Noel went to his friends in Wales. Before we parted I begged him to take his Antabuse tablets, and he gave me his usual promise. As usual I had misgivings.

Phyllis said, as she always did, smiling at me, 'Try to enjoy your holiday. Try not to worry. Try to relax. Try to laugh.'

It was spoilt, like the previous holiday, by Noel's breakdown and the news which reached me by telephone on the night I returned to London and settled into sleep at Cadogan Place. A strange voice informed me from Wales that Noel was in hospital. This time he had fractured his femur. How did he do it? He had been drinking at the local hotel. Outside, on the way home, he had slipped, I was told, or perhaps he had caught his foot in a pothole. I remember taking the name of the hospital, still half-asleep, and promising to visit Noel in Wales, or wherever the hospital was, as soon as I could get there by train.

I remember telephoning Phyllis, who said, speaking from her ballroom, 'Oh dear, poor Noel. How awful for both of you!'

But when I saw him I listened in angry silence to Noel's explanation, giving me the usual apologies. He had taken the Antabuse tablets and his friends at the bar, not knowing what they did, not understanding that Noel was an alcoholic, had pressed him to whisky. It may have been true about the pills. More likely not. I only knew that another holiday had been ruined for all three of us, and this time, after much suffering and grief, the story ended in death.

'I shall soon be all right,' Noel kept saying. 'It was a damn silly thing to do, but everyone makes mistakes. I shall soon recover, Nerina.'

He was in great pain but he managed to smile. With his hip held together by a metal pin, like an injured footballer, he would gradually learn to walk, using crutches, then a stick, and finally, he said, in a normal way. Of course there was no need to worry.

'Footballers do it. They even play football afterwards. It's a wonderful operation. I shall soon get well,' he kept saying.

I remembered the Christmas party, and Noel's old lady who was carried by a policeman up to my flat. She too had a fractured femur.

'Do you think you can possibly manage all those stairs, Noel?'

'Of course I can manage. It will only take a couple of months. I shall soon be home. I'm longing to get back to London, Nerina.'

Not once did I tell him how much I missed him. I knew poor Noel would insist on joining me, and this was not to be.

'Why can't I come home?' he used to say.

As I told him, again and again, the stairs made his return impossible. I pictured him, always in pain, drinking to forget his leg, falling head first, being found by one of us in the hall, this time with a broken neck.

At last I had to say: 'Noel, there are seventy-six stairs. I'm afraid you can never come home. This is the parting of the ways.'

Looking back, with sadness and regret, I wish I had found something kinder to say. Poor Noel. All his life the men and women who had loved him, or pitied him, had called him 'Poor Noel'. He was a man who needed help. My mother did her best. So did I. And during the last four months he lived in a country house in Sussex with Joan Venables, another friend who did her best. She was parted from her husband, Bernard Venables, a fishing friend of Howard's. Like Phyllis, she had always loved Noel.

It is sad to remember that he died in the Haywards Heath hospital of bronchial pneumonia. He hated hospitals. His death was very sudden. I was summoned by telephone, and when I arrived he looked at me without recognition. A few hours later he was gone.

In this way it ended, and when I came back to London, without him, after nine years of care, I knew that life must be started all over again. Loneliness must be conquered. An answer must be found, a way of life, a reason for living, a conclusion, a purpose, something for the questing mind. I thought I would never find happiness again.

I remember the times when I sat by myself in my lonely sitting-room. I watched television. I telephoned Phyllis. I tried to read. My eyes returned to Noel's empty chair. Sometimes they filled with tears. What would happen in the years to come? How would my story finish? Would my life soon end? Would I die alone?

A few years later, in the seventies, sharing every problem, large and small, my life became ecstatically happy. Phyllis was persuaded to live with me, as Noel had foreseen. It worked. Most of the time I had paying guests at Cadogan Place, two charming young men (one of them stayed with me for eight years), but I gave my bedroom (stuffed with dusty books) to Phyllis, and I slept in Noel's room, and because we all managed to like one another we were all able to share one small bathroom without coming to blows.

Phyllis said, 'I don't mind the bathroom problem. We can always go away for week-ends.'

This is exactly what we did. With the help of a mortgage, working in partnership, we managed to buy a thatched cottage in Buckinghamshire. It had to be painted inside and out. The roof had to be re-thatched. Trees had to be cut down, or their branches trimmed. The garden had to be dug and weeded and planted and pruned. A garage big enough for two cars had to be built after excavations in a high bank beneath a little wood of chestnut trees. In addition to all this we had numerous problems with plumbing and heating.

Most of the painting and gardening was done with my own hands while Phyllis was busy in her ballroom. After about six months of very hard work we moved in the furniture which belonged to Phyllis and paid for some very nice fitted carpets. My friend's bedroom was pale green. Mine was white. In the garden, in the spring, we discovered we had thousands of snowdrops, followed by primroses and bluebells in the little wood, not to mention several trees of lilac and laburnum loaded with blossom, followed in the summer by gorgeous old-fashioned red and white and pink roses, heavily scented.

Phyllis could hardly believe the beauty of it all, and neither could I.

'How can we go on holidays abroad? How can we leave the cottage?' we said to one another.

Needless to say we went on many holidays abroad. We went two or three times to Positano, without any further accidents, once or twice to the south of France, once to Corsica, once to Corfu, three or four times to Malta. I have many memories of my friend, always in the sunlight, always smiling, always beneath a blue sky dressed or partly dressed in blue. I felt radiantly happy on all these holidays, and so, I believe, did she. Most people thought we were sisters, a couple of English blondes, one more elegant than the other. When we returned to London there was much dancing for Phyllis, much writing and typing for me (in Noel's bedroom, where I managed to write three books), and every week-end a few peaceful days and nights at the cottage, among the flowers and the squirrels.

At Christmas-time we had snow and ice, I remember, and to walk from the kitchen to the garden gate was a dangerous proceeding because the path was so slippery and steep. The dignified Phyllis Haylor decided what to do. Wearing trousers and boots, she firmly sat down in the mud and slush, making her way to the gate, bumpety bump, on her muddy bottom. Then we began to laugh.

'I wish Noel could see us now.'

'Thank goodness he can't,' said my friend. 'No one but you has ever seen me like this!'

Christmas-time at the cottage became more wonderful than ever before.

When I lived with Noel I dreaded Christmas, owing to the drink problem, and today, having lost Phyllis, I find it a time of loneliness, but then, at the cottage, year after year, I looked forward with joy to the pile of presents, and the Christmas tree, beautifully decorated, and the sprigs of holly and mistletoe, and the flash of Christmas cards, hundreds of them it seemed, strung together with red ribbon and made to hang round the walls and over the mantelpiece in our colourful little sitting-room.

Every year Phyllis did all this, transforming the cottage. She always had many more cards and presents than anyone I had ever known (from fans in the dancing world), and as I sat on the floor beside the Christmas tree I handed her the presents, one by one, on Christmas morning when we returned from church. I loved watching her open her presents. I loved the small country church. Sometimes we gave a Christmas party for neighbours and friends. Sometimes we accepted invitations to cocktail parties. Best of all were the peaceful times at home, talking, laughing, exchanging ideas about my friend's work in the ballroom, or my own work, something half-written on the typewriter upstairs.

I had never been so happy in all my life. I had never laughed so much. The days and nights were filled with my love and happiness. I remember my smile of pleasure when Phyllis looked at me and said, as my mother might have said it: 'Your mouth used to turn down at the corners but now it turns up.'

'That's because you've made me so happy,' I said.

I can see now that my adoration was based on the need for motherly tenderness which only a woman can give to another woman. I had received it from Helen. I had given it to the little French girl when she had lost her reason. And now, late in life, Phyllis was giving it to me and I was giving it to her. It was like a marriage. We became passionate friends, and our friendship lasted until the day of her death.

During those golden years I was in constant touch with Helen and Andy, and Aimée Stuart, and also my Samaritan friends, and last but not least I still had a deep affection for my husband, whose letters continued although his beautiful handwriting began to deteriorate.

Of course I knew he was ill. I knew he suffered from

Parkinson's disease. I did not realize that each of his short letters, a page or two pages at most, required an immense effort, and that Howard would have to spend a whole day composing and writing a short note. He was very ill indeed. Even to cross the room unaided was difficult for him, partly because of his weight. He had many falls. He would suddenly crash to the ground. None of this did he tell me in his letters. When I sent him a copy of my latest book, *The Escapist Generations*, it pleased him very much because he found that he, my husband, was the hero.

It was published in 1973, and I am thankful that Howard read it before he died. The time sped by. One afternoon as I worked in the summer sunlight, planting marigolds, or something, in the cottage garden, I heard the telephone ringing. It was Howard's son, telling me that Howard was in hospital, and then, trying to break the news as gently as possible, that Howard was dead.

I remember feeling shocked and shaken, as though someone had hit me on the head. I remember giving the bad news to Phyllis, who gently said, 'Nerina, try not to feel miserable.'

'I feel I let him down.'

'Yes, I understand, but did you mean to hurt him?'

'No, of course not. I loved him.'

'Then try not to blame yourself. As Noel used to say, we all make mistakes.'

In my heart I am still blaming myself for hurting him, my dear, kind, heroic Howard, but the truth is I would do the same things again. As Renée would say: *'C'était plus fort que moi.'* As Helen would say: 'Husbands don't like the truth. You should never have told him the truth.'

Possibly, as I told Phyllis, I could have managed to enjoy both forms of love had I been clever enough to keep quiet about it. After all, without causing trouble, married women quite often have lovers. What is more, married women sometimes have female lovers.

'Perhaps you should have married a man like Noel,' my friend said, smiling at me, 'a man with no brains!'

'If I had stayed with Howard I would never have looked at another man.'

'I think you would have looked at me,' said Phyllis Haylor, still smiling.

Today, I believe, there are many lesbians in London but I am told they dislike women like myself who fall in love with men as well as with women. We are bisexual. We are ambisextrous, as Aimée Stuart would say. Lesbians accuse us of wanting the best of both worlds. Well, why not? Fifty years ago, when I was young and attractive, homosexuals were not acceptable as they are today. Will lesbians be acceptable in another fifty years? Will women be allowed to love both sexes? I wonder. I really do wonder.

Let us return to those golden years at the cottage, the happiest years of my life. They were also the most active years of my life. I am a slow writer, and during the years with Noel nothing was published, but later, with Phyllis, my happiness gave me the energy to write.

Following *The Escapist Generations*, I produced two books about London. The first was called *London Villages*, the second was called *More London Villages*. Then came *The Royal Family and The Spencers*, which needed a lot of research. I was still writing it in 1981, when Phyllis died.

In the seventies, in the active years, I had the energy to visit Paris every summer. There I found Renée, greatly changed, constantly confused, but delighted to see me.

'Je t'aime. Je t'adore. Tu es comme ma mere,' said my poor little French girl. Like Noel, she had fallen in the street and fractured her femur. She was living alone in a little room in Montmartre, spotlessly clean, the walls plastered with photographs of pretty girls and handsome men. I knew she had not long to live.

In my mind I could hear Noel saying: 'How sad! Is she in pain?'

'No, she has no pain. She still telephones me from Paris.'

'Does she really? Where does she get the money?'

'I don't know, but she does.'

Renée died at about the same time as Phyllis. At the end of the seventies I lost Helen, and Andy died a year later. Aimée Stuart, at the age of ninety, was still receiving me for week-ends at Brighton, dressing herself with extreme care in her prettiest clothes in order to please me. By this time her sight was very bad. She was almost blind. Then her woman friend died, and Aimée soon followed.

Most of my friends were older than myself, including Phyllis, and I could plainly see that my friends were leaving me, one by one. It seemed impossible that Phyllis would leave me too. Both of us were so active, and so healthy, and so happy.

But I do remember her saying to me: 'Please don't die first. I couldn't bear it. Please don't die first.'

'Don't let's talk about death,' I said.

We had so much to do. For her services to the ballroom dancing profession, my friend had received the Imperial Award and also the Carl Alan Award. In 1976 came another coveted award from the Ballroom Dancers Federation. With so much success and happiness why talk about death?

In 1979 we decided to move from Cadogan Place where I had lived for so many years. We found a delightful flat on Putney Hill, overlooking the river through a green curtain of trees and gardens, with a superb view, and lawns and flowers and squirrels, reminding us of the cottage.

Phyllis said, 'It feels like home,' as soon as she saw it.

'And anyway, I said, 'we've still got the cottage.'

The truth is that I sold Cadogan Place at a huge profit. Having bought a short lease for £8,500 I sold it, twenty years later, for £60,000.

Phyllis said, 'Clever Nerina!' in a smiling voice, and we laughed at the sheer delight of living together, and working together, and travelling together, and making love together. Such happiness would never come to an end. How could it possibly end? It lasted, as a matter of fact, for two more years. In October 1981 she died at the age of seventy-seven. On the last day of her life she spent a long afternoon at the Royal Academy, training her beloved students, and returned home at 5 p.m. quite radiant with pleasure because, as she proudly said, she had given a really good lesson, a remarkable lesson.

'Don't boast!' I said.

She was laughing as she gave me a kiss.

'I'll just have a rest on my bed, and then join you for drinks,' she said. A few hours later she had a heart attack. I telephoned for an ambulance, and held her hand, and went with her to Queen Mary's Hospital in Roehampton, where I waited in a crowded room for a doctor, or a nurse, someone to tell me what was wrong with the woman I loved.

I waited for only half an hour.

Then someone came to me and told me that Phyllis was dead.

I am still thinking about her, still grieving, still feeling lonely, still telling myself we had twenty-two years of friendship and happiness and love. Can anyone ask for more?